D1169416

Six dramatists in search of a language

Six dramatists in search of a language

Studies in dramatic language

ANDREW K. KENNEDY
Senior Lecturer in English, University of Bergen

CAMBRIDGE UNIVERSITY PRESS

Published by the Syndics of the Cambridge University Press
Bentley House, 200 Euston Road, London NW1 2DB
American Branch: 32 East 57th Street, New York, N.Y. 10022

Library of Congress Catalogue Card Number: 74-76572

ISBNS
0 521 20492 5 hard covers
0 521 09866 1 paperback

First published 1975

Printed in Great Britain
at the University Printing House, Cambridge
(Euan Phillips, University Printer)

For my Mother and Judy

ΟΡΕΣΤΗΣ
φεῦ φεῦ. τί λέξω; ποῖ λόγων ἀμηχανῶν
ἔλθω; κρατεῖν γὰρ οὐκέτι γλώσσης σθένω.

ORESTES:
God, what can I say – when words fail?
I can no longer curb my tongue.

Sophocles: *Electra*, 1174–5

For by thy words thou shalt be justified, and by thy words thou shalt be condemned.

Matthew, 12.37

It is not words that shake me thus. – Pish! – Noses, ears, and lips: – is't possible? – Confess!

Othello, IV, i, 41–2

Ravenous, the word tried its great lips
On the earth's bulge, like a giant lamprey –
There it started to suck.

But its effort weakened.
It could digest nothing but people.

Its era was over.

. . .

Ted Hughes: *Crow (A Disaster)*

CONTENTS

Acknowledgements – viii
Publisher's Note – ix
Preface – xi
Introduction – 1

1 Shaw – 38
2 Eliot – 87
3 Beckett – 130
4 Pinter – 165
5 Osborne – 192
6 Arden – 213

Conclusion – 230
Bibliography – 244
Index – 261

ACKNOWLEDGEMENTS

In the writing of this study I have been greatly helped by the critical encouragement of Ronald Gaskell, of the University of Bristol, as supervisor and friendly counsellor.

I also wish to thank Christopher Gillie and Professor John Northam (now at Bristol) for reading and discussing with me sections of the manuscript at a time when this was most helpful.

I owe a particular debt to librarians of the Universities of Cambridge and Bergen, and to the staff of the British Institute of Recorded Sound, for letting me listen to their excellent collection of recordings of drama in performance.

A generous grant from the Norwegian Research Council – Norges Almenvitenskapelige Forskningsråd – has enabled me to make good use of a year's leave of absence granted to me by the Department of English, University of Bergen.

My wife's typing converted into sense a manuscript she alone could decipher.

A.K.K.

PUBLISHER'S NOTE

The Publisher acknowledges the kind permission of the following to reproduce extracts from copyright material in their possession:

ARDEN: to Penguin Books Ltd and Grove Press Inc., for *Three Plays*, introduced by John Russell Taylor; to Methuen & Co. Ltd, for *Armstrong's Last Goodnight* and *Serjeant Musgrave's Dance*;

BECKETT: to Calder & Boyars Ltd, for *Molloy*, *Mollone Dies*, *The Unnamable*, and *Proust and Three Dialogues with Georges Duthuit*; to Faber & Faber Ltd and Grove Press Inc., for *All That Fall*, *Endgame*, *Happy Days*, *Krapp's Last Tape*, *Not I*, *Our Exagmination*, *Play and Two Short Pieces for Radio* and *Waiting for Godot*;

ELIOT: to Faber & Faber Ltd, for *Collected Poems 1909–1962* and *Collected Plays*; to Harcourt Brace Jovanovich Inc., for excerpts from the poetry, and for *The Family Reunion*, *The Cocktail Party*, *Murder in the Cathedral* and *The Confidential Clerk*, copyright 1939, 1943, 1950, 1954, 1963, 1964, by T. S. Eliot; copyright 1935, 1936, by Harcourt Brace Jovanovich Inc., copyright 1967, 1971, by Esme Valerie Eliot; to Farrar, Strauss & Giroux Inc., for *The Elder Statesman*;

OSBORNE: to David Higham Associates, for *The Entertainer*, *Epitaph for George Dillon*, *Inadmissible Evidence* and *Luther*; to Faber & Faber Ltd for *Look Back in Anger*; to Grove Press Inc., for *Inadmissible Evidence*;

PINTER: to Methuen & Co. Ltd, for *The Birthday Party*, *The*

Caretaker, *The Collection and The Lover*, *The Homecoming*, *The Room and The Dumb Waiter* and *A Slight Ache and Other Plays*;
SHAW: to The Society of Authors on behalf of the Bernard Shaw Estate, for *Arms and The Man*, *Back to Methuselah*, *The Doctor's Dilemma*, *Getting Married*, *Heartbreak House*, *Major Barbara*, *Man and Superman*, *Plays Unpleasant* and *Pygmalion*.

PREFACE

This study of the problems of language in modern English drama combines two critical approaches:

(1) dramatic theory – chiefly an inquiry into ideas relevant to dramatic language;

(2) practical criticism – testing the texture of the dialogue in the work of six dramatists on a linguistically informed but ultimately evaluative basis. The aim of this study is to avoid the schematisation to which the first approach is prone, when not constantly guided by renewed experience of particular works; and, conversely, to avoid the simplifications that so often go with the attempt to discuss nothing but the 'words on the page', particularly a dialogue sequence out of context.

Although any concentration on language in drama may seem a highly specialised interest, the present study is written out of a concern for drama as a whole. This is probably implicit in the tenor of the argument itself. More explicitly, certain methods of discussion follow from such a concern. First, in the more theoretical sections, I wished to focus on language as one of several interacting elements in drama, under pressure from changing formal and human needs; I was only indirectly concerned with the linguistic, philosophical or cultural points at issue. Secondly, in the specific dialogue criticism I have tried to remain aware of and, whenever possible, give an account of the structure as well as the texture of dialogue. I have offered critical readings only after attempting to experience each play as a whole – often in performance. Thirdly, after much reflection, I have preferred a dramatist-centred chapter division to a design based on stylistic categories, so as to preserve a greater sense of organic unity: the value of seeing the way one dramatist wrestles with the language in each play, and in the interrelated parts of his total work.

I had hoped, when first thinking about methods used in this study, to bring together approaches from three areas of inquiry: aesthetics, dramatic criticism and stylistics. But this has proved to be too ambitious. Although I have tried to fuse my awareness of these three areas, I have finally centred my discussion on drama, strictly rationing the discussion of general aesthetic questions ('representation' and 'expression' for example) on the one hand, and the use of the more rigorous methods of linguistic description on the other. Whenever one is forced to choose between methods, one discovers for oneself a hierarchy of levels: the dramatic function of language was the primary level, controlling the study of style, which in turn controlled the more detailed study of linguistic structures.

In general, I could only find use for stylistic methods that helped in understanding the specific dramatic effects of language, and which examined 'the expressive and suggestive devices which have been invented to enhance the power and impact of speech'.[1] For example, I found that Anselm Atkins' line-by-line study of Lucky's speech instantly illuminated an aspect of Beckett's dramatic language; while the description of tape-recorded samples of everyday conversation made by two linguists, Crystal and Davy – and which I was eager to test in my study of Pinter – turned out to be too space-consuming and microscopic for my purposes.[2] There are some linguistic methods which just do not seem to be promising – for example the statistical analysis of the peak usage of three-letter as against four-letter words at the beginning of each line of a play, a method that has been

1 Quoted from Valéry by Stephen Ullmann, 'Style and Personality', *Review of English Literature* (April 1965), pp. 21–31. The whole essay leads to this conclusion. See also Graham Hough, *Style and Stylistics* (London, 1969), pp. 53–8; and R.Wellek and A. Warren, *Theory of Literature* (1949), repr. Harmondsworth, 1963, pp. 174ff.

2 See below: p. 140 and p. 168, n. 8 respectively.

commended for the study of dramatic speech.[3] Perhaps in the course of the next half century or so a synthesis between rigorously descriptive and value-bearing methods will be achieved, or carried to a point that seems out of reach now.[4]

In the selection of drama for detailed study I have been guided by a number of considerations. In the first place, I have limited myself to English-language drama (with Beckett as an exceptional bilingual and cross-cultural writer whose plays, when not written in English in the first place, have been translated by Beckett himself with first-hand authenticity and freshness). It seems clear that in criticism so dependent on texts, the use of either translated or multilingual dialogue is unsatisfactory. In Eliot's words: 'in so nice a problem it is much safer to stick to one's own language' (*Selected Essays*, p. 37). The exclusion of Irish and American drama was more arbitrary: it was one way of avoiding 'infinity of inquiry'. The central emphasis on English drama is, then, a matter of economy and stylistic commonsense; it does not imply a belief in the special value of studying a 'national' area in modern drama where the cross-fertilisations, from several literatures, must be kept constantly in mind. My historical and critical bearings are, wherever relevant, taken from European drama as a whole.

The six dramatists studied in detail were chosen with two chief criteria in mind: intrinsic interest and special relevance to this study. The general interest is given in the introductory section of each chapter, while the subsequent section headings define specific approaches to the writer's dramatic language. (Chapter 6 has no such subdivision.)

The concentration on six dramatists inevitably meant excluding interesting and relevant work by many other dramatists. For example: Christopher Fry's verbal abundance; Ann Jellicoe's orchestration of a primitive, syllabic language in *The Sport of my Mad Mother*; Wesker's dramatisation of a social 'language gap' in *Roots* and other plays; the shift from naturalism to various kinds of post-Brechtian theatricality in Whiting's *The Devils*, Bolt's *A Man for all Seasons*, and Shaffer's *The Royal Hunt of the Sun*. Recent English drama, which – in the work of Stoppard,

3 C. B. Williams, *Style and Vocabulary, Numerical Studies* (1970), pp. 147ff.

4 I return to some of the critical tasks and problems in my Conclusion, pp. 237–48.

Bond, Storey and others – has begun to stretch our awareness in drama, could only be included in the general discussion. No criticism can aim at being comprehensive. I could only hope to reflect, within the limits of one selection, a concern for all drama.

A.K.K.

INTRODUCTION

I

The decision to study the problems of verbal expressiveness in modern English drama is not simply a methodological one – focussing on one element in drama so as to see it more clearly within discussable limits. This study is impelled by, and will attempt to demonstrate, the heightened critical consciousness about language in drama, which is already *there* – makes itself felt or is 'encoded' – in the achieved work of our representative dramatists. *Criticism* and *crisis* are related in the development of all the arts (the etymology and the common adjective are a pointer): critical awareness is 'fed back' at an accelerating rate into separate acts of creation that may result in a crisis of expressiveness.

There seem to be three main areas of critical self-consciousness about language in drama:

(1) The dramatist's awareness of naturalism as a tired or exhausted style which yet survives – since the dramatist cannot wholly lose touch with everyday speech without sterility – as a constant pull towards mimetic dialogue.

(2) His awareness of a whole 'imaginary museum' of possible languages, usually conjoined with a self-imposed and restless search for a 'new' language, worked out in and for his own drama.

(3) His awareness of the shrinking uses and powers of language itself, as the mediator of thought and feeling, and as the meaningful counterpart of action.

Only a brief, simplified gloss can be given here of each of these complex areas of critical awareness, aspects of a single theme that runs through this whole study.

It is no news that naturalism has imposed a severe limitation on the resources of the word in the theatre. But the crisis of verbal expressiveness, as I see it, is not found in classical naturalistic drama as much as in the peculiar stylistic problems a dramatist experiences when he attempts to go 'beyond naturalism' – whether through an enriched theatrical language (prose rhetoric, liturgy, the parodistic use of former styles or archaic speech), or through pushing the verbal poverty of naturalism itself, with conscious artistry, towards a fragmented or minimal language. It is not just that naturalism has established itself as the dominant modern style which could not be ignored, could only be reacted to with a conscious aesthetic purpose – an explicit or implicit personal poetics – involving a rethinking of the function of language in drama. Even more significantly, a dramatist cannot leave behind the 'living speech' of his age in the radical way in which an abstract artist can leave the human figure out of his canvas or his sculpture.

The 'living language' keeps pressing with peculiar tenacity on the 'shaping imagination' of the dramatist. Yet the dramatist who is critically conscious of the shortcomings of an imitative language in drama may become a highly conscious critic of everyday language itself. Many of the most interesting attempts at creating new patterns of dialogue based on everyday speech (for example Eliot in *Sweeney Agonistes*, Beckett in *All That Fall*, Pinter in much of his work) gain their expressive vitality partly through a built-in critique of everyday speech – through the patterns of parody, exposing *homo loquax* in his struggles with the curse of language. There is, then, a danger that the language-conscious dramatist will lose the art of creating a non-parodic or natural-sounding dialogue – the language of men speaking to men.

The rich spectrum of possibilities which the post-naturalist dramatist has 'before' him for creative use may be seen as a source of great potential stylistic freedom (comparable to that enjoyed by the Modernist poet and novelist). Yet it is bought at the cost of a language-consciousness which is limiting in certain crucial ways. In a sense the dramatist is aware of too much – modes of language from the past, the multiple styles of his own age, countless experimental possibilities. Conjoined with the urge to innovation – 'making it new' – this sets up a taboo on repetition, including self-repetition; and it imposes on the dramatist the burden of re-creating the language for himself, possibly for each new play, and for a splintered audience which has to be *taught*, by the work itself, to respond to the unfamiliar language, as if it were a new code to be deciphered, within a strict limit of time (and all the other limitations of a stage performance). To take only one characteristic situation: when a dramatist revitalises his language through 'borrowing' a language from the past – Eliot using the rhythms of *Everyman* for sections of *Murder in the Cathedral*, or Arden using sixteenth-century Scots in *Armstrong's Last Goodnight* – he is working through a much more self-conscious, critical-creative situation than the dramatist who inherits, among other conventions, a central yet flexible dramatic language.[1] He is (though such spatial metaphors can do no more than approximate) 'outside' rather than 'within' his verbal medium. He is reframing this or that language, a subtle practitioner of parody and pastiche, a linguistically conscious ventriloquist.

An awareness of the 'sickness' or all-pervasive inadequacy of language[2] can add a new dimension to the more formal problems of using words in post-naturalist drama. Critical concepts interact with painful personal experience: the intense awareness of failing words may have a mystical source (as in Eliot), or it may absorb a philosophical critique of language (Beckett), or it may manifest itself as a more general weariness or despair concerning

[1] Allardyce Nicoll points out that Shakespeare inherited four chief stylistic modes for his dialogue: blank verse; prose; rhymed ten-syllable and rhymed shorter lines – each with its own distinct function, which the audience immediately recognised. *The Theatre and Dramatic Theory*, London, 1962, pp. 157ff.

[2] I shall briefly trace the literary-dramatic context for this 'sickness of language' in the section on Symbolist and related ideas, pp. 22ff. A sentence from Ernst Cassirer seems to epitomise 'the conclusion which the modern sceptical critics of language have drawn: the complete dissolution of any alleged truth content of language, and the realisation that this content is nothing but a sort of phantasmagoria of the spirit'. From *Language and Myth* (1925), translated by Suzanne Langer, London, 1946. (This quote via Ellmann and Feidelson, *The Modern Tradition*, New York, 1965, p. 636.)

the value of language. Only detailed discussion can show the extent to which the texture of dialogue in particular works is moulded by such radical thinking about language. The tension between words and the Word, fallen speech and the promptings of illumination, cut through Eliot's technical struggles, 'the intolerable wrestle with words'. Beckett, who used to read Mauthner's *Critique of Language* aloud to Joyce,[3] has woven a far-reaching epistemological scepticism about all language into all his texts; and his dialogue is shot through with the pathos of man's insuperable need to go on talking without end, despite the ultimately self-cancelling feeling that 'there is nothing to express, nothing with which to express'. Pinter, influenced by Beckett, had to overcome a sense of 'paralysis' or 'nausea' induced by words;[4] but he went on to develop a technical refinement of dialogue, 'a language where under what is said another thing is being said'. When the tormented language-consciousness combines with new techniques in dialogue (and both Beckett and Pinter went further here than Eliot) then a *theatre of language* comes into being which, unlike the traditional theatre, presents not just 'the psychological relationships which language only translates...' but sets up 'a dramaturgy of human relations at the level of language itself'.[5]

2

Historically, these types of language-consciousness have made themselves felt comparatively late in the English theatre – many years after they had begun to germinate in European culture. There seems to be no radical questioning – in London, early in the century – comparable to Yeats' asking whether it is possible to make a play that will live, a work of art, 'out of a dying, or at any rate a very ailing language' (*Samhain*, 1904);[6] or Hofmanns-

3 Richard Ellmann, *James Joyce*, New York, 1959, p. 661. For 'there is nothing to express...' see my Ch. 3, pp. 134ff.

4 Cf. Ch. 4, p. 172.

5 Jean Vannier, 'A Theatre of Language', *Tulane Drama Review* (Spring 1963), p. 182. (See also p. 169, n. 11.)

6 *Explorations*, 1962, p. 167. The whole context is relevant, because Yeats is here expressing hope for a language 'as much alive as if it were new come out of Eden'. See also the section on Symbolism in this Introduction.

thal's asking, in his 'Lord Chandos' Letter (1902), whether language, when it fails in connecting and in being speakable, should not be abandoned altogether.[7] One has to bear in mind here a number of things: the innate artistic conservatism of the theatre in England at the turn of the century, including, among other things, the unquestioning faith in the language of imitation of a dramatist like Pinero, and the relative timidity of Henry James in his dramatic years. Above all, the scene was dominated by the 'naive' and robust creativity of Shaw, who became conscious only gradually and partially of some of the things he was doing in drama: that his language was not Ibsenite; that 'verbal music' tended to work against mimetic speech. It was only late in his long life that Shaw explicitly declared that the theatre 'does not develop, and it has, in the evolutionary sense, no future that will not repeat the past'. And it was towards the end of his life that he argued, retrospectively, that his early and 'furious' opposition to Pinero and the School of Paris (including Sardou, whom Henry James admired) made him go 'back to Shakespeare, the Bible, Bunyan, Walter Scott, Dickens, Dumas *père*, Mozart and Verdi' – in short, an all too miscellaneous 'imaginary museum'.[8] And Shaw only became troubled by the absurdity of words sporadically and in the old, confident, pre-modern sense of the absurd.

The problems of language in modern drama were crystallised – as problems – in the early dramatic criticism of Eliot (from 1919 onwards).[9] And one might single out Eliot's celebrated rejection, in 'Four Elizabethan Dramatists' (1923), of William Archer's over-simple faith in the progress of drama based partly on the affirmation that the *language of imitation* has a natural ascendancy in modern drama.

Archer's late book *The Old Drama and the New* (1923) includes something like a doctrine on dramatic language, which has the clarity of assertions made by someone who thinks he is standing firmly on the top of the ladder. Even the tone is triumphant

[7] Hugo von Hofmannsthal, 'Ein Brief', *Werke: Prosa II.*, Frankfurt, 1959, pp. 7–20. (English translation in *Selected Prose*, London, 1953.)

[8] The two Shaw quotes are taken, respectively, from *Shaw on Theatre* (ed. E. J. West), pp. 217 and 268; the dates are 1933 and 1946. See also Ch. 1, pp. 39–40, with further quotes. The statement at the end of the paragraph is the subject of a section on pp. 75ff.

[9] Cf. Ch. 2, n. 4 especially.

whenever Archer celebrates the substitution of 'the true accent of human speech for inflated rhetoric'[10] and, in his grand exordium,

> the sloughing off from drama of the lyrical and rhetorical elements, both tragic and comic, and of the conventions associated with them, until we reach a logical and consistent art form, capable of expressing, by means of pure imitation, not only the social but the spiritual life of the modern world.[11]

The comfort of this doctrine, from Archer's point of view, is that it works both retrospectively (all drama of the past points to this state of technical refinement in dialogue) and, as it were, prophetically (there is no reason why 'progress', so defined, should not continue). Between the two primary sources of all drama – imitation and passion – the former has at last come into its own; and it follows that rhetorical, lyrical, 'cothurnate' speech is, in modern drama, an aberration.[12]

For a dramatist who wrote in keeping with Archer's doctrine the writing of the dialogue would present only, or largely, technical problems – problems of economy, timing, appropriateness, 'speaking in character'. Such things do demand great and consistent creative attention, but they are usually free from the kind of tensions we find in the work of the dramatist who sets out to re-create a dramatic language.

Looking back, we may briefly recall that two such very different early contemporaries of Shaw as Pinero and Henry James seem to have accepted the ascendancy of the language of imitation, without any critical questioning. Pinero once wrote an essay to explain the failure of Robert Louis Stevenson as dramatist (1903),[13] in which he criticises Stevenson for 'deliberately imitating outworn models'. In this respect Stevenson

10 William Archer, *The Old Drama and the New*, London, 1923, p. 124.

11 *Ibid.* pp. 24–5.

12 My sentence, made up of terms repeatedly used by Archer.

13 'Robert Louis Stevenson: The Dramatist', extracts reprinted in Barrett H. Clark, *European Theories of the Drama*, New York, 1929, pp. 454–7. My own quotes are taken from the fourth and final paragraphs. Pinero objects to Stevenson's imitation of the 'absurdities' of the stage – precisely what happens later in parodistic theatricality. As for 'progressive' drama, this came to be opposed by deliberate 'regression' to primitive modes.

was like the many poets and novelists, starting with the Romantics, who had broken what is 'perhaps the only universal rule of the drama...that you cannot pour new wine into old skins'. This amounts to a failure to realise that the art of drama is *progressive*. Stevenson had failed to master the new technique of compression, the art of making the characters 'say nothing very remarkable, nothing you think...that might not quite well have occurred to you'. The 'problem of language' from that standpoint is tantamount to the effort of writing such compressed dialogue: 'every page of the play has cost more care, severer mental tension, if not more actual manual labour, than any chapter of a novel, though it be fifty pages long'.

Henry James's agonised struggle to write a few dramatic masterpieces – his love of the 'drama', hatred of the 'theatre', that 'unholy trade' – has been reconstructed, in masterly detail, by Leon Edel in several studies.[14] We are made to re-experience the peculiar ambiguities of a reluctant lover for a questionable art form; we see James spending twenty years or so in conscious preparation for drama in Paris and London; we see how preoccupied he was by the conditions of the theatre of his time, with what circumspection he chose the *subjects* and thought about the *structure* of his plays. ('The fine thing in a real drama, generally speaking, is that, more than any other work of literary art, it needs a masterly structure...The five-act play...is like a box of mixed dimensions and inelastic material, into which a mass of precious things are to be packed away. It is a problem of ingenuity and a problem of the most interesting kind...') Yet in all his writing about drama, James – the subtle master of verbal nuances and the creator of the 'dramatic method' in the novel – seems to have given no critical attention to his dialogue, or to dramatic language in general. Neither does he seem to have considered the possibility of choosing or creating a theatrical style in opposition to the dominant style of his time.

Thus Pinero, the successful non-literary dramatist, and James, the unsuccessful literary dramatist, virtually shared the assumption

[14] (1) *Henry James: Les années dramatiques*, Paris, 1931. (2) Introduction to *The Complete Plays of Henry James*, London, 1949. (3) Introduction to Henry James, *Guy Domville*, London, 1960, pp. 13–121. The bracketed quotation is from Henry James' review of Tennyson's *Queen Mary* (1875), quoted by Edel (3), pp. 39–40.

that the problem was learning to write dialogue, in accordance with the dominant, the progressive style of the day. Wholly new kinds of stylistic tension arise in the work of the dramatist who refuses to accept the language of imitation as *the* style, who becomes aware of an extended spectrum of possible dramatic languages.

3

In examining this extended spectrum, let us consider first of all the limits of possibility for *any* dramatic language – the point where it ceases to be a language. For it is no longer enough simply to recall the old truism that all dramatic speech is more than words; that the words of any play – except, perhaps, in intentional closet drama – are written to be spoken and enacted; that there is in drama, and only in drama, a permanent tension between verbal and non-verbal elements (since poetry and the novel cannot, even at extreme points, experiment beyond words). We must be aware, further, that this unique interaction between word and non-word – from the single gesture to the whole concert of signals on stage – has itself been put under pressure by the heightened critical questioning of the value of the word in the theatre. In brief, the quickest escape-route from the internal tensions of language – which we shall chiefly consider – is the enlargement of the area of wordless drama: mime and ballet, music and sound effects, the promised freedoms of physical expressiveness: the actor's body, the 'events' on the stage, the spontaneous instants of performance. The very word language – which we shall consistently restrict to the verbal element, the forms of speech and dialogue – has been extended to include almost anything: we might hear about the language of movement, about action-language. This extension is interesting; it is partly metaphorical, partly influenced by the modern structuralist approach which sees every system of signs, from menus and garments to ways of pointing, as a language.[15] In the

[15] Roland Barthes can be tentative and declaratory in turn concerning *language/speech* as 'a general category...which embraces all the systems of signs'. See *Elements of Semiology* (1964), London, 1967, pp. 9 and 25. In the context of the theatre, he sees the words spoken by the actors (with gesture) as 'turning' signs in a whole polyphony of signs. *Essais critiques, Littérature et signification*, Paris, 1964, p. 258.

present context, the appeal to non-verbal 'languages' as in some sense more creative or more vital than words in the theatre should help to define the pole of wordless drama. And we need this definition even if the 'aesthetics of sight and sound' may appear to cut the ground from under our feet. Here then is an extract from Antonin Artaud's manifesto attacking verbal drama, and extolling the 'language of space and movement', and a 'language half-way between gesture and thought' in *The Theatre and its Double* (1938).

This language cannot be defined except by its possibilities for dynamic expression in space as opposed to the expressive possibilities of spoken dialogue. And what the theatre can still take over from speech are its *possibilities for extension beyond words*, for development in space, for dissociative and vibratory action upon the sensibility. This is the hour of intonations, of a word's particular pronunciation. Here too intervenes (besides the auditory language of sounds) the visual language of objects, movements, attitudes, and gestures, but on condition that their meanings, their physiognomies, their combinations be carried to the point of becoming signs, making a kind of alphabet out of these signs. Once we are aware of this language in space, language of sounds, cries, lights, onomatopoeia, the theatre must organise it into veritable hieroglyphs...[16]

Clearly, this is a creed rather than a critical statement; and Artaud nowhere examines how literary dialogue works in, or in counterpoint with, a performance. The attack on articulate language ultimately assumes that the reader, including the potential dramatist, will share a general weariness with *all* the conventions of dramatic speech – poetic, rhetorical, and naturalistic; and beyond that lies the reaction against the linguistic habits of Western culture, nothing less. The position is, as intended, extreme, although not all that new. (One thinks of Gordon Craig discovering the clue to the Art of the Theatre in a notice he saw at the stage door of a Munich theatre: *Sprechen streng verboten.*[17] And 'pure theatre' can be traced back to the

[16] This manifesto is reprinted in *The Theory of the Modern Stage* (ed. Eric Bentley), Harmondsworth, 1968, pp. 55–6. For a full contrast between '*langage concret*' and '*langage articulé*' see Antonin Artaud, *Le Théâtre et son double* (1938), Paris, 1964, pp. 53ff.

[17] Edward Gordon Craig, *On the Art of the Theatre*, London, 1911, p. 131. Cf. 'Über-marionettes and wordless plays and actorless dramas are the obvious steps to a far deeper mystery', quoted in Eric Bentley, *The Playwright as Thinker*, New York, 1955, pp. 17ff.

non-verbal gags of the clowns, to the *commedia dell'arte* and, ultimately, to the vulgar mime-plays of antiquity.[18]) Then the text may become a 'pretext' – or it is reduced to something provisional and minimal, a scenario (as in the hands of the Living Theatre of our time). The words – if words – are to serve as an 'auditory language of sounds', intonations, cries, onomatopoeia; the syllable, or the isolated word, replaces the sentence; incantatory rhythm imposes abstraction. As a potential direction non-verbal drama shifts the whole spectrum of dramatic language away from those modes of drama – particularly Greek and Elizabethan – where the text fully controls enactment.[19]

A less radical idea may be briefly considered: the idea that non-verbal action – mime for instance – can express the words in a play. Thus Arthur Miller, a dramatist with limited verbal gifts whose plays are, nevertheless, hardly the stuff for a dumb-show, writes:

> *A very great play can be mimed and still issue forth its essential actions and their rudiments of symbolic meaning*; the word, in drama, is the transformation into speech of what is *happening*, and the fiat for intense language is intensity of happening.[20]

Despite the question-begging 'very great play' and the seeming confusion of 'essential' and 'rudiments', a point is made: words can be transposed into wordless action, which is in some sense primary. Does Miller think that mime could be a direct 'translation' of the words – a correspondence? Presumably not. Mime

18 See Martin Esslin, *The Theatre of the Absurd*, revised ed., Harmondsworth, 1968, pp. 318–29 (drawing on the partly disproved work of Hermann Reich).

19 Cf. Raymond Williams, *Drama in Performance*, London, 1968, pp. 175ff.

20 Arthur Miller, *Collected Plays*, London, 1958, Introduction, p. 8. (My italics for sentence, Miller's for 'happening'.) Cf. the more extreme sounding 'The greater and chief part of playwriting has nothing to do with words' – Elder Olson in *Tragedy and the Theory of Drama*, Detroit, 1961, p. 9. Such statements look Aristotelian at first sight. But Aristotle balanced his view that 'the plot is the first principle' (*Poetics*, VI, 14) by the view that the words, when they are spoken, should be irreplaceable: 'the effects aimed at in speech should be produced by the speaker and as a result of the speech. For what were the business of a speaker, if the Thought were revealed quite apart from what he says?' (*Poetics*, XIX, 3, Butcher's translation).

can only render the curve of action in a play. In a mimed performance of *Macbeth*, for example, the pattern of ambition would reach us forcefully and, probably, less crudely than through the dialogue of the gangster film version *Joe Macbeth*. But no mime could render central transactions which depend on close-knit dialogue. For example, there is the intense pressure built up by the way the word 'man' is modulated in the exchange between Macbeth and Lady Macbeth in Act I scene vii: the way in which the connotations of 'human' and 'humane' are counter-used to rebound as 'not manly', and to insinuate 'not virile'; the way in which the brutally spare, unmetaphorical lines:

> And, to be more than what you were, you would
> Be so much more the man.

become charged with the essential action: a dehumanising act is made to appear 'supermanly' through the duplicity of words. This is as un-mimable as complex metaphorical language.

Even if we do not accept either the radical idea of wordless drama, or the suggestion of mime-for-word translation, we can recognise an increasingly powerful pull towards non-verbal expression in drama. Mime is one example. Pure mime – with its own expressive code, at once physical and metaphorical, the art of Barrault and Marceau – is a classically clear convention. But the mime-scene has grown from a carefully limited, almost illustrative, scene in a complex play into an essential component of the verbal texture of the play. One thinks here of the difference between the function of the 'dumbshow' in *Hamlet* and the 'pantomime' in Strindberg's *Miss Julie* (1888); the latter is a deliberate attempt at making the dumb action part of a dialogue which is thought of as a musical composition (as Strindberg's Preface to the play makes clear). In later modern drama mime tends to be further extended, to take over where words manifestly fail, in a climax beyond words, or to suggest that essential experience is 'unspeakable'. Thus extended, the 'mute theatre' can be exploited to redeem the supposed impoverishment of the verbal resources of drama.

Wordless drama as a potential direction, an inward pull, may be more important in the work of a dramatist than any actual mime-plays or mime-scenes he has created. Beckett has only written two mimes proper – *Act Without Words* I and II (1957,

1960)[21] – but the pressure of mime against words can be felt in all the plays: from the silent-cinema acts of *Godot*, and the long mime-opening of *Krapp's Last Tape*, to the image of Winnie, in *Happy Days*, buried first to the waist, then to the neck, an extreme counterpoint to speech. It is as if Beckett's dialogue had to pass through the medium of silent action before it can emerge as dialogue; even the famous pauses gain their power from the implicit feeling that they might never end. There is a radical conception of mime at work in Beckett's drama, which goes with a quasi-mystical reaching out towards new creation out of silence, to counteract the limitations of syntax and vocabulary as mere reflexes.

Beckett is probably unique in making silent action the ultimate context for every text; but mime has become a recurrent method of replacement for words even in the work of dramatists dependent on full-bodied dialogue, or explicit discussion. In the post-war drama even a playwright like Wesker, close to surface speech, invents non-verbal 'demonstrations', like the mime-scene in the first act of *Chips with Everything* (1962) – the silent raid into the coke yard – and the ballet-like making of apple strudel in *The Four Seasons* (1965) which lasts about ten minutes, and is being explicitly offered as a 'very dramatic' process, accompanied by a page of culinary notes, and by an Epilogue which discusses the difficulty of avoiding both the pseudo-poetic and the impoverished current English dialogue.[22]

The distance from Beckett to Wesker itself provides a wide range, but examples could be multiplied – for a large number of post-naturalist plays embody a search for non-verbal expression. Further, if one took certain acts of 'extension beyond words' for comparative study, one could show, first, the extent to which a particular dramatist's inventiveness in mute or predominantly visual scenes affects his dialogue technique and, secondly, the extent to which the function of such scenes has become enlarged since the drama of early naturalism. Consider, briefly, the dance

21 That these mimes should have been *written*, in close verbal detail, is of some interest. The rhythmic sequences – projecting gesture and movement – suggest Beckett's characteristic word-sequences rather than choreography, or visually conceived patterns.

22 *New English Dramatists*, 9, Harmondsworth, 1966, pp. 173–4; and pp. 188ff.

that brings to a climax the third Act of Arden's *Serjeant Musgrave's Dance* (1959). A visual scene – accompanied by frantic drum-beat and song – is the central image of the play; and its deliberate pictorial primitivism links up with Arden's attempt to exploit a pre-rational picture-language through ballad and folk-song and outlandish dialogue.[23] And that demoniac stamping around the suspended corpse in uniform is not just more violent, but also structurally more emphatic than, say, the tarantella scene in *The Doll's House* (1879) Act II, or the Captain's dance to the Entry of the Boyars in *The Dance of Death* (1901) Act I scene i.

To take another example: the drum-scene at the end of the first Act of *The Birthday Party* (1958). Within the action of the play it is the first climactic point where words break down and the march around the table to the savage drum-beat takes over. It foreshadows Stanley's speechless giggle after blind man's buff (end of Act II), and his total reduction to inarticulate sounds at the end. Physical scenes – games – are synchronised with the failure of words. At the same time, it is worth reflecting on the distance of that drum-scene from Shaw's Bacchic–Salvationist drum in the operatic climax of the second act of *Major Barbara* – which depends on a verbal medley – and its relative nearness to Eliot's idea of the primitive drum as the essential dramatic rhythm.

I have said little about music here because the relationship between words and music will be discussed at relevant points, in considerable detail: the operatic 'verbal music' of Shaw; the rhythmic liturgy of Eliot; the vestiges of the Symbolist 'musicalising' of language – the contest between text and music, reaching abstract finality in Beckett's *Words and Music* (1962); and the post-Brechtian English attempts at dramatic song – these are merely headings and pointers.

4

The spectrum of dramatic languages is very wide: potentially the modern dramatist has a creative choice ranging from complete 'verisimilitude' to 'abstraction', from the detailed imitation of 'appearances' to the compressed expression of 'essences'. Why

23 Arden has also attempted to write a virtual mime-play, *Friday's Hiding* (1965), which appears to be a failure.

then should one talk about the critical limitations of language in modern drama, over and above the limitations of language in traditional drama?[24]

Every attempt at pushing back the limits of art goes with the discovery of limits beyond which it seems impossible to go. This seems to apply to the limits of possibility for language in drama. At one pole, the dramatist may seem to be reaching for complete 'tape-recording fidelity' to actual talk, developing the techniques of mimesis to the point of hyper-naturalism, the record of minutiae and gaps in conversation. Moving towards the other pole, the dramatist may aspire to the 'condition of music', imposing patterns and rhythms on the language, diminishing what is translatable or denotable, what is personal or local, in speech, for the sake of intensified expressiveness.

These polar extremes of 'representation' and 'expression' are more hypothetical than actual creative possibilities. For dramatic language is – as one experiences it in every examined play – dual: mimetic-expressive. It can hardly be like the raw speech-flow (like an unedited tape-recording of random conversation), nor can it go all the way to abstraction (language as sound-and-rhythm). The patterning of language begins in the act of writing within or towards a dramatic situation; a one-act comedy by Chekhov or a seemingly overheard revue-sketch by Pinter is 'patterned mimesis'.[25] Conversely, speech remains, as a medium, much less malleable than the 'language of music';[26] many kinds of patterning are inhibited by the obstinate concreteness of *one* language – its syntactic, lexical, and phonetic attributes, let alone its imagery, its literary and communal 'memories'. The language

24 Thomas van Laan, *The Idiom of Drama*, Ithaca, N.Y., 1970, Ch. 1, discusses some of the limitations of dramatic speech in traditional drama, and, in particular, the Greek chorus and the 'Spokesman' in Shakespeare as devices to transcend the speech of individual characters in dialogue.

25 Cf. Ch. 4, pp. 175–6 below.

26 Deryck Cooke, in *The Language of Music*, Oxford, 1959, pp. 25ff., briefly contrasts the scope of musical and verbal expression from a different angle. Roger Fowler has recently argued that 'semanticity' differentiates music and poetry absolutely, but an analogy between the 'grammar' of musical and linguistic works is possible. 'Structure of Criticism and Languages of Poetry', *Contemporary Criticism* (ed. M. Bradbury and D. Palmer), London, 1970, pp. 179–81, reprinted in Roger Fowler, *The Languages of Literature*, London, 1971.

that drama can use is a conservative medium; it cannot be shaped or orchestrated beyond a certain point. Even the rhythmic crescendo of Beckett's *Play*, to take an extreme example – where the first cycle is not intended to be caught by ear or mind – keeps throwing up recognisable fragments of a fading interpersonal battle in words (coming from limbo or hell, where language, though transmuted, survives).[27]

Eliot once wrote: 'In genuine drama the form is determined by the point on the line at which a tension between liturgy and realism takes place.'[28] Eliot's 'line' can be applied to dramatic language: in genuine drama the language is created at some point on the line at which a tension between 'imitation' and 'patterning' takes place. In our culture in general, and in post-naturalist drama in particular, this tension tends to be worked out at a highly conscious level, a historically conscious level. Many of the most significant plays written during this century embody stylistic tensions that go back to the original, late nineteenth-century Naturalist/Symbolist bifurcation, point back to those opposed modes of language (rooted in opposed metaphysics, objective/subjective ways of trying to reach reality). But it is not the split between these two languages – the 'false alternatives' of Edmund Wilson[29] – which we need to trace now, but rather the way in which a limited dramatic language (whether naturalist or symbolist in its germinal aesthetic) is modified or transcended, and the way these modes of language interact.

5

A limited dramatic language is no more than a first step towards that internalised, self-conscious limitation which may be called a critical dramatic language. The language of classical naturalism – above all the work of Ibsen and Chekhov – offers a clear idea of a limited language: it formally inhibits a gamut of expressive possibilities: verse, incantatory rhetoric, palpably stylised dia-

[27] See Ch. 3, pp. 132 and 151.

[28] Introduction to *Savonarola: A Dramatic Poem*, by Charlotte Eliot, London, 1926, p. x.

[29] Edmund Wilson, *Axel's Castle* (1931), London, 1959, pp. 232–5. He looks beyond 'false dualisms' – and the infinite specialisation and divergence of the arts and sciences, predicted by Valéry – to a convergence of styles in the future.

logue, and so on. At the same time, such drama begins to explore, as part of its human concern, certain taboos on self-expression (in the manner of Lopahin's trivial, evasive talk when he fails to propose to Varia near the end of *The Cherry Orchard*), and even certain states of dissatisfaction with the existing theatre offering 'the tritest words' (Konstantin, in *The Seagull*).[30] The 'naturalistic' and the 'natural' – the formal and the human – limitations of dramatic speech are connected, and the failures of language are still seen as merely local in the perspective of the whole play.

In many significant post-naturalist plays the formal limitations are deliberately taken further – are underlined or parodied – for the sake of intensified expressiveness. At the same time, the human limitations – the comedy and pathos of failing expression – becomes more central; they are reflected in the texture of the *whole* play. (Pinter's *The Caretaker* is an example of the relatively simple extension of these limitations.) Or else the internal critique of verbal expressiveness becomes the substance of the play, and a source of creative energy. (In *The Seagull* (1896) the fragmented lyricism in Konstantin's anti-naturalist play-within-the-play remains, in the context of the whole play, and from Chekhov's point of view, a sympathetic satire on an etiolated dramatic language. In *Krapp's Last Tape* (1958) the fragmented lyricism of young Krapp, the would-be writer, is mocked in the very act of being endlessly replayed from a mechanically rotating tape; yet Beckett uses Krapp's 'poetic moments' as still points of authentic expression against an otherwise fossilised language.[31]) In these and other ways, language is used to draw attention to itself – in communication and self-expression, in dialogue and monologue. A limited dramatic language still 'holds as 'twere the mirror up to nature'; a critical language holds, as it were, the mirror up to itself.

30 Chekhov, *Plays* (transl. E. Fen), Harmondsworth, 1959, p. 123, immediately followed by Konstantin's demand for 'new art forms', and later in the same act by the performance of his play (also referred to in this section). Contrast Chekhov himself insisting that what should be shown on the stage is people in 'life' – not 'clever sayings every minute', but 'talking nonsense', talking of the weather. Full statement quoted by David Magarshak, *Chekhov the Dramatist*, New York, 1960, p. 84.

31 Cf. Ch. 3, pp. 148–9.

We may now turn to some of the key ideas of classical naturalism as a limited language, and point to their creative effects in later drama. Here it is necessary to draw on European drama as a whole, to point to the key definitions and plays. (Incidentally, these definitions should guard against a loose use of the word 'naturalistic' and related terms in later discussion.)

First, then, Ibsen's famous decision to turn, after *Peer Gynt* and *Brand*, to '*the very much more difficult art of writing the genuine, plain language spoken in real life*'.[32] Historically, this decision made possible a dramatic language which had been envisaged long ago by Castelvetro's neo-classic concept of consistent naturalism: 'dramatic speech must be, or seem to be, *exactly what the speaker would use* if he were to come to life miraculously outside the theatre in the given situation'.[33] Metaphorically, Ibsen might have been his own phonographer, building up a vast collection of *records* – actual conversations – to be played and replayed in selections. In practice, Ibsen created a limited language that is under constant poetic pressure. The spare economy of the conversational dialogue is selectively patterned: in the early prose plays through the use of key words in successive contexts; in the late plays, from *Rosmersholm* on, through making characters converse in metaphors, so that 'people's inter-relationships are changed through language rather than through plot-motives'.[34] In the late plays in particular, Ibsen's limited language has a subtle texture and an intense verbal expressiveness.

32 Letter dated 25 May 1883 (my italics). This translation (which has become well-known and is acceptable): Mary Morrison (ed.), *The Correspondence of Henrik Ibsen*, London, 1905, pp. 367–8. Cf. 'den ulige vanskeligere kunst at digte i jaevnt sandfaerdigt virkelighedssprog', Ibsen, *Samlede Werke*, Oslo, 1946, XVII, pp. 510–12. Cf. also letter on not wanting human beings to talk 'the language of the Gods' (15 Jan. 1874), *The Correspondence*..., p. 269; *S.W.* XVII, pp. 122–3.

33 Bertram L. Joseph in article on Drama (I 4) in the *Encyclopaedia Britannica* (1968), discussing Castelvetro's *La Poetica di Aristotile volgarizzata* (1570) – my italics.

34 Inga-Stina Ewbank, in 'Ibsen's Dramatic Language as a Link Between his "Realism" and "Symbolism"', *Contemporary Approaches to Ibsen I*, Oslo, 1966, and *Henrik Ibsen* (ed. James McFarlane), Harmondsworth, 1970, pp. 308–12. See also Mrs Ewbank's equally interesting later essay: 'Ibsen and "the far more difficult art of prose"', *Contemporary Approaches to Ibsen II*, Oslo, 1971.

Nevertheless, Ibsen was a naive dramatist, in Schiller's unpejorative sense of the naive – a writer at work before the age of full critical awareness. A sentence from a letter in translation should not be construed too closely. Yet it is worth noting that each of the adjectives Ibsen uses would, for a later, more radically style-conscious writer, present doubts and ambiguities. A 'plain language' = doubts about expressive power (Synge called Ibsen's works 'joyless and pallid', in one characteristic reaction to naturalism); a 'genuine...language' = doubts about the 'authenticity' of language (the increasing use made by dramatists of a language of roles, 'appearances', self-dramatisation and parody, from Shaw, Pirandello and Eliot to our time); 'real life' = metaphysical or epistemological doubts (Eliot and Beckett). And all these doubts, often overlapping and fusing, have entered into the story of the 'difficult art of writing' dialogue.

The second key to understanding the limited language of classical naturalism is the idea of spoken action. In 1899 Pirandello, who admired Ibsen, defined his ideal of dramatic dialogue as:

> *spoken action, living words that move, immediate expressions inseparable from action*, unique phrases that cannot be changed to any other and belong to a definite character in a definite situation: in short, words, expressions, phrases impossible to invent but born when the author has identified himself with his creature to the point of seeing it only as it sees itself.[35]

Pirandello himself came to write as much *against* as *within* this mode of dialogue.[36] In *Six Characters...* (1921) we find something like a critical parody of the fine economy where word and situation are one. What we have instead is a split between these two; for instance, the Father's desire for potentially infinite self-expression is pressing against the fixed limits of verbal imitation; there are either too many words or too few, they sprout in luxuriance or else wither away.

35 Luigi Pirandello (1899), translated by F. Melano, in *The Theory of the Modern Stage*, pp. 154 ff (my italics). Cf. also Eric Bentley, *The Life of the Drama*, London, 1965, pp. 96–8, for the line from Ibsen to Pirandello's *azione parlata*.

36 See my '*Six Characters*: Pirandello's Last Tape', *Modern Drama* (May 1969), pp. 1–9.

Shaw, who came to drama as an ideological 'Ibsenite' writing quasi-naturalistic thesis-plays, had little of Ibsen in his dialogue from the start. As he developed, he came to exploit more and more a backward-looking rhetorical expressiveness: speech arias and ensembles transpose much of the dialogue. Writing retrospectively, as late as 1923, Shaw acknowledged that he had never been a 'representationist', but had always been 'in the classic tradition recognising that characters must be endowed by the author with conscious self-knowledge and power of expression...'.[37] This led to a hyper-articulate heightening from without, directly opposed to the word-economy and inner pressure of 'spoken action'. But Shaw could not fully control the various tensions between 'natural' and 'theatrical' speech; and his dramatic language exhibits, among other things, the comic pathology of word-excess, man the language animal in a theatre of shrinking action.

When Eliot decided, with full critical consciousness,[38] to 'enter into open competition with (naturalistic) prose drama', he tried to create a transparent, almost subliminally working 'verse for other voices', which could 'stand the test of dramatic utility' – a form of spoken action in verse. (He even paid a somewhat cryptic tribute to Ibsen and Chekhov at this stage.) Yet not only did Eliot find it difficult to achieve the density of 'spoken action' in practice; he was still haunted by the 'unattainable ideal' of a dramatic poetry that could reach barely definable feelings 'beyond the nameable, classifiable emotions and motives of our conscious life when directed towards action ...'. Something of Eliot's linguistic dualism[39] – the felt opposition between 'endless palaver' and a potentially 'perfect order of speech' – has survived into his final phase, pointing to the distance between the now accepted limited language and that ideal dramatic language: beyond action, reaching towards the unnameable, into silence. The specific problem is the thinly textured 'subliminal' verse; the fundamental problem seems to be the decay of spoken action.

[37] *Shaw on Theatre* (ed. E. J. West), p. 185. For fuller quotation, reference and discussion see Ch. 1, pp. 53ff.

[38] All quotations from 'Poetry and Drama' (1950), second section. For further discussion see also Ch. 2, n. 5 and pp. 95–6.

[39] See Ch. 2, pp. 108–10.

It is as if a new 'dissociation of sensibility' had set in – tending to disjoin speech and action. Such a disjunction becomes something like a creative principle – and the source of several technical innovations in dialogue – in the plays of Beckett, Pinter and others. The famous ending of *Waiting for Godot* – 'Yes, let's go.' *They do not move.* – epitomises one kind of speech–action counterpoint. And we shall study in detail the way Beckett weaves a semblance of dialogue out of monologue, words moving through the intensities of non-action.[40] Pinter underscores his conception of 'unverifiable' action by giving this or that character elaborately evasive bravura speeches, a 'torrent of language'.[41] The old Pirandellian definition might then have to be rephrased in some way like this: spoken approximation to potential action or non-action. . . unique phrases that can change to any other though they seem to belong to one non-definite character seeking to define a situation.

We come now to the idea of *subtext* – the third and probably clearest definition of naturalism as a limited language, which eventually developed towards a critical language. We know that the idea of the subtext was, in Stanislavski's conception, first of all a practical way of teaching the actor to speak the words of a play – Chekhov in particular – through discovering

> *the inwardly felt expression* of a human being in a part, which flows uninterruptedly *beneath the words of the text*, giving them life and a basis for existing. The subtext is a web of innumerable, varied inner patterns inside a play. . .[42]

It is (I paraphrase) the interaction of text and context, the latter involving a connected and inward reading of the whole play. Now it is perfectly possible to see in this method primarily an early example of a partial retreat from words, the historic first step of extending the non-verbal end of the spectrum. Stanislavski himself says, further on in the same section, that

> the printed play is not a finished piece of work until it is played on the stage by the actors and brought to life by genuine human emotions; the same can be said of a musical score. . .[43]

40 Ch. 3, pp. 153–64.

41 Cf. Ch. 4, especially remarks on the verbal smokescreen, n. 7; pp. 180–1; reference in n. 36.

42 Constantin Stanislavski, *Building a Character* (transl. E. R. Hapgood), London, 1949, p. 113 (my italics).

43 *Ibid.* p. 114.

and Raymond Williams has made a revealing study[44] of Stanislavski's 'production score' for *The Seagull* chiefly to bring out the diminished control of dramatic speech. At the same time, no one can miss the repeated emphasis on *inwardness* in Stanislavski ('a theatre of inner feelings'); the sustained refusal to let any phrase, even if trivial-seeming, become merely mechanical, stereotyped stage speech; the desire to let each word, and the whole consort of words, have full value. Clearly, this cannot be just a matter of directing and acting, however sensitive the interpretative artists are. It is Chekhov's text itself that creates the subtly interconnected patterns: 'the idiomatic dialogue turned into evocation',[45] a limited language intensified by its placing and internal counterpointing.

For our immediate purpose what matters most is this: the nature of subtext in dialogue was hardly understood by dramatists writing in English before Pinter.[46] But in the dialogue of several post-war dramatists, Pinter in particular, subtext is not only exploited but pushed towards new and systematic subtleties, sometimes at the cost of mannerist obliqueness. Thus, we have been rightly told that Pinter's dramatic language can be seen as a development from Chekhov, and Stanislavski's method; his 'reliance on multiple and conflicting subtexts poses the main problem for understanding his dialogue, especially in reading the mere words of the printed text'.[47] To this a few brief observations may be added. Pinter writes a quasi-naturalistic dialogue as if he had linguistically trained aural perception; but the seemingly accurate 'real language' phrasing is consciously patterned to show up the inadequacies – idioms as idiocies – and the failures of language. The technique of pauses and the elliptical sayings; the repetitions and circumlocutions; the language-games and

44 In *Drama in Performance*, Chapter 6.

45 David Magarshak, *Chekhov the Dramatist*, p. 162. Cf. also John Gassner, Introduction to *20th Century Russian Drama*, New York, pp. 4–5.

46 This point overlaps with what has just been said concerning Shaw and Eliot. For further discussion see also Shaw, Chekhov and *Heartbreak House*, Ch. 1, pp. 56–7 and 59–61; and Eliot's explicitness, Ch. 2, pp. 95–6; and – in the context of the 'unsayable' – pp. 123ff.

47 John Russell Brown, 'Dialogue in Pinter and Others', *Critical Quarterly* (Autumn 1965), p. 234. This study was further developed in the same author's *Theatre Language*, London, 1972, Ch. 1. (This book appeared after completion of my own work.)

cliché-catalogues; further, the play on stress and rhythmic nuances – all these amount to a linguistic naturalism which has, clearly, grown into something else. Here we have, again, a progression from a limited to a critical language.

In sum, one reaction to the crisis of naturalism – the language of imitation increasingly felt to be *both* impoverished and over-explicit – was an intensification or distortion of originally naturalistic methods. 'Spoken action' then gives way to showing the falling apart of speech and action; and the 'subtext' serves to stylise the rhythms of evasion and the misuse of speech.

6

Classical naturalism had a built-in propensity towards the less than articulate and the unspoken; but it was the Symbolist poets and dramatists who first explored a potentially self-annihilating language: language not as a medium of communication (since it palpably fails as such) but as a barrier that must be broken down in each act of expression. First music, and then silence – which have affinities with the mystic's discipline in attempting to reach communion beyond the noise or obstruction of words – became the ultimate analogies for verbal expression. The desire to 'purify' the language, to make it 'say' less, and suggest or intimate more, to exploit the inner relations and undertones in a language – all these are part of the aspiration towards a 'language within the language'.[48] From the point of view of previous concepts of what is 'dramatic' such aspirations tend to a static and lyrical, a non-mimetic language.

The Symbolists, and the poet-dramatists who came under their influence, essentially distrusted the facility of 'talk' and 'rhetoric' alike, and, ultimately, all the *public* functions of language. Rimbaud, in his quest for the unknown, for 'unutterable, unnameable things', proclaimed the need for a new and universal language – instinctively opposed to the academician's dictionary – a language 'of the soul, for the soul, containing everything, smells, sounds, colours'.[49] And Mallarmé, in defining

[48] See also Laurence Lerner, *The Truest Poetry*, London, 1960, Ch. VI (using Valéry's ideas and his phrase 'un langage dans le langage').

[49] In the letter to Paul Demeny (1871), French and English text in *Rimbaud* (ed. Oliver Bernard), Harmondsworth, 1962, pp. 7–17 (quote from p. 13).

the expressive powers of allusion, of subtly distilled essences, claimed that 'thought itself is no longer expressed in merely common language' and that 'speech is no more than a commercial approach to reality'.[50]

It has been said that the long-term legacy of Mallarmé can be detected wherever there is 'the effort to overcome the mediocrity of purely representational drama through musicality and suggestiveness in both language and dramatic design...through a reduction of the role of narrative, and through an interiorization of dramatic action'.[51] A new element – diagnosed by Lukács as early as 1906 – enters into and transforms the texture of dialogue:

> What is said becomes ever more peripheral to what is not expressible. ...the openly spoken [is ever more submerged] in the allusion, in silence, in effects achieved by pauses, change of tempo, etc. For the process which proceeds exclusively within, which will not even seek for words, which *can* not, is better expressed by word groupings than by their sense, and better by their associative power than by their real meaning, by their painterly or musical...energy. The more lonely men in drama become (and the development is ever more in this direction, or at least toward awareness of it) the more dialogue will become fragmented, allusive, impressionistic in form rather than specific and forthright.[52]

The inner connection between the ideal of purified and inward language and the pull towards *inarticulate* speech is significant. As Yeats said (in a somewhat different context) '*The human voice*

50 'Crise de Vers' (1886–95). This translation by B. Cook, quoted from Ellmann and Feidelson, *The Modern Tradition*, pp. 108ff. Cf. Mallarmé, *Œuvres complètes*, Paris, 1945, pp. 360ff ('[la pensée] qui ne se réclame plus seulement de l'expression courante' and 'Parler n'a trait à la réalité des choses que commercialement', pp. 365–6). Cf. Mallarmé on inventing a language when starting to work on his play-fragment *Hérodiade* (letter to Cazalis, 1864): 'Peindre, non la chose, mais l'effet qu'elle produit.' See also Mallarmé on ballet and on mime in 'Crayonné au Théâtre' (1887), *Œuvres complètes*, pp. 303–7, 310.

51 Haskell M. Block, *Mallarmé and the Symbolist Drama*, Detroit, 1963, pp. 131ff. Professor Block gives a longish and insufficiently qualified list of dramatists who came under the Symbolist influence, including Hofmannsthal, Yeats and Beckett.

52 Georg Lukács, 'The Sociology of Modern Drama' (transl. Lee Baxandall), *The Theory of the Modern Stage*, p. 443. (Lukács gives no examples.)

can only become louder by becoming less articulate, by discovering some new musical sort of roar or scream.'[53] Many post-naturalist dramatists are haunted by the idea – a fusion of critical concept and intuitive exploration – that inarticulate voices are more expressive than any available form of articulate speech. The inarticulate offers an escape, partly from the stereotypes of speech (including the over-explicit conversation in the drawing room), partly from the whole rationalising structure of dialogue that keeps offering clues to itself (the background and motivation of what is being said by the characters). More important is the promise of a greater intensity, of an inner integrity found through the disintegrating language. This is probably linked, psychologically, with the energies sometimes released by human breakdown or loss, and, formally, with the principle of 'less is more', whereby a medium of art is developed towards greater compression and implicitness. At a certain point of development – most consistently in the work of Beckett[54] – the attempt is made to re-create language in and through its decay.

The creative uses of pathologically inarticulate speech are also extended, taken well outside any traditional perspective. Shakespeare used inarticulate language principally to represent madness – real or feigned. Poor Tom's language is a magnificent example of intensification which reflects, beyond the local interest of feigned-mad language, the denatured world of *King Lear*; yet it is controlled by a hierarchy of values and styles in the whole play (*pace* Jan Kott's post-Beckett interpretation of the play). In nineteenth-century European drama – including naturalism – the inarticulate element is still held in perspective. Büchner's *Woyzeck* (1836) was probably the first play to make an inarticulate character central, and to show the experience of breakdown through language; yet Woyzeck is seen to be reduced to madness, step by step, by the voices of the other characters, in a psychosocial framework that illuminates the process of disintegration. By contrast, Lucky's breakdown in *Waiting for Godot* is not only shown through language, it dramatises the breakdown of language itself: the stages of an aphasiac's regression into total silence point to a more general 'sickness of language'. In a less extreme

53 W. B. Yeats, 'Certain Noble Plays of Japan' (1916), *Essays and Introductions*, London, 1961, p. 223 (my italics).

54 See also Ch. 3, particularly pp. 134–5, 138ff.

form, pathologically inarticulate speech is repeatedly exploited; it is the language of Aston and his numbed and fragmented way of speaking (at the end of Act II of *The Caretaker*), that exposes his condition – language is used as a symptom.[55]

There is a critical problem here which is inadequately faced by those one-sided responses one keeps meeting: by the heady avant-gardist hope invested in 'drama which says more in mumbles, mutters and broken phrases than has been said in generations of literary articulateness',[56] or by the facile rationalist dismissal of the 'cult of dumbness'.[57] What is needed is a critical awareness of the power of the inarticulate, its intensity and immediacy. We shall ask, further, how this power is related to the diminishing returns of certain types of verbal explicitness (rhetoric in Shaw for example). At the same time we must bear in mind the risk that 'normal' speech – supposing we accept the concept of linguistic norms – may come to be exhausted for the purposes of drama, may come to be heard as banal or inauthentic.

We come back to the realisation that dramatic language may be subject to an inner movement from explicit statement to implication, suggestion, minimal speech. Koestler in *The Act of Creation* calls this process *infolding*:

> The intention is not to obscure the message, but to make it more luminous by compelling the recipient to work it out by himself – to recreate it. Hence the message must be handed to him in implied form – and implied means 'folded in'. To make it unfold, he must fill in the gaps, complete the hint, see through the symbolic disguise.[58]

From the Symbolists to Beckett's *Play* or Pinter's *Landscape* and *Silence*[59] such a principle of inner economy is at work. It is one response to the feeling that a particular dramatic language has

55 For further discussion of Lucky's speech and Aston's speech see Ch. 3, p. 140, and Ch. 4, pp. 183–4 respectively.

56 Charles Marowitz, originally writing for the little magazine *X* (Dec. 1960), quoted in 'The Cult of Dumbness' (see n. 57).

57 'The Cult of Dumbness', editorial, *The Times Literary Supplement* (23 Dec. 1960). Reprinted in John Gassner, *Directions in Modern Theater and Drama*, New York, 1965. Gassner is himself one-sided in his assessments.

58 Arthur Koestler, *The Act of Creation*, London, 1964, pp. 337–8.

59 See also Ch. 3, p. 132, and Ch. 4, pp. 188–91.

become exhausted through over-use; an attempt at making each play offer an occasion for language to re-create itself, as it were, out of nuclear particles of word-sound, from within.

There are various, probably overlapping, ways in which one may account for such a development: the deflation of value-bearing language under the pressure of war and barbarism;[60] the analysis of abstract ideas into no-sense by critical philosophy from Berkeley (whom I take to be one of Beckett's masters) to Wittgenstein; the familiar Hegel–Marx theory of man's progressive alienation in Western society; the technologically enforced shrinking of the area of language in our culture; and the older, perhaps over-simplified, idea that urban English is an impoverished language (Synge in the Preface to *The Playboy of the Western World*). We shall have to remain aware of all these accounts. But the sharpest focus must be on what is peculiar and even unique in dramatic language: its simultaneous dependence on slowly changing everyday speech and on the increasingly short cycles of decay and renewal in art.

We must remain aware, further, of the way we get tired of a dramatic language when we may not get tired of a whole range of spontaneous human communication – the way we live through words. It is possible that the exhaustion of naturalism is different in kind from the exhaustion of any other dramatic language – say blank verse – for it may ultimately make everyday language itself less accessible as a source of renewal to the dramatist.

We still have dramatists who turn to a new speech area to find new patterns of dialogue: 'make it new' by discovering the language of one particular 'tribe' (as Synge claimed to be doing when he listened to the servants' conversation through the chink in the floor). But even here the concern with rhythmic expressiveness is primary, and it is the distancing – from the hybrid, almost polyglot English of educated people – that is striking. One recent example is David Rudkin's *Afore Night Come* (1963), where the use made of various West Midland dialects is as ritualised as Eliot's low-class London speech in *Sweeney Agonistes*. Rudkin's patient recording of 'the type of language used by these people' is a deliberate attempt to solve a problem of dramatic language: 'It is no longer possible to be

60 See, for example, Gide on Dada, quoted in Ch. 1, p. 80, n. 80.

blunt and direct in the exploitation of language, to be a purely poetic dramatist, without a highly conventional play.'[61] It is no longer possible, in the post-naturalist drama, to pin one's hopes on the naive naturalist as Yeats, in effect, did in his capacity as script-reader for the Abbey Theatre: he found in certain plays written by uneducated people – 'all eye and ear' – an antidote to the plays with 'no sense of dialogue, all literary second-hand'; for these plays came direct from the tape-recording ear; 'written out by some man who had admired good dialogue before he had seen it on paper'.[62]

The naive dramatist here envisaged is less and less likely to exist; while the critically conscious dramatist can hardly remain immune from the critique of naturalism which, so to speak, alters his perception, his selective hearing of everyday speech. One result is that there are more and more dramatists, as will be seen, who hear the 'literary second-hand' in everyday speech: rhetorical echoes, cliché-literacy, the linguistic debris of an old culture. It is as if the 'living language' had itself become a dead language for such a dramatist. To illustrate this aspect of the crisis of dramatic language we may briefly recall the language-pains of Mrs Rooney, in Beckett's *All that Fall* (1957). Mrs Rooney has been spending the whole morning vainly trying to communicate with the people who try to help her on a weary journey to the station. Part of her frustration comes from the way her simplest words are deflected, turn bizarre, unnatural, literary. This becomes explicit when her blind husband takes her up on a phrase ('till we come safe to haven', in a naturalistic context) and says that she is 'struggling with a dead language'. At that point they are startled by the urgent bleating of sheep – that still unexhausted, natural, rural sound. And Mrs Rooney remarks, with pained literary nostalgia: 'Theirs has not changed since Arcady.'[63]

7

The inward-looking theatre goes with an infolding language within the language; against this may be set a new theatricality

[61] From an interview with David Rudkin, *The Guardian* (21 July 1964).
[62] 'A People's Theatre, A Letter to Lady Gregory', III (1919). This quotation is from *Yeats: Selected Criticism* (ed. A. Norman Jeffares), London, 1964, p. 184.
[63] *All That Fall*, London, 1957, pp. 31–2.

which extends and externalises, breeding composite languages out of old ones, as style breeds style in Malraux' *musée imaginaire.*[64] These might be called dramatic collage-languages, exploring the interaction between 'real' and 'theatrical' speech.

Making theatre out of the theatre goes back to the Renaissance and Baroque feeling for the subtle interplay between 'reality' and 'appearance', world and stage, following the development of a self-contained and secular theatre, the play as illusion.[65] Then, as in Elizabethan and Jacobean drama, the theatrical nature of life ('All the world's a stage') is explored through all kinds of play metaphor, through devices like the play-within-the-play, the actor-spectator or the actor-character. We then have plays where several perspectives and several modes of language interact. Thus, the delightful collision of planes of action in *A Midsummer Night's Dream* is made concrete through the polyphonic interplay of discordant languages (Bottom against Titania; the clown-players against both the would-be play *Pyramus and Thisbe* and the witty lines of the stage audience).[66] Among the many strands of theatricality in *Hamlet*, the imaginative interaction between the Player and Hamlet (himself an actor of his 'antic disposition') stands out: it probes into the precarious borderline between 'acting' and 'action', through the ambivalent and contagious power of histrionic rhetoric.[67] In short, the juxtaposition of styles and the use of a specifically stage-conscious language may be considered the chief linguistic resources of theatricality.

In Pirandello's 'theatre in the theatre' and in Brecht's epic theatre, we have the two main sources of modern theatricality, as vision and as language. In several Pirandello plays the character struggles to compensate for the limitations of the role, in part the limitations of a naturalistic language.[68] In Brecht's anti-illusionist

64 This point was first made by me in an article, 'Old and New in London Now', *Modern Drama* (Feb. 1969). Malraux's ideas were related to poetry by Donald Davie in 'The Poet in the Imaginary Museum', *The Listener* (11 and 18 July 1957).

65 Cf. Anne Righter, *Shakespeare and the Idea of the Play*, London, 1962, Ch. 3 especially.

66 Cf. C. L. Barber, *Shakespeare's Festive Comedy*, Princeton, 1959, pp. 148–57.

67 I would support this by a close reading of *Hamlet* II, ii, 430–617, in the light of Hamlet's histrionic speeches throughout the play.

68 Discussed in my article on *Six Characters*; see n. 36.

drama the direct address to the audience is restored, and the way is open for the use of a wide range of languages, catch-phrases from the street, proverbs, the ballad, the cabaret, histrionic expressiveness. (Among many examples we may recall one: Arturo Ui – Hitler – prepares for his role by taking lessons in acting.) One can see more than a local relevance in the Actor who mutters – in the dialogue on 'The Removal of Illusion and Empathy' – 'So it's back to asides, to "Honoured Sirs, behold before you King Herod"'.[69] The Actor has grasped the argument about the demolition of 'the fourth wall'. These are points of reference we shall need in studying theatricality in modern English drama.

The theatricality we are concerned with is emphatically verbal, opposed as much to the extremes of anti-verbal theatre – sufficiently indicated by Artaud's 'extension beyond words' – as to the limited and minimal languages which are the joint legacy of Naturalism and Symbolism. We shall be dealing with the exploitation of *theatricality in and through language*: plays in which man's public voices are, as it were, primary material. The relevant dramatists aspire to plays as lasting *works*, as distinct from scenarios or improvised verbal events. Thus Shaw's well-known attack on the nineteenth-century actor managers – on their 'gorgeous stage ritualism' at the expense of the text – is inseparable from his propaganda on behalf of the *published text* of a play, and his insistence that 'it is drama that makes the theatre and not the theatre drama'.[70] Such a position is paralleled in our own time by Osborne's public attacks on the theatre of *happenings*, the affirmation of 'a great allegiance to words':

They may be dispensed with, but it seems to me that they are the last link with God. When millions of people seem unable to communicate with one another, it's vitally important that words are made to work. It may be very old-fashioned, but they're the only things we have left.[71]

69 Bertolt Brecht, *The Messingkauf Dialogues* (transl. J. Willett), London, 1965, pp. 51–7. There is an excellent discussion of the formal elements in theatricality (other than language) in Oscar Büdel, 'Contemporary Theater and Aesthetic Distance', *P.M.L.A.*, LXXVI (1961), reprinted in *Brecht* ('Twentieth Century Views'), Englewood Cliffs, N.J., 1962, pp. 59–85.

70 Preface to *Three Plays for Puritans* and Preface to *Plays Unpleasant*. (This quotation from Penguin edition (1946), pp. xi–xii and pp. ix–x, respectively.)

71 Second interview with Kenneth Tynan, *The Observer* (7 July 1968).

John Arden's attempt to create a popular poetry-in-the-theatre is (in his own critical writing) related to a literary tradition – 'Chaucer, Skelton, Shakespeare, Jonson, Defoe, Gay, Dickens, Hardy, Joyce'.[72] And we find in his work the familiar paradox of a conscious literary use of a seemingly pre-literary or, at all events, pre-sophisticated language[73] – the ballad with its promise of 'primary colours'. In short, Arden's search for a popular drama is inseparable from his language-consciousness, from his concern for the power of the word in the theatre.

In verbal theatricality even the clichés of the popular theatre – ranging from Victorian melodrama and farce (Shaw, Arden, and others) to the music hall and contemporary 'show business' (Osborne) – are, at least in intention, used to re-create an old language, a form of folklore, in a new frame of art.

We may now define the distance between verbal theatricality and an inward or minimal dramatic language through an over-statement:

> the player's exhibitionism, with the exaggerations and deformities that accompany it, belong to an eternally-recommenced game of mimic self-realisation. The only provision is a theatre diametrically the reverse of Stanislavski's, not a muted theatre of naturalism, of fragmentary utterance and groping gesture, but a palace theatre, of pompous phrase and imperial movement, where art completes and magnifies life – a theatrical theatre, in short, as distinct from the anti-theatrical theatre of Stanislavski and Beckett.'[74]

Here 'diametrically the reverse' should be qualified, since there are interesting cross-fertilisations, chiefly in and through Beckett's theatricality. But a polarisation of dramatic language *has* taken place. There is the progressively restricted language of the room tending to be further internalised in solipsistic talk, the speaker, like Pascal in Valéry's fine image, 'talking to himself on the brink of the void, where he looks exactly as if he were on the

[72] John Arden, 'Telling a True Tale', *Encore* (May–June 1960) and *The Encore Reader* (ed. Charles Marowitz), London, 1965, pp. 125–6. See also Ch. 6 below.

[73] Brecht is here the catalyst. See also 'the view that literature needs constantly to renew itself by "re-barbarization"'. Wellek and Warren, *Theory of Literature*, p. 236 (and their reference).

[74] Jonas A. Barish, 'Exhibitionism and the Anti-Theatrical Prejudice', *E.L.H., A Journal of English Literary History* (March 1969), p. 28.

edge of the stage, reasoning with the spectre of his self in front of the world'.[75]

And opposed to that there is the extendable language of the stage *as* this or that public stage: platform, pulpit, rostrum, scaffold and the rest, where the 'hypocrite' actors play a part, make a scene, or dramatise a dubious self, through speaking their lines. We have several interchangeable metaphors here; and the theatre lends to public 'stages' a language that may then be returned to the theatre. Shaw wrote at the turn of the century:

> modern civilisation is rapidly multiplying the class to which the theatre is both school and church. Public and private life become daily more theatrical; the modern Kaiser, Dictator, President and Prime Minister is nothing if not an effective actor; all newspapers are now edited histrionically...The truth is that dramatic invention is the first effort of man to become intellectually conscious. No frontier can be marked between drama and history or religion, or between acting and conduct ...[76]

The hypothesis that the theatre and public life directly interact – that they have a kind of symbiotic relationship – can be found at work behind most forms of verbal theatricality. (It even informs Eliot's speech-of-appearance for actor-hypocrites in the later plays.) Potentially, the post-war dramatist knows more about the function of language in role-enactment than Shaw could have known. Certain radical insights into the working of language – both its power and impotence – are now widely diffused. From politics comes what might be called the post-Hitler insight: that incantatory theatrical rhetoric can totally transform a human situation; and from less lethal languages of propaganda and advertising – accompanied by litanies of reiteration – comes the knowledge that public languages are 'pre-fabricated', and that such languages in turn fabricate 'roles'. From psychology comes a growing understanding of the *persona*, the masked or false self, tending to pathological dissociation from the inner

75 Paul Valéry, *Variété* (1924), reprinted in Pascal, *Pensées*, Paris, 1965, p. 153: 'il se parle sur la marge du néant, où il paraît exactement comme sur le bord d'un théâtre, et il raisonne devant le monde avec le spectre de soi-même' (my translation).

76 Preface to *Plays Pleasant*, Penguin ed. (1949), pp. 11–12, Standard ed. p. xi.

self.[77] The speech of the old *dramatis personae* could express authentic inwardness as well as public roles; the speech of the persona tends towards a willed projection, making use of the nearest language available for 'the game of mimic self-realisation'.

I have coined the term 'costume speech' with these and other considerations in mind. On the simplest level, it is a theatrical language that functions somewhat like costume jewelry: it is more ostentatious than the 'real' thing, but just right for display and illusionism. In this sense costume language works like the old epideictic rhetoric, display oratory or playful ostentation (which de Quincey distinguished from eloquence).[78] But it is a language that has many gradations from the tirade – the bombast speeches – to 'the really fine rhetoric...where a character in the play *sees himself* in a dramatic light'.[79] And we shall sometimes have to make the difficult distinction between 'tirade' and the ambiguous sincerity of feeling in self-dramatisation, say in an Osborne character. For it is for the dramatist to control – and for the critic to judge – the theatricalised voice of the actor-character, who listens to himself and who requires a stage audience. If the metaphor 'costume' suggests something 'put on', then in modern theatricality we move from the hypocrite actor-language of a Jonson or Molière character, to the precarious camouflages of self-expression, when a person's identity is itself in question.

[77] Jung's term *persona* is, of course, itself a borrowing from the theatre: originally the mask worn by an actor. But in the new conception it illuminates in a very precise way what we find in so much externalised speech: 'The persona is the individual's system of adaptation to, or the manner he assumes in dealing with, the world. Every calling or profession, for example, has its own characteristic persona...One could say, with little exaggeration, that the persona is that which in reality one is not, but which oneself as well as others think one is.' C. G. Jung, *The Archetypes and the Collective Unconscious*, in *Collected Works*, London, 1963, vol. 9, Part 1, pp. 122ff. For the 'false self' see R. D. Laing, *The Divided Self* (1959), Harmondsworth, 1965. Lionel Trilling, *The Opposing Self*, London, 1955, makes use of a related idea intermittently, best seen in the Preface and in the contrast between Keats and Kafka in their sense of identity (pp. 38ff).

[78] See Kenneth Burke, *A Grammar of Motives and A Rhetoric of Motives* (1945 and 1950), New York, 1962, pp. 594ff and 650.

[79] Eliot discusses such a development in rhetoric from Kyd to Shakespeare in '"Rhetoric" and Poetic Drama', *Selected Essays*, pp. 37–42 (quoted from p. 39). Cf. also Ch. 2, n. 2, and Ch. 5, pp. 204ff.

Verbal theatricality may exploit the most public elements in the language, the resounding clichés, the famous speeches, the known quotations and styles – in short, the stereotyped voices of man. At its most conscious it becomes a parasitical language, living on an old style which is made new through such devices as ironic counterpoint, parody, and pastiche.

It is partly the conscious use of a language in quotation marks that makes verbal theatricality another *critical* language. When Shelley wrote pastiche-Jacobean for *The Cenci*, 'with Lamb's *Specimens of the Dramatist* at his elbow', he was not writing a language in quotation marks, merely borrowing. Such a procedure could not solve Shelley's problem of dramatic language: he could neither use his own poetic voice, nor accomplish what he proposed in the Preface: 'in order to move men to true sympathy we must use the familiar language of men', thus doing for his age what the old English poets did for theirs.[80]

The degree of conscious control in using an old language is an essential issue, which will exercise us repeatedly – it is, for example, a key point in the discussion on Shaw's use of rhetorical expressiveness through parody and pastiche. When Eliot introduced contemporary political jargon into the Knights' speech in *Murder in the Cathedral* – leaning out of the play – he knew exactly what he was doing: fusing the method of direct parody (borrowed from Shaw) and the modernist technique of a montage of styles. Much of contemporary theatricality amounts to parodistic montage – not necessarily satirical or 'debunking' – but critically conscious: a play with or on received languages. But it is Joyce rather than Eliot whom one might consider the indirect master of modern theatricality: the delighted sampling of languages from the museum, the serious parody unhampered by one-sided ideological commitment. A playful relativist attitude to all styles may be inseparable from verbal theatricality. For instance, in *Rosencrantz and Guildenstern are Dead* – the most self-consistent contemporary example – there is a double parody: the new frame around the passages from *Hamlet* and the mannered

[80] *The Complete Poetical Works of Percy Bysshe Shelley*, Oxford, 1907, pp. 274–5. Cf. also George Steiner, *The Death of Tragedy*, London, 1961, pp. 147–50. But Dr Steiner holds that in *The Cenci* 'pastiche is carried to the level of art'. (The phrase about Lamb is Edmund Blunden's; Lamb's book was in fact *Specimens of English Dramatic Poets.*)

word-play that runs through the 'meta-play''s idiom: the speech of university wits who have read Beckett.[81]

An old style can be exploited in a new way rather as an old myth (the material, not so much the language) has been exploited: the House of Atreus untold times. It has often been said that only a limited number of myths are available for drama; it is probable that there are only a limited number of dramatic languages, and that we have heard most of them before. A new dramatic language is then a new combination of known styles. We have seen this happen in all the arts: in poetry (*The Waste Land*); in painting (Picasso's variations on Velazquez' 'Las Meninas'); in music (Stravinsky's Handel chords in *The Rake's Progress*); in film (Godard's *Une femme est une femme* with 'its loving pastiches of Hollywood musicals...a kind of exhibitionist demonstration that a film is a film is a film').[82] Yet it has taken a long time for the theatre to be recognised as a living museum of speech where – in Malraux' sense of the imaginary museum – dialogue itself becomes increasingly a dialogue between this or that language. Once this is recognised, we respond to the overtones and resonances of a theatrical language as we respond, in music, to 'the jazzy rhythm, the folksy tune, the march, the hymn, the minuet; they all evoke clusters of cultural resonances which we do not have to have explained'.[83] For in our culture, language is backward-looking and the bearer of long memories; certain words, phrases, and rhythms are charged with resonances which, in the theatre, can be distinctly heard.

The ultimate aim of the dramatist who makes use of a 'stock' language – theatrical rhetoric, or the English ballad, for example – is to remake that language in a new context in such a way that the traditional and modern resonances are heard in counterpoint. In other words the dramatist aims at re-creation out of a fusion of old and new elements (somewhat in the manner of Lévi-Strauss' *bricoleur*).[84] The potential choice – the ways in

81 Cf. my study of this play in *Modern Drama* (Feb. 1969), pp. 439–42.

82 Penelope Houston, *The Contemporary Cinema*, Harmondsworth, 1963, p. 104.

83 E. H. Gombrich, *In Search of Cultural History*, Oxford, 1969, pp. 44–5.

84 'The creations of the *bricoleur*' (or do-it-yourself man) 'always really consist of a new arrangement of elements'...like the creations of mythical thought. Claude Lévi-Strauss, *The Savage Mind* (1962), London, 1966, pp. 16–33 (quoted from p. 21).

which languages can be combined – is very great. And the method of revitalising the language of drama through the use of this or that stock language seems to free the dramatist from the burden of having to 'invent' a language; it seems the chief alternative to re-creating a limited language from within, through methods that intensify and subtilise. Yet there is a risk of imitating or echoing a former style too externally, of merely using 'the stock of expressions of feeling accumulated'[85] in a language of the surface. When the purpose of playing is to hold, as 'twere, the mirror up to the theatre, there is a risk that it will chiefly show the very age and body of the time its love of mirrors.

8

Value judgements on the opposed dramatic languages just outlined must await supporting practical criticism of texts. Yet one cannot contemplate the polarisation of language in drama without becoming aware that such a development is making it increasingly difficult for a dramatist to create, within one play, a language that is both inward and public, 'sacred' and 'profane', participatory and spectatorial.

At the beginning of the Christian era the gospel narrative spontaneously created a dialogue which, as Erich Auerbach argued,[86] is both personal and communal, everyday and for all time – less stylised than anything in classical literature, including the dialogue (stichomythia) of Greek tragedy. Peter's betrayal is re-created from within by turning *direct speech*, for the first time in literature, into the living dialogue of a dramatic moment. The power of the Peter story manifests itself through 'the gestures and words of inwardly moved persons', without any conscious

[85] Eliot's phrase, when distinguishing the poetry of *surface* from the *essential* poetry in the essay on Ford, *Selected Essays*, pp. 203–4. The essential poetry appears to be defined there as 'the pattern, or we may say the undertone, of the personal emotion, the personal drama and struggle' and as a profound purpose whose absence makes drama tend towards mere sensationalism.

[86] Erich Auerbach, *Mimesis, Dargestellte Wirklichkeit in der Abendländischen Literatur*, Bern, 1946, II, pp. 45–55. My précis is based on pp. 52–3; the brief quotation is taken from p. 53 (*erscheint...sich in den Gesten und Worten der innerlich bewegten Menschen offenbart*). English transl. by W. R. Trask, Princeton, 1968, pp. 40–9.

attempt at imitation or art. One can accept the uniqueness of the gospel occasion, and still feel that in the dialogue of great drama similar occasions occur – approximating an absolute authenticity of utterance, re-created from within a seemingly local event which is yet made significant, through gestures and words, as a universal experience. It is an ideal conjunction which we can find hardly anywhere in the specialised languages of modern drama.

The limitations of rationalised or forensic theatricality are almost caricatured in Shaw's complaint that the gospel narrative is keenly disappointing because, in effect, there is so little dialogue or debate in it: 'on the stage the dumb figure' of Jesus cannot be accepted; 'it is to him that we look for a speech that will take us up to heaven'.[87] And Shaw proceeds to eke out the deficiencies of the meeting between Jesus and Pilate as recorded, by offering us a cadenced eight-page disputation. An extreme example perhaps. But, from one point of view or another, various dramatic languages in our time have the mark of a strained inventedness about them; the language of a play can become so specialised that it functions for one play only.

It is possible for a dramatist to react against all 'invented' languages, and seek authenticity in a 'given' language, in words taken from testimonies or all kinds of source material, from newspapers and memoirs. It is a search for a 'central core of evidence' in words actually spoken, at a precise point in time, by some men for all men. A 'documented' language is then used much more exclusively than it is in the old conventions of historical drama. Peter Weiss' *The Investigation* (*Die Ermittlung*, 1965), for example, makes use of trial records in a new way (the difference in kind and degree can be measured in comparison with Shaw's *Saint Joan* or Miller's *The Crucible*). The whole play is a selection and arrangement of what was spoken by nine witnesses and eighteen defendants (nameless in the play) at the Auschwitz trial at Frankfurt; the formal division of the work into eleven cantos, and the breaking up of the speeches into verse-like lines is unobtrusive when heard (though on the printed page the prose–verse draws attention to itself in places as a dubious literary device). Essentially one of the extreme limits

[87] Preface to *On the Rocks*, in *Too True to be Good* (etc.), Standard ed. pp. 176ff.

of human experience comes across in a language so 'transparent' that it takes us straight into the event witnessed:

Judge: Could you see anything through the hatches in the door
Witness 7: The people pushed against the door
and climbed up the columns
Then came the suffocation
as the gas was thrown in[88]

There is a different kind of authenticity in the robust theatrical collage *Oh What a Lovely War* (1963). Within the framework of a pierrot show – the popular theatre of the past – the play represents episodes from the First World War through songs, slogans, documents-as-cartoon, speeches quoted and parodied. (One local effect 'frames' a letter from Shaw read out from a pacifist platform by Mrs Pankhurst, so that Shaw's eloquent alliterative nouns acquire a certain air of literary impotence.[89])

Such plays are unlikely to solve the problems of dramatic language for many writers; and they raise difficult further questions about 'authenticity' as a value. The intention here is merely to point to such possibilities of using a 'given' language in the attempt to regain some primary meaning for drama: a language that directs attention away from itself to the centre of a communal experience. As in the dialogue which embodies the verbal core of Peter's betrayal, our attention (even the attention of the most language-conscious reader or listener) is redirected to the signified event, and held there. Then verbal analysis and the problems of expressiveness are seen in perspective; every attempt to focus on language is concerned, as is the dramatist, with a search for significance.

88 Peter Weiss, *The Investigation* (English version by Alexander Gross), London, 1966, p. 190. I take the phrase 'central core of evidence' from Peter Weiss' Remarks, *ibid.* p. 10.

89 *Oh What a Lovely War* by Theatre Workshop, Charles Chilton and the members of the original cast, London, 1965, Act II, p. 68.

1: Shaw

Construction, he owned with engaging modesty, was not his strong point, but his dialogue was incomparable.
(Shaw to William Archer, before he started writing plays. *Prefaces*, p. 699)

Now it is quite true that my plays are all talk, just as Raphael's pictures are all paint, Michael Angelo's statues all marble, Beethoven's symphonies all noise.
(Shaw in the year of his death. *Shaw on Theatre*, p. 290)

There are other reasons than mere prominence for making Shaw the starting point in this study. There is the simple level of interest that precedes close questioning, Shaw as a representative type, the word-intoxicated dramatist who made language – high-toned, seemingly verbose, always explicit – the pivot of dramatic action. Even this simple level of interest is at once cut through by the ironic knowledge that the emphasis on 'talk' as action – which seemed to Shaw a revolutionary innovation – may seem to us to yield a more backward-looking dramatic language than the economy of classical naturalism (Ibsen's structured minimum speech, Chekhov's orchestrated fragments); and the hyper-articulateness of Shaw has a distinctly pre-modern feel about it when set against the dominant modes of twentieth-century drama. Merely to name the century is to be reminded of one of the most conspicuous of Shaw's personae: the would-be dispenser of Twentieth Century Treatises, like the celebrated Mrs Clandon's household works in *You Never Can Tell*. Yet the energy put into dramatising what were intended to be 'Twentieth Century Creeds' left him, as a dramatist, essentially parasitical on certain worn-out nineteenth-century conventions (romance, melodrama, farce) both in the structure and in the language of his plays.[1]

The tensions in Shaw's work are more interesting than the

[1] This is conclusively shown in Martin Meisel, *Shaw and the Nineteenth-Century Theater*, Princeton, 1963.

failures, even where these are seen and redefined. At the same time, new knowledge about Shaw's theatre as a whole as well as a certain hindsight make us ask new questions about him. Was Shaw's ceaseless search for new expressiveness – to embody a genuinely changing vision – checked, above all, by an inability to evolve a new dramatic language? Was the famed 'evolutionary appetite' blunted by language – something more conservative than either ideas or dramatic form? Or may his theatrical eclecticism – the shifts of style within particular plays as well as the arc of development in his whole work – now be seen as a valid alternative to stylistic possibilities Shaw found uncongenial? An alternative to the mechanical language of the 'well-made play' and the *mere* comedy of manners; to the inward language of 'art-drama'; and to the disciplines and limitations of naturalism. And if this is so, what prevented Shaw from developing a more radically stylised dramatic language – as Brecht did after him – for his ambitious parables of the theatre?

Further, Shaw's tendency to play parodistic variations on inherited styles may today throw light on a question we keep asking throughout this study: how does the literature of the past affect dramatic language? Shaw made constant use of what may be called the 'imaginary museum' of speech, but in a 'naive' (critically half-conscious) and improvisatory fashion. Witness the way Shaw tended to compile impressive-sounding but not quite authentic artistic pedigrees for himself as a dramatist, culminating in the all-purpose genealogy with which he looked back on his work at the end of his life:

> The truth was that I was going back atavistically to Aristotle, to the tribune stage, to the circus, to the word-music of Shakespeare, to the forms of my idol Mozart, and to the stage business of the great players I had actually seen acting...I was, and still am, the most old-fashioned playwright outside China and Japan.[2]

The 'atavistic' going back may now be seen as a strategy, even if half-improvised, for extending the resources of his verbal theatricality: drawing in 'voices' beyond the range of both everyday language and a more 'univocal' style.

We may also see more clearly now the tension between

[2] (Reprinted from *New Statesman and Nation*, 6 May 1950.) *Shaw on Theatre* (ed. E. J. West), London, 1958, p. 294.

naturalism and rhetorical expressiveness which runs through Shaw's entire work. One need only recall, in advance of detailed discussion, that Shaw once saw himself as an 'Ibsenite' while, in so far as he took note of Ibsen's language at all, he found the text too limited or inexplicit (complaining that 'what he [Ibsen] hasn't said he hasn't said'). On the only occasion when Shaw wrote expressly to offer advice on the subject of dramatic dialogue, he pointed to some indefinable method – which eluded Henry James in the theatre – whereby literary language was made *audibly* intelligible:

> It [audible intelligibility] is not missed through long words or literary mannerisms or artificiality of style, nor secured by simplicity. Most of the dialogues that have proved effective on the English stage have been written either in the style of Shakespeare, which is often Euphuistic in its artificiality, or in that of Dr Johnson, which is, as Goldsmith said, a style natural only in a whale. Ben Jonson's *Volpone* is detestably unreadable; yet when spoken on the stage it is a model of vivid dialogue...Speech does not differ from literature in its materials. 'This my hand will rather the multitudinous seas incarnadine' is such a polysyllabic monstrosity as was never spoken anywhere but on the stage; but it is magnificently effective and perfectly intelligible in the theatre. James could have paraphrased it charmingly in words of one syllable and left the audience drearily wondering what on earth Macbeth was saying.[3]

In this letter, as so often in the 'composition' of a dialogue sequence, Shaw is concerned with the human voice as an instrument for which the dramatist must write a score; it is a quasi-operatic approach. The other essential feature of his verbal theatricality is an awareness of man as a language animal, bravura speech-maker, fantasist, mock-poet and so on. In this awareness we now perceive an affinity between Shaw and certain contemporary dramatists. And we are probably better tuned in than we used to be to hear in Shaw's dialogue the parody of articulate verbalisation itself, the comic-pathetic inadequacy of words in their abundance. At all events, the development of drama, our understanding of language, and critical scholarship have combined to enable us to respond to Shaw's dialogue with greater understanding.

[3] *Ibid.* pp. 165–6 (*The Times Literary Supplement*, 17 May 1923).

Ambiguities of 'style'

Shaw never quite made up his mind whether what he called 'art' was an essential element in drama or merely a by-product of having something urgent to say. A tension – not simple contradiction – runs through his theorising, as it does through his whole creative work. Right at the beginning he proclaimed *Widowers' Houses* as 'a propagandist play – a didactic play – a play with a purpose', yet he simultaneously insisted that the play should be judged 'not as a pamphlet in dialogue, but as in intention a work of art as much as any comedy of Molière's is a work of art'.[4] And this insistence was accompanied by a kind of lament on the way all the vulgarities of the age ('the people do not speak nobly', among other things) combined against 'beauty' and 'art'. A little later, in his most sustained defence of the 'problem play', he argues with overtones of regret that the age has forced 'poets...to turn the theatre into a platform for propaganda and an arena for discussion'; and he looks foward to a more orderly civilisation where writers 'will not need to spend their energies in trying to teach elementary political economy'; or devising 'object lessons' – like Ibsen – instead of writing 'great and enduring dramatic poems'.[5] Again, dramatising his own critical tension between 'art' and 'didacticism', he offers a double justification of *Arms and the Man*: the play uses the method of Cervantes (burlesque); but for good measure Shaw proceeds to publish the documentary 'verification' for his exposition of soldiering. Quotes from the memoirs of generals are used to 'underwrite' the dialogue.[6]

By the turn of the century Shaw had begun to advertise himself as an 'artist-philosopher', as if the hyphen could resolve his art/anti-art dilemma. A careful rereading of his seemingly robust early statements on drama and on 'style' reveals precarious ambiguities, relevant to Shaw's attitude to dramatic language. For example, in the well-known 'Better than Shakespear?' sequence[7] Shaw underpins one of his key arguments – 'It is

4 Preface to *Widowers' Houses* (1893), Independent Theatre series, *The Complete Prefaces*, London, 1965, pp. 702–3.

5 'The Problem Play – A Symposium' (1895), *Shaw on Theatre*, pp. 58–66.

6 'A Dramatic Realist to his Critics' (1894), *ibid.* pp. 18–41.

7 Preface to *Three Plays for Puritans* (1900), concluding section (my italics).

the philosophy, the outlook on life, that changes, not the craft of the playwright' – by claiming, for himself, that it is a new vision that has seemingly made new the otherwise old elements in his drama. All his powers

'availed me not until I saw *the old facts in a new light*. Technically, I do not find myself able to proceed otherwise than as former playwrights have done. True, my plays have the latest mechanical improvements: *the action is not carried on by impossible soliloquies and asides...*'

But Shaw claims that 'my attempt to substitute the new vision, natural history for conventional ethics and romantic logic may so *transfigure* the eternal stage puppets' that even the older playgoer cannot recognise how old, or old-fashioned, the plays are. Even so, Shaw predicts that the time will soon come when:

my twentieth century characteristics will pass unnoticed as a matter of course, whilst *the eighteenth century artificiality* that marks the work of every literary Irishman of my generation will seem antiquated and silly...What the world calls originality is merely an unaccustomed method of tickling it.

Such disarming modesty does not altogether compensate for Shaw's failure to make clear, to himself and concerning his own drama, how seeing the *old facts in a new light* relates to his own attempts at using *an old style in a new frame* (starting with the ten plays written before this Preface). Yet, this is one of the crucial questions – the attitude to 'style' – bearing on the language of his more ambitious later plays, as will be seen. At this stage, Shaw seems satisfied with the notion that the new idea/outlook will, for a time, 'transfigure' a play. A play may then be provisional, perhaps an example of *Gebrauchskunst*: when the new 'outlook' is absorbed, it leaves behind only...'artificiality'. And drawing attention to 'the eighteenth century artificiality' in his work, just after having claimed a superficial naturalism (no soliloquies and asides) goes with a still casual, almost haphazard, doubleness in the language of the plays.

The central ambiguity of Shaw's thinking about 'style' can be read between the lines of the 'Epistle Dedicatory' to *Man and Superman* (1903), one of the high points of Shaw's own 'creative evolution' as a dramatist. At first sight, the following passage looks anything but ambiguous: a manifesto against 'aestheticism', a defence of didactic drama, seen by Shaw as being in direct line of succession from *Everyman* and Bunyan:

[But] for art's sake alone I would not face the toil of writing a single sentence. I know that there are men who, having nothing to say and nothing to write, are nevertheless so in love with oratory and with literature that they delight in repeating as much as they can understand of what others have said or written aforetime. I know that the leisurely tricks which their want of conviction leaves them free to play with the diluted and misapprehended message supply them with a pleasant parlor game which they call style. I can pity their dotage and even sympathise with their fancy. But a true original style is never achieved for its own sake: ...*effectiveness of assertion is the Alpha and Omega of style.* He who has nothing to assert has no style and can have none: *he who has something to assert will go as far in power of style as its momentousness and his conviction will carry him. Disprove its assertion after it is made, yet its style remains.* Darwin has no more destroyed the style of Job nor of Handel than Martin Luther destroyed the style of Giotto. All the assertions get disproved sooner or later; and so we find the world still full of *magnificent débris of artistic fossils, with the matter-of-fact credibility gone clean out of them, but the form still splendid.*[8]

There are a number of points to note here. First of all, there are the overtones of feeling that work against the conscious message about 'conviction': that almost Gautier-like creed, 'Disprove (its) assertion after it is made, yet (its) style remains'; that nostalgic rhetoric on the art of the past: 'magnificent débris of artistic fossils'...'the form still splendid'. One begins to get the feel of art/anti-art tension in Shaw: the probable origin of his ambivalent attitudes to the 'poet' and the 'artist' as reflected in those flawed characterisations – Marchbanks and Dubedat in particular – where divided sympathy leads to uncontrolled pastiche. And one understands the 'Platonic' urge behind the Ancients' contempt for art in *Back to Methuselah* V (where 'works of art' are in effect equated with the Automata that speak like stage-figures). Shaw's dialectical love–hate relationship with 'art' – coloured by his early personal link with the Pre-Raphaelites[9]

8 *Man and Superman*, Penguin ed. p. xxxvii; Standard ed. pp. xxxiv–xxxv (my italics).

9 *Candida* (1894) is the key play for Shaw's ambivalent attempt to 'distil the quintessential drama from Pre-Raphaelitism' (Preface to *Plays Pleasant*, fourth paragraph), and *John Bull's Other Island* (1904)

and his conflict with aestheticism – affects his whole approach to drama; and, in his language, creates a recurrent need to poetise and/or parody 'poetical' voices.

There is, further, a revealing contradiction in Shaw's talk of 'magnificent...fossils'. The idea of 'form' emptied, in the course of time, of 'meaning' itself reveals a risky antinomy. And we may associate 'fossils' with dead exhibits in the imaginary museum. Can the dramatist, we may ask, make creative use of such fossils – like the 'style of Job' – after Darwin? Presumably not, for (in the passage that immediately follows the one quoted) Shaw attacks academic art and the 'academic copier of fossils': his villain is the 'man of letters' who 'thinks he can get Bunyan's or Shakespeare's style without Bunyan's conviction or Shakespeare's apprehension'. Later we shall see what happens when Shaw himself makes use of one of these fossil-styles – for example Bunyan's prose – in *Major Barbara* (cf. pp. 69ff.). Here we note again the failure to think out, at a crucial stage in his development, the inward relation between 'conviction' and 'style'; and between the old style in the imaginary museum, and its possible uses for the dramatist. And, as far as one can see, this particular lack of clarity affected all his work.

But that is not all. Shaw's idea of 'conviction' works against his real needs as a dramatist, particularly as a dramatist who, at his best, finds the stuff of his dialogue in the dialectic of opposed

dramatises a conflict with 'the spirit of the neo-Gaelic movement' which Shaw considered 'only a quaint little offshoot of English Pre-Raphaelitism'. (Preface to this play, Standard ed. pp. 13 and 41.) See also:

(*a*) Elsie B. Adams, 'Bernard Shaw's Pre-Raphaelite Drama', *P.M.L.A.*, LXXX (1966), pp. 428–38 – excellently documented (stressing Shaw's debt to the anti-academic, 'back to nature', and religious–didactic aspects of Pre-Raphaelite art) but far-fetched in regarding all the 'Life-Force' plays – from *Man and Superman* to *Saint Joan* – as 'Pre-Raphaelite drama'.

(*b*) M. J. Sidnell, 'John Bull's Other Island – Yeats and Shaw', *Modern Drama* (Dec. 1968), on the celebrated clash of positions between Shaw and Yeats (and the Abbey Theatre) over this play.

The language of *John Bull's Other Island* in itself points, I think, to the aesthetic distance between Shaw and Yeats. The play sets up an ironic counterpoint of many voices – a clash of styles centred on Shaw's dialectic of England/Ireland, 'efficiency'/'dream' – as opposed to an inwardly conceived and univocal language.

attitudes: in the ironic collision of ideas as voices rather than in any one 'conviction'. Shaw's theatricality requires what can only be called a multiple standpoint – as can be seen in the ideological self-parody of John Tanner, Revolutionary; in the interplay between the voices of 'reality' and 'fantasy' in *Heartbreak House*; and in the many-angled historicism – leading to a collage of styles – in *Saint Joan*. In his study of Shaw's *non-dramatic* prose Richard M. Ohmann recognised a stubborn tendency to be 'inhospitable toward conceptual ambiguity';[10] when 'conviction' enters drama in this sense – as a one-pointed rhetorical stance – it is inhospitable towards a genuinely 'dialectical' dialogue.

The creative power attributed by Shaw to 'conviction' also calls for comment. 'He who has something to assert will go as far in power of style as its momentousness and conviction will carry him.' To say that 'conviction' will 'carry' a writer into power of style suggests a quasi-organic view: as if the language were moulded from within, by the pressure of thought (as it may be in much modern poetry, but not in the rhetorical convention which tends to 'clothe' thoughts in suitable words).

A critic who has given particular attention to Shaw's aesthetic assumptions throws light on the peculiarity of Shaw's 'organic' ideas:

> Shaw is hard to place in the literary tradition partly because his idea of literary form is pre-romantic while his idea of literary value is post-romantic; 'poetry' was decoration, 'prose' was organic. He might think of poetry somewhat as did Johnson, but 'organic form' was as important a critical principle to him as it is to Sir Herbert Read. Shaw absorbed this idea through biological rather than literary interests – from Butler rather than Coleridge...[11]

10 *Shaw: the Style and the Man*, Middletown, Conn., 1963, p. 81. Ohmann's own one-phrase summary of points made in Ch. 1.

11 Bruce R. Park, 'A Mote in the Critic's Eye: Bernard Shaw and Comedy', *Texas Studies*, XXXVII (1958), reprinted in *G. B. Shaw, A Collection of Critical Essays* (ed. R. J. Kaufmann), N.J., 1965 (quote from pp. 49–50). This essay is also illuminating on the distinction between one-dimensional, discursive, synonym-accumulating language (Shaw's), and the modernist exploitation of language in *depth*. Park concludes that certain critical approaches – e.g. those applied to poetry by 'the most influential of our serious modern critics' – are inappropriate to Shaw's comic theatre.

and among the quotations given in support of this view is what Cashel Byron says of the musician: 'Every man has to grow his own style out of himself.' It is certain that Shaw wanted his dramatic language to be *carried* into 'power of style'; and he did at times allow his speech-rhapsodies to be *carried* by a Shelley-like afflatus. With this goes a tendency to exult over his spontaneity in writing plays, what he called 'hallucination':

> I find myself possessed of a theme in the following manner. I am pushed by a natural need to set to work to write down the conversations that come into my head unaccountably. At first I hardly know the speakers, and cannot find names for them.[12]

It is possible to see both the value and the risk of such a 'romantic principle' of play-writing: it is, on the one hand, part of Shaw's revolt against the mechanical construction and language of the well-made play; but it can also go with lack of stylistic control, as in the indulgent or even capricious transitions in the later plays. It is as if fertility and a relative critical un-selfconsciousness were inseparable in Shaw's work; from this point of view he is, in Schiller's sense again, a 'naive' dramatist.

We have said that the art/anti-art tension in Shaw's attitude to style was strongly coloured by his ambivalent recoil from 'art for art's sake'. In this respect his stance resembles Brecht's later attack on art-literature (for example on Stefan George and 'all those quiet, refined and dreamy men') and on the drama of empathy and feeling.[13] For Shaw even the didactic urge was only part of a larger urge to create a drama with an extended range of reference, with a fast-moving dialogue taking in a wide range of themes and tones. The idea of a *static* – or an inward and univocal – drama was the exact antithesis of what Shaw wanted from the theatre. When Yeats objected to Shaw's 'inorganic, logical straightness' – to which he opposed the 'crooked road of life' – he really defined a central antithesis in drama, one to which we shall keep returning. What matters here is that

12 'On the Principles that Govern the Dramatist', Letter to *The New York Times*, 2 June 1912, reprinted in *Shaw on Theatre*, pp. 116ff. Cf. also pp. 50 and 75 (with n. 68) in this chapter.

13 Marianne Kesting, *Bertolt Brecht*, Hamburg, 1959, p. 39 (my translation) and Ronald Gray, *Brecht*, Edinburgh and London, 1961, pp. 60–3.

Shaw in his characteristic insistence that 'static sensation' was insignificant, that only 'sensations of irresistible movement to an all-important end'[14] merited artistic expression, was really opting for a language of arrow-like movement in a willed direction. (The exact opposite of Zeno's arrow, or still-motion, which could be taken as the figure of Beckett's language.) And Shaw's Faustian, continuously forward-thrusting, linear language did not really change – as will be seen – despite his attraction to seemingly different aesthetic ideas. In *In Good King Charles's Golden Days* (pp. 78ff.) the artist (Kneller) proclaims that 'the line of beauty is a curve' against the straight lines of Newton's space and time. But – even if the artist is thus shown to be as advanced as Einstein's idea of a curved universe – the Shavian line of rhetoric remains straight. As will be seen, the language of Shaw's late plays was not remoulded – had no 'curve' in its syntax or rhythm – even under the pressure of inter-war disillusionment and questioning.

The theatre as temple, and word-music

Shaw had something like his own religion of art. We cannot study his dramatic language without taking into account his committed view of the theatre as a 'temple' and his serio-comic exploitation of music *in* words. One might expect both the ritualistic and the operatic elements in his drama to work as much against linear stage rhetoric as they work against naturalistic talk. For the approximation of language to music can be – like gesture, mime and silence – a way of transcending 'normal' speech, an attempt to pass beyond the translatable verbal notation. But then in Shaw's temple the sermon is more important than any liturgy; and what he understood by word-music is, in essentials, the opposite of the Symbolist idea of 'musicalising' language – it is to import the energies of the aria and vocal ensemble into rhetoric.[15]

14 These quotations are taken from Shaw's relatively late attack on the 'aesthetes' – in the person of Clive Bell – in the *New Republic*, XXIX (22 Feb. 1922). Quoted from *Shaw on Theatre*, pp. 151–2. See also Shaw and word-music, particularly p. 51 below. (For Yeats quotation see n. 22.)

15 We may note this curious retrospective statement: 'I have never aimed at style in my life: style is a sort of melody that comes into my sentences by itself. If a writer says what he has to say as accurately

One's first reaction to Shaw's Wagnerian aspirations to drama as ritual is to take them with a large pinch of salt. One tends to assume that all that Shaw had in mind in talking of the theatre as a temple was to make use of the pulpit: bringing people to 'conviction of sin', as he said in the preface to *Man and Superman*. Yet some of Shaw's statements imply much more: for instance when he claims – in the introduction to his collected dramatic criticism for the *Saturday Review* – that the theatre 'is as important as the Church was in the Middle Ages and much more important than the Church was in London in the years under review. A theatre to me is a place "Where two or three are gathered together"'.[16] And again: 'The theatre is really the week-day church; and a good play is essentially identical with a church service as combination of artistic ritual, profession of faith and sermon.'[17]

The Wagnerian note – both the religion-substitute and the craving for *Gesamtkunstwerk* – seems to be present in such a view of the theatre; and if a 'profession of faith' were synonymous with created work Shaw's theatre would have to be placed somewhere near Bayreuth if not the Festival of Dionysus. Indeed, J. Percy Smith, in dissenting from Francis Fergusson's confinement of Shaw to the drawing room and clearly with the above passages in mind, declares:

> the performance in the theatre is the celebration in miniature of the mysterious working of the Life Force, in which the spectators participate as surely as the actors. In a word, it is ritual. If for Shakespeare all the world is a stage, for Shaw the stage is all the cosmos.[18]

While this is overstating the case, we should at least recognise 'ritual drama' as a potential direction in Shaw when we examine relevant scenes in the plays, for example the irruption of the

and as effectively as he can, his style will take care of itself, if he has a style. But I did set up one condition in my early days. *I resolved that I would write nothing that would not be intelligible to a foreigner with a dictionary, like the French of Voltaire; and I therefore avoided idiom.* (Later on I came to seek idiom as being the most highly vitalized form of language...)' From the Preface to *Immaturity* (1921), *Prefaces*, p. 677 (my italics).

16 *Our Theatres in the Nineties*, vol. 1, 'The Author's Apology', p. vi.

17 *Ibid.* vol. 1, p. 264.

18 J. P. Smith, *The Unrepentant Pilgrim*, London, 1966, p. 203.

chorus from *The Bacchae* in the second act of *Major Barbara*, the 'mystic' voices in *Saint Joan* and the strains of *Back to Methuselah* conceived on the analogy of Wagner's *Ring* cycle.

The direct effect of operatic modes of composition on Shaw's dialogue – the debt to Mozart, Verdi and *opera buffa*, more persistent in the end than the Wagnerian aspirations – is very well-documented.[19] From *Mrs Warren's Profession* to *The Apple Cart* we are repeatedly aware of scoring for voices, the distribution of dramatic lines according to voice quality; and the operatic climaxes probably represent the most immediately recognisable non-naturalistic elements in Shaw's plays. It is almost certainly what the ordinary playgoer has in mind when he says, about Shaw's characters, 'they talk so artificially'. But before looking at the specific effect of Shaw's operatic dialogue, let us briefly state a general critical point.

The best solution for a dramatist who wishes to combine music and drama in serious comedy appears to be the radical one: unity of form like Aristophanes' *The Birds* or Brecht's *Threepenny Opera*, where speech and song are an integral part of the comic-satiric design and yet distinct. (This is to assume that the Musical – a form Shaw spurned while alive and posthumously served as an unwitting librettist – is not adequate for serious comedy.) Such stylisation – or open theatricality – frees the dramatist from the constraint of having to *hide* 'beneath his superficially colloquial and "natural" dialogue the grandiose and declamatory elements he acquired from Rossini and Verdi, as well as from Shakespeare'.[20] But Shaw could not be as radical as Brecht in this respect, partly because he saw himself as a conscious opponent of the various Victorian mixtures of speech and song, particularly the operatic element in melodrama, or melo-drama. So, instead of exploiting a whole range of theatrical possibilities – song, for example, or deliberate rather than half-naturalistic recitation – Shaw tended to resort to what he himself called 'word music'.

19 Meisel, *op. cit.* Ch. 2, is particularly valuable. See also: 'Opera taught me to shape my plays into recitatives, arias, duets, trios, ensemble finales, and bravura pieces to display the technical accomplishments of the executants...' *Shaw on Theatre*, p. 294.

20 From a running commentary on William Irvine's *Universe of G.B.S.*, New York, 1949, p. 13. Quoted by Meisel, *op. cit.* p. 433.

Shaw's early desire to reject music-in-drama while consciously writing verbal music for his plays is the source of another tension in his dialogue. For Shaw tends to be carried away by what he wants to resist. He regards music in dramatic speech as dangerous enchantment (the fear of art as 'magic'), or a threat from the absurd; and yet 'music' is the chief source of rhetorical rhythm in Shaw, used to emphasise 'meaning' – as in the main speeches of such central characters as John Tanner/Don Juan, Undershaft and Barbara, and Joan, among others. This dualism of meaning/music, fact/absurdity runs through all his most ambitious plays. More precisely – and more harmfully – he is 'hampered by the certainty of becoming absurd if he does not make his musically arranged words mean something',[21] something explicit. Such tension is probably the clue to dialogue that sounds like a form of rationalised automatic writing: there is an abandon, an apparently irresistible flow of words, as in the early poetry of Shelley; and yet this excess of words is over-rationalised – speech after speech is added for emphasis. This is what happens in the supposedly Mozartian speech arias in *Don Juan in Hell*, where Shaw is most consciously exploiting his first-hand knowledge of music. The word-music has become a word-flood. It is as if Shaw piled word upon explanatory word into that dangerous solution 'music', so as to oversaturate it with 'meaning'.

[21] This early (1894) statement is typical: 'The fact is, there is a great deal of feeling, highly poetic and dramatic, which cannot be expressed by mere words – because words are the counters of thinking, not of feeling – but which can be supremely expressed by music. The poet tries to make words serve his purpose by arranging them musically, but is *hampered by the certainty of becoming absurd if he does not make his musically arranged words mean something to the intellect as well as to the feeling.*

For example, the unfortunate Shakespeare could not make Juliet say:

O Romeo, Romeo, Romeo, Romeo, Romeo;

and so on for twenty lines.' And then Shaw goes on to contrast the dramatist with the enviable tone poet who can make Tristan say nothing but 'Isolde' five or more times. Wagner may 'reduce the words to pure ejaculation' or 'substitute mere roulade vocalisation, or even balderdash for them, provided the music sustains the feeling which is the real subject of the drama'. *Music in London* (1890–4), III, pp. 133–4. Cf. Meisel, pp. 41–2. (My italics.)

As it happens, we have on record the judgements of two poets – each in his different way involved in poetry and music – saying apparently contradictory things about Shaw and music. Yeats, in his famous comment on Shaw as a 'sewing machine that clicked and shone', makes the stylistic character of this nightmare quite unmistakable; for Shaw, like his master Samuel Butler, has made the 'discovery that it is possible to write with great effect without music'.[22]

By contrast, W. H. Auden, a full generation later, considered Shaw's devotion to music as 'perhaps the clue to his work'; for Shaw's 'writing has an effect nearer to that of music than the work of any of the so-called pure writers'.[23] But Yeats and Auden are, in this context, opposed poles: for Yeats is one of the 'pure' writers for whom 'music' meant intimacy; while Auden recognised that word-music in Shaw was 'superabundance of energy'. And the latter, we may add, has the stamp of rational rhetoric even when a character like the Mayoress – alias the pythoness on the tripod – speaks, in a state of trance, words that seem to come to her out of music:

> We spent eternity together; and you ask me for a lifetime more. We possessed all the universe together; and you ask me to give you scanty wages as well. I have given you the greatest of all things; and you ask me to give you little things. I gave you your own soul: you ask me for my body as a plaything. Was it not enough? Was it not enough?[24]

It is this speech that Eric Bentley described as a musical climax – not a climax of plot – in the play.[25] Yet such 'music' has little inwardness; those symmetrical or antithetical personal pronouns are carried by a robustly demonstrative syntax.

Outside the plays, the ambivalence of Shaw's attitude to word-music (his term) can best be gauged from some of his statements, made over half a century, on Shakespeare's dramatic verse. From something like total hostility to 'Shakespeare's

[22] *Autobiographies*, London, 1955, p. 283. (Another quotation from the same passage, a comment on the first performance of *Arms and the Man*, is used in the art/anti-art discussion, p. 46.)

[23] W. H. Auden, 'The Fabian Figaro', *Commonweal* (23 Oct. 1942). Quoted by Eric Bentley, *Bernard Shaw*, London, 1950, p. 153.

[24] *Getting Married*, p. 338.

[25] Eric Bentley, *op. cit.* p. 155.

extraordinary artistic powers'[26] as unintelligent and amoral, Shaw moved in mid-career to an ironic defence of Shakespeare's 'orchestral passages' which were not to be considered obscure since 'there never was any wit or meaning in them...any more than there is wit or meaning in the clash of Wagner's cymbals or the gallop of his trombones in the Valkyries' ride'.[27] And then, towards the end of his life, he announced in effect that Shakespeare was one of his singing-masters: 'I was going back atavistically...to the word-music of Shakespeare' (see p. 39, n. 2). How, one may ask, has 'the word-music of Shakespeare' – for so long seen as external, decorative, enchantment, or else fustian – come to be seen as a model for the rhythms of Shaw's prose rhetoric? The answer must be that Shaw regarded Shakespeare's dramatic poetry (mistakenly) as just verse rhetoric, 'resonant with the thrills a master of language can produce by mere artistic sonority'; in short, 'orchestral verse',[28] an instance of the operatic mode in dialogue. It is probable that Shaw – who once claimed that he had 'never lost touch with the Jacobean language'[29] – thought of his own dramatic language as inviting comparison with Shakespeare. In *Shakes versus Shav*[30] – the puppet play he wrote at the end of his life – Shav pits against his antagonist's *King Lear* Captain Shotover's rhythmic chant from *Heartbreak House*, as proof of verbal mastery. This tournament in

26 *Shaw on Shakespeare* (ed. E. Wilson), London, 1962, p. 221 (reprinted from *Saturday Review*, 2 Jan. 1897). 'Shakespeare wrote for our theatre because, with extraordinary artistic powers, he understood nothing and believed nothing.'

27 *Shaw on Theatre*, p. 123 (reprinted from *Fortnightly Review*, Aug. 1919). (Cf. the ironic defence of Shakespeare's 'Echolalia' in 'The Sanity of Art', *Major Critical Essays*, p. 319.)

28 *Major Critical Essays*, pp. 140–1. (The immediate context refers to *Othello*.) In *The Dark Lady of the Sonnets*, Shakespeare is portrayed noting down musical phrases and 'cadences' from the guard and from the Queen. See also Shaw's attack on 'rhetoric and stage pathos' in *Antony and Cleopatra*, Preface to *Three Plays for Puritans*, Penguin ed. p. xxx; Standard ed. p. xxvii.

29 'The Dying Tongue of Great Elizabeth', *Saturday Review* (11 Feb. 1905); *Shaw on Theatre*, p. 100. But Shaw seems to admit that his real link is with the language of a later century: 'as an Irishman [I] have for my mother tongue an English two centuries earlier than twentieth century cockney'. (Cf. 'eighteenth century artificiality', quoted on p. 42.)

30 *Shakes versus Shav* (1949), reprinted in *Shaw on Shakespeare*, pp. 265–9.

words is only a skit. Yet we realise that the aspiration to word-music as an attribute of poetic power was a genuine aspiration in Shaw. And this aspiration went with operatically conceived shifts to heightened language; and with a recurrent indulgence in rhythmic speech-making – 'atavistic' rhythms. There is some irony in the conclusion of this playlet where the puppet Shav makes up a 'musical' speech from a cento of Shakespearian blank verse, to the reproach of the puppet Shakes: 'These words are mine, not thine.'

Shaw and naturalism

Shaw only gradually recognised his distance from naturalism in his attitude to dramatic language – explicitly only relatively late in his development. In 1927, he wrote:

> Neither have I ever been what you call a representationist or realist. I was always in the classic tradition, recognising that stage characters must be endowed by the author with a *conscious self-knowledge and power of expression*...and a freedom from inhibitions, which in real life would make them monsters of genius. It is the power to do this that differentiated me (or Shakespeare) from a gramophone and a camera. The representational part of the business is mere costume and scenery.[31]

Here Shaw comes near to claiming the kind of expressive power that Dryden had in mind when he stated that 'serious plays ought not to imitate conversation too nearly'. Though Shaw may have been the first dramatist to exploit the comic potentialities of a phonograph on stage, he certainly had less use for that invention than any of the great prose realists. Not that the latter reproduce conversation, but they write from and against the felt pressure of 'men speaking to men'. Despite differences, this is true of Ibsen and Chekhov; and Synge's eavesdropping or Pinter's 'ear for dialogue' does, at one level, mean storing in the mind speech fragments ready for patterning in dialogue.

[31] Letter to Alexander Bashky, *Shaw on Theatre*, p. 185 (written in 1923, published in *The New York Times*, 12 June 1927). (My italics.) Cf. historical characters 'endowed...with enough consciousness to enable them to explain their attitude to the twentieth century audience' – making them explicit, 'more intelligible than they would be in real life'. Preface to *Saint Joan* (1924), 'The Inevitable Flatteries of Tragedy' Penguin ed. p. 64.

Instead, Shaw carried in his mind a prodigious gallery of known rhetorical models ready to be drawn on for 'power of expression'. It is a process of heightening from without, essentially different from Pirandello's definition of *spoken action*: 'immediate expressions inseparable from action...words, expressions, phrases impossible to invent but born when the author has identified himself with his creature to the point of seeing it only as he sees himself'.

This takes us to the essential distinction between 'spoken action' and 'verbal theatricality', discussed in the Introduction.[32] The former goes with authentic self-expression under the pressure of action; the latter with 'endowing' a character 'with conscious self-knowledge', or costume-speech. At its simplest this takes the form of comic-didactic bravura speech for a 'ventriloquist' like Doolittle, in *Pygmalion*, Act II. Shaw first prepares a kind of rostrum for such a character, the stage directions announce that he has 'a remarkably expressive voice' and that he adopts a *pose* on entry. Next a link is established with superficial naturalism; Higgins savours one of Doolittle's early flourishes:

> This chap has a certain natural gift for rhetoric. Observe the rhythm of his native woodnotes wild. 'I'm willing to tell you: I'm wanting to tell you: I'm waiting to tell you.' Sentimental rhetoric! that's the Welsh strain in him.

Finally Doolittle is told the 'floor is yours', and the dialogue gives way to the dustman's tirades, including the well-known disquisition on middle class morality.[33] ('What am I governors both? I ask you what am I? I'm one of the underserving poor: that's what I am'). Here Shaw is exploiting, with the gay linguistic consciousness that fits in well with a comedy on the mechanics of speech,[34] the simple comic tension in 'natural...

32 Pp. 18–19 with n. 35; and p. 29.

33 Shaw himself compared Doolittle's disquisition on middle-class morality to Falstaff's discourse on honour. *Shaw on Theatre*, p. 132.

34 Shaw writes from the standpoint of a superior Higgins: Received Pronunciation versus eccentric dialects. Compare Higgins' disgust with the non-standard diphthongs in the alphabet (film version of *Pygmalion*, Harmondsworth, 1941, pp. 65–6) with Shaw himself wanting to shoot the teacher every time he hears the children chant 'Ay-ee, ba-yee' etc. instead of the standard sounds. (Preface to R. A. Wilson, *The Miraculous Birth of Language*, London, 1942, p. xxix.) Shaw's linguistic stance finds an easy outlet in parody,

rhetoric', vulgar eloquence. It does not wear well – it is too obvious – but it is certainly controlled. But in Shaw's more ambitious plays the pull of verbal theatricality against naturalism goes with a complex and often imperfectly controlled tension.

Shaw's inability to distinguish critically between naturalism (or 'natural history') as an ideology and naturalism as a style has, it seems, never been noted. It is widely recognised that in *The Quintessence of Ibsenism* Shaw misunderstood Ibsen; it is less well-known how difficult Shaw found it to understand his own art. The *Quintessence* – the first (1891) edition, that is – was, after all, intended to be nothing but a vigorous defence of the 'realist' *Weltanschauung*; there was no confusion there, only a conscious if mistaken omission of 'Ibsen the poet'. Similarly, whenever Shaw talks about the basis of the new drama as a new 'natural history'[35] the stress is, deliberately, on the message, not the medium. It is in the later writing, in the chapters added to the enlarged edition of *The Quintessence* in 1913, that we can discover how central – and once again how unresolved – is the tension between the 'naturalist' vision and the non-naturalistic language in Shaw. (The discussion of Ibsen's four last plays, with its sympathetic awareness of how Ibsen's art had changed, and its insight into the the death-in-life of the aged Ibsen 'like a child trying to learn again how to write', in itself demonstrates a characteristic duality in Shaw even in the years before the First World War: he writes of disturbed modes of being and language with the old robust symmetry.[36]) But it is the ten-page argument

most often using lower-class accents as *buffa* voices in operatic scoring – Burgess (*Candida*), 'Enry the polytechnician, and the revolutionary tramps in *Man and Superman*; the Irish peasants of *John Bull's Other Island*; Boanerges, the stupid trade unionist, in *The Apple Cart*, etc. The underlying linguistic ideology is perhaps best summed up by Shaw's desire to 'nationalise...the existing class monopoly of orthodox speech', in *Morning Leader* (16 Aug. 1901), reprinted in *The English Language*, vol. 2 (ed. W. F. Bolton and D. Crystal), Cambridge, 1969, pp. 80–5.

35 (1) Preface to *Plays Pleasant* (1898) – conclusion.

(2) Preface to *Three Plays for Puritans* – conclusion.

(3) Preface to *Three Plays by Brieux*, London, 1911, pp. xiiiff, where the context is scientific factuality against 'romance' and writing on hitherto tabooed subjects – including sex.

(4) Preface to *Heartbreak House* – conclusion. Cf. also p. 42 above.

36 Cf. my section on 'The Absurd and the Hyper-articulate' (pp. 75ff).

entitled 'The Technical Novelty of (Ibsen's) Plays' that tells us most about the tension we are concerned with. For it is here that Shaw singles out *discussion* – as first manifested in the final act of *Doll's House* – as the principal innovation of the post-Ibsen drama; and, in effect, he equates the drama of discussion with a minimum of the bad old theatricality (not just Scribe, but Othello's handkerchief and even the tragic *dénouements* of Ibsen[37]). Indeed, the play Shaw now most admires for its absence of forced stage action is *The Cherry Orchard*, written by a 'hand no less deadly than Ibsen's because more caressing'. No doubt Shaw was at this time feeling his way towards a new creative method – the *supposed* Chekhovian elements in *Heartbreak House* – and he can so far forget his own actual practice as to define the post-Ibsen drama as 'really the inevitable return to nature which ends all the merely technical fashions. Now the natural is mainly the everyday; and its climaxes are, if not everyday, at least everylife, if they are to have importance for the spectator.'[38]

But what kind of dialogue does Shaw envisage in this 'return to nature' in dramatic art? The answer is the use of 'what has been used by preachers and orators ever since speech has been invented...rhetoric, irony, argument, paradox, epigram, parable'. And as if to underline how final this answer is, the chapter ends with a resounding restatement of what is to be substituted for the 'old stage tricks': 'a forensic technique of recrimination, disillusion, and penetration through ideals to the truth, with a free use of all the rhetorical and lyrical arts of the orator, the preacher, the pleader, and the rhapsodist'.[39]

It is really the case that Shaw was, simultaneously, drawn to versimilitude and driven to all the known forms of eloquence in dialogue by a contrary impulse. The linguistic gap that separates 'the natural that is mainly the everyday' and 'the free use of all the rhetorical and lyrical arts' fairly epitomises the duality found in all the plays. That is why one finds a hesitancy under the seemingly robust critical statements; and we are enabled, as

37 In the Preface to *Three Plays by Brieux*, Shaw more than half agrees with Judge Brack's comment on Hedda's suicide: 'people don't do such things'. He prefers 'slices of life' as the material for the dramatist; and yet, he says, 'life as it occurs is senseless' (pp. xvii and xxvi).

38 *Major Critical Essays*, p. 139.

39 *Ibid*. p. 146.

if reading a code, to see how, whenever Shaw makes the attempt to come near to everyday speech, the dialogue is soon transposed into quite another key.

This is true even in those plays which are most nearly naturalistic in intention. Thus *Widowers' Houses*, the nearest thing in Shaw to the thesis-play, was, in Shaw's own words, 'distorted into a *grotesquely realistic* exposure of slum landlordism';[40] and to the stylistic incongruity Shaw himself noted in his apprentice work, we may add an early example of dialogue where theatricality repeatedly triumphs over Shaw's intention to expose reality and move the audience to 'conviction of sin'. Sartorius, for example, reels off this little litany of objects as he defends the view that his tenants are not fit to live in proper dwellings:

My young friend: these people do not know how to live in proper dwellings: they could wreck them in a week. You doubt me: try it for yourself. You are welcome to replace all the missing banisters, handrails, cistern lids and dusthole tops at your own expense; and you will find them missing again in less than three days: burnt, Sir, every stick of them. I do not blame the poor creatures: they need fires...(Act II, *Plays Unpleasant*, Penguin ed., 1946, p. 69).

A 'Dickensian' voice in a supposedly 'Ibsenite' play; yet in the first Preface Shaw explains – has to explain – that Sartorius is no Pecksniff but a typical citizen; and elsewhere he argues that 'the Dickens–Thackeray spirit is that of a Punch-and-Judy showman...in contrast to Ibsen's power to move through every character'.[41] If we turn to a sociological play with a markedly personal centre – *Mrs Warren's Profession* – we find that in such scenes as the confrontation between mother and daughter in the final act, the personal emotion is diluted by Shaw's preservation of melodramatic speech in a play written against melodrama. Mrs Warren – naturalistically portrayed as the high-class prostitute and conventional woman – speaks with the posed voice of 'the fallen woman' and 'the grief-stricken mother'.

40 Preface to *Plays Unpleasant* (1898), Penguin ed. (1946), pp. x–xi; Standard ed. pp. x–xi. Shaw goes on: 'The result was revoltingly *incongruous*...*The farcical trivialities* in which I followed the fashion of the times became silly and irritating beyond all endurance when intruded upon a subject of such *depth, reality, and force* as that into which I had plunged my drama.' (My italics.)

41 *Prefaces*, pp. 701–6; and *Major Critical Essays*, pp. 131ff.

The violent style-shifts from quasi-naturalism to hybrid modes of heightened expression can best be seen in *Major Barbara* and *Heartbreak House*, two central plays in Shaw's search for a theatre of parables. More extended study would show how the texture of either play is made up of continuous, and sudden, modulations from one key to another; the principle of selection is often arbitrary, for Shaw is relying, above all, on what Francis Fergusson has called the 'perpetual-motion machine of the dialogue', and on his own expectation that the plays will be interpreted by actors displaying 'great virtuosity in sudden transitions of mood'.[42] Here two scenes must suffice to clinch the point. The shelter scene in *Major Barbara* (Act II) starts with superficial naturalism, including the attempt at authentic Cockney accents; and Shaw's descent from the Edwardian conversation scene (of Act I) into the world of the socially damned might make one expect something approximating Gorky's *Lower Depths*. But the language of the poor turns out to be melodramatic stage-Cockney – Bill Walker derives from Bill Sikes. As for the climax of the scene, we had better look at it before attempting to say what it is:

Barbara: (*almost delirious.*) I can't bear any more. Quick march!
Cusins: (*calling to the procession in the street outside.*) Off we go. Play up, there! Immenso giubilo. (*He gives the time with his drum...*)
Mrs Baines: I must go, dear. You're overworked: you will be all right tomorrow. We'll never lose you. Now Jenny: step out with the old flag. Blood and Fire! (*She marches out through the gate with her flag.*)
Jenny: Glory Hallelujah! (*flourishing her tambourine and marching.*)
Undershaft: (*to Cusins, as he marches out past him easing the slide of his trombone*). 'My ducats and my daughter!'
Cusins: (*following him out.*) Money and Gunpowder!

42 Francis Fergusson, *The Idea of a Theater* (1949), New York, 1953, p. 194, and *Shaw on Theatre*, p. 185, respectively (see p. 53, n. 31, for context). Since writing this I have seen new productions of *Major Barbara* (R.S.C. Oct. 1970) and *Mrs Warren's Profession* (National Theatre, Dec. 1970), and I feel bound to report that in each play the posed and the personal, the melodramatic and the natural tone were given a unity. The very scenes and speeches I have discussed were controlled by the *authentic-sounding* melodramatic tone of the leading actress (Barbara/Judi Dench; Mrs Warren/Carol Browne). The climax of *Major Barbara*, Act II, is interpreted as genuinely Dionysiac by Margery Morgan in *The Shavian Playground*, London, 1972, pp. 142ff.

Barbara: Drunkenness and Murder! My God: why hast thou forsaken me? *(She sinks on the form with her face buried in her hands. The march passes away into silence. Bill Walker steals across to her.)*
Bill: *(taunting.)* Wot prawce selvytion nah?

Caught up in a whirl of 'scoring' we have here in quick succession: the voice of Barbara's anguish; brisk colloquial orders and the cue to a wedding march from Donizetti; a clash of slogans over drum, tambourine and trombone ('Blood and Fire' versus 'Money and Gunpowder' being central to the play); the slogans merge into ironic quotation (Shylock's line) and despairing quotation (the words from the Passion which, in another context, sum up an entire culture's tragic sense); and finally the Cockney phrase of Bill which, three times repeated in the scene, is used like one of the Cries of London. What is intended? Almost certainly a theatrical equivalent for what an earlier stage direction calls a 'convulsion of irony' at the spectacle of Undershaft (whom Cusins calls 'Mephistopheles! Machiavelli!' in an *aside* in the same scene) buying the Salvation Army. What is the effect? The potential personal reality is killed (Barbara's anguish, requiring 'empathy'); for there is no centre, phrases are used like stage properties. At the same time the irony (requiring more classic detachment or 'alienation') overflows into the orchestrated clash of voices, the operatic *tour-de-force*.[43]

But if in *Major Barbara* (1905) Shaw still used melodrama as a ground bass for the 'Socratic dialogue' structure of the play, in *Heartbreak House* (1913–16) he is for the first time consciously aiming at a play – fusing leisurely discussion, 'fantasia' and parable – with a natural-sounding dialogue, dependent – in his own words – on 'nuances and subtleties'. Indeed, any good production of the play confirms that much of the dialogue has a spontaneity, a casual yet compelling rhythm, rare in earlier plays by Shaw. Yet in the presumably central scenes dealing with

43 In a comparative study of Shaw and Brecht I would argue that Shaw needed a cooler principle of alienation for his drama of parables; and that the romantic irony – and the intrusion of personal–melodramatic language – in a play like *Major Barbara* cuts across his intention to demonstrate that it is a mistake to be either poor or merely charitable. But then Brecht in *St Joan of the Stockyards* – which is derived from *Major Barbara* – also fails to give any degree of reality to either the capitalist or the workers. (Cf. Ronald Gray, *op. cit.* pp. 51–2.)

felt experience – the sequence of heartbreaks and the sense of being stripped naked – Shaw cannot decide whether to give such experience natural or posed expression. For example, Ellie, the *ingénue* turned Shavian heroine, is intended to speak with the voice of authentic experience, as in her long duologue with the Captain in Act II where she makes this inward discovery after a heartbreaking experience: 'I feel now as if there was nothing I could not do, because I want nothing.'[44] Yet in the same Act we have Mangan's writhing and sobbing heartbreak in the midst of the trilling voices of the Captain's demon daughters (Hesione invoking the 'night in Tristan and Isolde'); and in Randall's shouting–foaming–weeping, Shaw falls back on an *opera buffa* heartbreak. The transitions from the expression of feeling to its parody are very precarious. And throughout the play the voices of personal experience are stylised in a manner barely distinct from the love-poses of the 'equestrian classes' – their galloping language predominates. (As Hector says, 'In this house we know all the poses.')

The 'spiritual marriage' of Ellie and the sleeping Captain is another operatic climax.[45] First a quartet of voices exclaiming all together 'Bigamy!' and asking lucid questions that merge into stage 'rhubarb'; then Hector intoning Shelley:

> Their altar the grassy earth outspread,
> And their priest the muttering wind.

There follows Ellie's vow:

> Yes: I, Ellie Dunn, give my broken heart and my strong sound soul to its natural captain, my spiritual husband and second father.

And, as the Captain awakes, Ellie intones a litany of blessings:

> There is a blessing on my broken heart. There is a blessing on your father's spirit. Even on the lies of Marcus there is a blessing; but on Mr Mangan's money there is none.

Of this incantation Ellie herself says that she does not understand it, though she knows it means something. It seems that Shaw intends to switch from the ironic operatic mode to something

44 *Heartbreak House*, Penguin ed. (1964), pp. 130–1; Standard ed. p. 115.
45 *Ibid.*, Penguin ed. pp. 148–50; Standard ed. pp. 131–2.

like a personal epiphany. But he is only master of the operatic mode, as in the *Götterdämmerung*-like ending, with the desperate yet frivolous voices celebrating the explosion. If the 'extravaganza' or 'fantasia' elements are stressed, as in the theatre they often are, the play lives; if the personal theme is stressed, we find a waste of spirit in an expense of words. The inwardly controlled *subtext* and expressiveness of Chekhovian comedy, half-attempted by Shaw, are not within the range of his dramatic language.

After *Heartbreak House* Shaw's drama becomes, with a few exceptions, much more deliberately non-naturalistic. But the exception, *Village Wooing* (1933), is worth brief consideration. For in this play Shaw does attempt to reproduce conversation; the playlet is a succession of three conversations. But what is striking is, firstly, that these duologues are between two cyphers: A, a literary gentleman who becomes a grocer, and Z, a bored young lady who becomes his 'slave' in the village shop; secondly, where the naturalistic dialogue has most vitality it anticipates Ionesco's later use of clichés in cross-talk as an assault on human reason:

Z: I never cared much for geography. Where are we now?
A: We are on the Red Sea.
Z: But it's blue.
A: What did you expect it to be?
Z: Well, I didn't know what colour the sea might be in these parts. I always thought the Red Sea would be red.
A: Well, it isn't.
Z: And isn't the Black Sea black?
A: It is precisely the colour of the sea at Margate.
Z: (*eagerly*) Oh, I am so glad you know Margate. There is no place like it in the season, is there?
A: I don't know: I have never been there.
Z: (*disappointed*) Oh, you ought to go. You could write a book about it.
A: (*shudders, sighs, and pretends to write very hard.*)
A pause.
Z: I wonder why they call it the Red Sea.[46]

By the Third Conversation the conversational dialogue is too much for Shaw. And without any apparent change in the situation,

[46] '*Too True to be Good*', '*Village Wooing*' & '*On the Rocks*', Standard ed. p. 112.

merely letting A draw on his being 'a poet' and not a 'materialist', the key changes into:

A: We shall get quite away from the world of sense. We shall light up for one another a lamp in the holy of holies in the temple of life; and the lamp will make its veil transparent. Aimless lumps of stone blundering through space will become stars singing in their spheres. Our dull purposeless village existence will become one irresistible purpose and nothing else. An extraordinary delight and an intense love will seize us. It will last hardly longer than the lightning flash which turns the black night into infinite radiance...[47]

The emphatic rhythm, the repetition and balance, the near-pastiche poetic diction in A's speech all emerge from the conversation piece. Such a transition is almost an indulgence; an uneasy mixture between 'the thrilling voice' of the higher love in *Arms and the Man* and the earnest speculative rhetoric in *Methuselah*.

That Shaw had aspirations to naturalism is clear; it is equally clear that his attempts at naturalism were deflected by his emphatically different use of language. The early documentary plays turned into something else; melodrama when inverted – or used as the basis for a discussion play – left solid blocks of melodramatic dialogue in an otherwise changing form. And in his most memorable play on a contemporary theme, the rhythms of contemporary speech are like one thin voice in a many-voiced assembly.

To command many voices is one of the primary talents of the dramatist. (Children begin by mimicking voices and gestures.) All tension, and comic tension in particular, springs from a clash of discordant worlds, unexpected collisions. A dramatist who has more than one style is potentially able to voice every style of speech, to present or parody every voice. But the crucial question in Shaw is the extent to which he can *command* his mixture of styles; the extent to which his use of traditional rhetoric in an art of parody and pastiche is controlled.

Parody and pastiche

There are several reasons for focussing attention on this topic. In the first place, the gift for parodistic language would seem to

[47] *Ibid.* pp. 137–8.

be the exactly 'right' gift for the comic-didactic dramatist: the gift of making ideas and attitudes *heard* as verbal gestures, wrong ideas as false speech-making. Parody is an essential element in the great tradition of comedy, and when we want to test the extent of Shaw's control over words – whether, for example, it makes sense to charge him with uncontrolled parody and pastiche – we have at the back of our minds such classic examples of total control as *Les précieuses ridicules* and *A Midsummer Night's Dream*, the latter including in its rich, polyphonic interplay of opposed styles the parody of the language of romantic love as well as burlesque of a specific genre (the play performed by Bottom and his company) with appropriate bits of romantic–tragical–satirical pastiche. These are recognisably Shavian methods. But Shaw is, as Eric Bentley remarked[48] – through his dependence, in the early plays, on taking an established convention and turning it inside-out, romance into anti-romance and so on – 'parodistic in a way, or to an extent that Plautus, Jonson and Molière were not'. What we must add and stress in the present context is parody as verbal expressiveness. The vocabulary, the rhythms, the voices are taken over from a burlesqued convention and amount, to use one of our key phrases again, to costume-language. At its simplest level, as when we hear the voices of higher love in the posing duologue between Sergius and Raina, we have what might be called direct, classic parody, wholly unambiguous in its control. Shaw is attacking 'strenuous, eloquent, trumpet-tongued lying'.[49] A problem of judgement arises only when we appear to find the strenuous eloquence ambiguously employed in trumpet-tongued truth-telling.

Secondly, it follows from what has been said that parody and pastiche show one way out for the double-minded dramatist who is a naturalist in his ideology ('natural history') but who is progressively driven to non-naturalistic language. For parody and pastiche are, as they work in the theatre, ways of smuggling in eloquence or heightened speech through putting words in a frame or in quotation marks: as samples of 'romantic' or 'melodramatic' rhetoric. Certainly, the prose dialogue of most great comedies is patterned speech; in English drama alone one

[48] 'The Making of a Dramatist (1892–1903)', reprinted in *G. B. Shaw, A Collection of Critical Essays*, pp. 57–75 (quotation: p. 62).

[49] Preface to *Plays Pleasant* – conclusion.

need only look at a page of Congreve or Sheridan or Wilde.[50] The sheer concentration of witty language (and concentration = *Dichtung* in Pound's forced bilingual equation) is enough to remove it from everyday speech, whether we have epigrammatic ping-pong dialogue or elaborate set speeches depending on mere words, in the manner of Mrs Malaprop's ten malapropisms in one speech when speaking 'in moderation'.

Bergson defined verbal comedy as 'the transposition of a natural expression into a different tone',[51] and this can hardly be bettered. But Bergson then went on to distinguish between parody – transposition of the solemn into the familiar – and exaggeration; and this, on reflection, cannot be accepted. Perhaps parody is something that 'expands or contracts, changing shape like a fish under water, the water being one's own particular notion of the fish';[52] but that is too slippery. In the present context parody is best understood as the mimesis of distorting mirrors, they minimise *or* they magnify. Smuggling in eloquence by the back-door is one effect. Pastiche is the specialised technique for imitating a past style, very often an elaborate style. Parody and pastiche can do without one another, but they are often parasitical on the past in a similar way – certainly in Shaw. One must add that these devices are eminently theatrical: the tone and manner of a speaking voice is amplified; the expression is masked. Further, to be parodistic is to be eclectic, many-voiced. Add to this the argument of the previous paragraph – that an ideology can be shown up through a voice – and the attractions of parody for Shaw should be clear.

Finally, to put it the other way round, we shall be able to see the relevance of Shaw to parody and pastiche when discussing the characteristically modernist use of these devices in later drama. As it is, we can see that Shaw at least foreshadows the later extensions of the use of parody in fantasy, role-playing, and in underscoring the fragile relativity of all things said. But, in

50 See Nicoll, *The Theatre and Dramatic Theory*, London, 1962, pp. 152ff. (But Nicoll's emphasis on sound effects, like concealed alliteration, is overdone.)

51 Henri Bergson, *Le Rire* (1900), Ch. II, Section II, subsection ii: 'On obtiendra toujours un effet comique en transposant l'expression naturelle d'une idée dans un autre ton.' (This quote from Paris ed., 1912, p. 125.)

52 Dwight Macdonald, *Parodies*, London, 1961, p. xi.

revaluing parody as a style-substitute that is itself a style, we remain aware that parody can also be evasion: neither the language of experience, nor the authentic utterance of the creative dramatist.

Here, to help definition, is a reminder of how fully controlled, direct (classical) parody works:

Raina: (*Placing her hands on his [Sergius'] shoulders as she looks up at him with admiration and worship.*)
My hero! My king!
Sergius: My queen! (*He kisses her on the forehead.*)
Raina: How I have envied you Sergius! You have been out in the world, on the field of battle, able to prove yourself there worthy of any woman in the world...
Sergius: Dearest: all my deeds have been yours. You inspired me. I have gone through the war like a knight in a tournament with his lady looking down at him!
Raina: And you have never been absent from my thoughts for a moment. (*Very solemnly.*) Sergius: I think we two have found the higher love.
Sergius: My lady and my saint! (*He clasps her reverently.*)

Arms and the Man, Act II

Unambiguous – certainly. The language of the two poseurs is so simplified that, on the printed page and in isolation, it looks facile. But it *is* successful in its own terms: the words are the exact equivalent of posed gesture; the audience can recognise and 'debunk' the attitude and style amid laughter; and yet that romantic vignette 'a knight in a tournament' is sufficiently real to connect with the mother's *meant* enthusiasm for the cavalry charge in Act I:

our gallant splendid Bulgarians with their swords and eyes flashing, thundering down like an avalanche and scattering the wretched Serbians and their dandified Austrian officers like chaff.[53]

The light parody links the ideas, the props and the voices that glorify love-and-war. If anything, the language of the play goes flabby because there is too much explicit debunking, not letting the audience do enough of its own parody-spotting, as in

[53] *Plays Pleasant*, Penguin ed. (1949), p. 20.

Bluntschli's realistic counter-speech on the same hero still in Act I:

He did it like an operatic tenor. A regular handsome fellow, with flashing eyes and lovely moustache, shouting his war-cry and charging like Don Quixote at the windmills. We did laugh.[54]

In a finer economy it should have been enough to make us hear the operatic tenor in a war-cry speech.

Still more interesting is the method of conscious self-parody that takes us one step nearer to the unconscious variety. We find it, for example, in *Man and Superman* where the speeches of John Tanner, and his dream-state emanation Don Juan, exhibit the comic pathology of verbal excess. Both his roles, the reluctant lover and the would-be ideologue, are archetypes for the Talker. One may see these roles as carriers of the virus of logo-mania – Shaw's complaint.

Here is one passage:

Ann: I love my mother, Jack.

Tanner: (*working himself up into a sociological rage.*) Is that any reason why you are not to call your soul your own? Oh, I protest against this vile abjection of youth to age! Look at fashionable society as you know it. What does it pretend to be? An exquisite dance of nymphs. What is it? A horrible procession of wretched girls, each in the claws of a cynical, cunning, avaricious, disillusioned, ignorantly experienced foul-minded old woman whom she calls mother, and whose duty it is to corrupt her mind and sell her to the highest bidder. [. . .] The law for father and son and mother and daughter is not the law of love: it is the law of revolution, of emancipation, of final supersession of the old and worn-out by the young and the capable. I tell you the first duty of manhood and womanhood is a Declaration of Independence: the man who pleads his father's authority is no man: the woman who pleads her mother's authority is unfit to bear citizens to a free people.

Ann: (*watching him with quiet curiosity.*) I suppose you will go in seriously for politics some day, Jack.

Tanner: (*heavily let down.*) Eh? What? Wh-? (*collecting his scattered wits.*) What has that got to do with what I have been saying?

Ann: You talk so well.

Tanner: Talk! Talk! It means nothing to you but talk.

Man and Superman, Act II[55]

[54] *Ibid.* p. 31.

[55] Penguin ed. (1946), pp. 102–3.

Tanner is unconscious, but the dramatist is fully conscious of the parody, which is the right relationship between patient and pathologist. The comic situation allows for the thick underlining of 'talk-talk' in the dialogue that follows Tanner's set speech, repeated in the famous last words of the play. (Ann: 'Go on talking.' Tanner: 'Talking!' *Universal laughter.*) However, the reader or sophisticated audience will respond to the quality of Tanner's tirade long before the comic climax. The rhetoric is used to mock itself exactly enough: first a rhetorical question, then an Oh-exclamation, then the speaker answering his own questions with a musical phrase ('exquisite dance of nymphs') and a catalogue of invectives ('mere words', for the mother figure is quite impersonal across the two formal relative clauses) rising to the balanced cadences of political oratory: manifesto and windbaggery in one breath.

In such a speech the sense of commitment – elsewhere Shaw's – is deflected into 'mere words'. It is a more ambiguous method than the showing up of an ideology through a voice; parody is now used to suspend belief in something the dramatist wishes to advocate rather than 'debunk'.[56]

At its best, conscious self-parody goes with creative scepticism. It is taken as far as it will go – and sometimes beyond that point – in the detachable 'Shavio-Socratic dialogue', *Don Juan in Hell*. (The fact that it is detachable is a weakness in form connected with the runaway automatism that much of the dialogue suggests.) The most satisfying way of reading, and probably of playing, this exuberant piece is a parody of the dialogue form, and of dialogue itself. The virtuoso scoring for voices, the verbal music turned word-flood (see p. 50), the

[56] For the relationship of *Man and Superman* to Shavianism see Robert Brustein, *The Theater of Revolt*, Boston, 1964, pp. 218–20. The key point is that 'By distancing himself from the Shavian Tanner, Shaw can demonstrate how Shavianism, being mainly intellectual and theoretical, is really inadequate to the thing it describes.' *Note*: That Shaw was intentionally relativist at this stage can be seen from his comment on the way opinions are expressed by his Don Juan and other characters in the play: 'They are all right from their several points of view; and their points of view are, for the dramatic moment, mine also. This may puzzle the people who believe that there is such a thing as an absolutely right point of view, usually their own.' *Man and Superman*, Epistle Dedicatory, Penguin ed. p. xxviii.

disproportion of speech in relation to what can be said, all work towards this. The controlling factor, as far as one can detect it, is in the conscious excess that stamps such a speech as logomania; such speeches are also 'framed' ironically by the surrounding dialogue. There are many examples of this: the alliteration pile with the crescendo of manic adjectives:

The Statue: Not that I see any prospect of your coming to any point in particular, Juan.

Don Juan: (*somewhat impatiently.*) My point, you marble-headed old masterpiece, is only a step ahead of you. Are we agreed that Life is a force which has made innumerable experiments in organising itself; the mammoth and the man, the mouse and the megatherium, the flies and the Fathers of the Church are all more or less successful attempts to build up that raw force into higher and higher individuals, the ideal individual being omnipotent, omniscient, infallible and withal completely and unilludedly self-conscious: in short, a God?

The Devil: I agree, for the sake of argument.

The Statue: I agree, for the sake of avoiding argument...[57]

Then there is the litany on the devil's friends which takes an antithetical formula ('They are not beautiful: they are only decorated') and repeats it, with one syntactic variant, just under thirty times and provokes an explicit discussion on Don Juan's 'flow of words' and the vanity of talk; and there is the repeated suggestion in the sequence of speeches on the Life Force that Don Juan's speeches are – perhaps as a mark of Hell – infinite.

When we understand the move from direct parody – the voice of the debunked old hero – to conscious self-parody – the new Shavian anti-hero made to show up his old-style rhetoric – we are given a new key to understanding unconscious parody and pastiche. In the incessant speech-making of John Tanner/Don Juan there is, already, an element of loss: the intensity of feeling under the issues presented can hardly surface; or rather, the experience is one of intense verbal energy. The language of parody can be a way of having it both ways – the escape from passion into the intellect's Life to Come is both *meant* and *mocked*. But what

57 *Man and Superman*, Act III, Penguin ed. p. 158; Standard ed. p. 109. At the end of this exchange Don Juan elegantly withdraws the reference to Fathers of the Church as being dragged in 'purely for the sake of alliteration'.

language is left for Shaw when a particular experience is *meant* to communicate a central conviction or an inward experience? As a practical test one may compare these passages:

(1) D.J.: No: I sing, not arms and the hero, but philosophic man: he who seeks in contemplation to discover the inner will of the world, in invention to discover the means of fulfilling that will, and in action to do that will by the so-discovered means.

(2) B.: (*transfigured.*) I have got rid of the bribe of bread. I have got rid of the bribe of heaven. Let God's work be done for its own sake: the work he had to create us to do because it cannot be done except by living men and women. When I die, let him be in my debt, not I in his; and let me forgive him as becomes a woman of my rank.

C.: Then the way of life lies through the factory of death?

B.: Yes, through the raising of hell to heaven and of man to God, through the unveiling of an eternal light in the Valley of the Shadow.

(3) D.: I believe in Michael Angelo, Velasquez and Rembrandt; in the might of design, the mystery of colour, the redemption of all things by Beauty everlasting, and the message of Art that has made these hands blessed. Amen. Amen. (*He closes his eyes and lies still.*)

(4) S.: (*weirdly chanting.*)
I builded a house for my daughters, and opened the doors thereof
That men might come for their choosing, and their
betters spring from their love...

(5) L.: I can wait: waiting and patience mean nothing to the eternal. I gave the woman the greatest of gifts: curiosity. By that her seed has been saved from my wrath; for I also am curious; and I have waited always to see what they will do tomorrow. [...] I say, let them dread, of all things stagnation; for from the moment I, Lilith, lose hope and faith in them, they are doomed. In that hope and faith I have let them live for a moment; and in that moment I have spared them many things.[58]

[58] (1) *Man and Superman*, Act III. (Penguin ed. p. 160; Standard ed. p. 110.)
(2) *Major Barbara*, end of Act III.
(3) *The Doctor's Dilemma*, Act IV. (Penguin ed. p. 174; Standard ed. p. 163.)
(4) *Heartbreak House*, end of Act I.
(5) *Back to Methuselah*, Part V, concluding speech by Lilith.
The respective dates for these plays are: 1901–3; 1905; 1906; 1913–16; 1918–21. The passages thus came from plays that represent

These passages should speak for themselves to a considerable extent. We need only note some essentials before attempting a new value judgement. The first passage fits in with what has been said about parody in *Man and Superman*: but this time the explicit use of the mock-epic manner draws attention to the parodist's debt to a well-tried pattern. (Pastiche with parody.) In the second passage, Barbara is given, for the expression of her conversion to her new religion, a set speech made up of a nun's catechism-derived cadences – with an ironic twist – followed by Bunyan romanticised. (Pastiche – for emotional climax.) Dubedat's death-bed speech draws on the creed formula. (Pastiche; pathos laid on.) The fourth passage, with its quasi-Biblical poetic prose, forms part of a carefully orchestrated chorus at the end of Act I of *Heartbreak House*, the ritual chant of a family reunion. (Pastiche; search for a new dramatic language.)[59] In the final speech Lilith, given creative power, speaks the language of God as mediated by the Authorised Version. (Pastiche; search for 'that of which one cannot speak'.)

What these speeches have in common, with the exception of the Superman's creed, is their lack of distancing – we are to 'empathise' rather than judge. Shaw is attempting to give poetic power to a persona or 'message' he finds important; or rather, elements taken from melodramatic rhetoric, from the Authorized Version, from the Apostles' Creed, and other public property, are used to create lyrical excitement at a given climax in a play. Pastiche is not now the appropriate verbal clothing for a pose, but appears to be used to express something authentic and inward. When so used it tends to be felt as the language of pseudo-experience.

Shaw's central development: both the continuity and 'creative evolution' of his dramatic art. With *Saint Joan* (cf. pp. 72ff.) these are the plays where Shaw is most clearly trying to extend the resources of his drama, from comedy and the discussion play to parable; where there are uncertainties of control in the dialogue there is a corresponding lack of definition in the search for a new form – a theatre of parables.

59 For what Shaw thought of this speech see *Shakes versus Shav* (1949) and p. 52 above. Brustein (*op. cit.* p. 222) thinks it is a 'foretaste of the kind of choral technique T. S. Eliot will use in *The Family Reunion*'. I think it is the operatic grand finale used to heighten expressiveness – a significant experiment.

Yet, another reading – and playing – is possible: one that brings out the theatricality of pastiche and plays down what is left of the naturalistic approach in Shaw, with expectations of 'felt life' and 'spoken action'. Instead, we can see in Shaw's recurrent recourse to pastiche an early example of dramatic collage – old rhetoric pasted into new frames in a language for roles. We can then read the death-bed speech of Dubedat (3) as a moment of make-believe pathos, the words of Immortal Art a flawed character turns on himself, like a spotlight. In technique, as in the text, the creed-formula is remarkably close to the intermixed Shakespeare quotes which B.B., in his embarrassment over forced pathos, strings into a cento:

> Out, out brief candle:
> For nothing canst thou to damnation add;
> The readiness is all.

Dubedat and B.B. are both collage artists in words, like Broadbent in *John Bull's Other Island* to whom, as Desmond MacCarthy noted as early as 1904, 'the works of Ruskin and Shelley are merely pots of romantic paint...wherein he finds colours with which to daub his own undertakings'.[60] Barbara's conversion speech (2) makes sense as the new role assumed by a person who still speaks with her old voice, as if the old role were ghost-writing the speech for her, drawing on previously acquired 'hot-gospelling' stock phrases. The speech has about the same value as the intrusion of Dionysus via Gilbert Murray's version of the *Bacchae* in Act II: the emotion is externalised, converted into a theatrical counter. This fits in with the operatic element in the play briefly discussed in the previous section; the main material for Shaw's operatic libretti is, precisely, pastiche. Similarly, Captain Shotover's chant (4) fits in well with the language of histrionic attitudes and fantasy we stressed in that play: it is one air in the medley.

Shaw is reaching towards a poetry of the theatre that is – like costume jewelry – made up of intrinsically non-precious materials. One concludes that what is wrong in these plays is not the recourse to pastiche, but its uneven or un-radical use. For just

[60] Desmond MacCarthy *Shaw*, London, 1951, p. 30. For Dubedat and uncontrolled pastiche see also Appendix *Note*, p. 85, example 2, and art/anti-art, pp. 93 ff.

as Shaw chose to conceal 'beneath the superficially colloquial and "natural" dialogue' his operatic propensity (cf. p. 49, n. 20) – instead of an open form with explicit stylisation – so he used pastiche fitfully instead of systematically in plays that began with and kept returning to the naturalistic manner. The systematic solution would have been that expressionistic theatricality to which Shaw's work does indeed point: a drama of roles where the personae *can* speak, and necessarily speak, through speech appropriated for the occasion.

In coining the term 'costume speech' there was no specific reference to historical plays. Yet there is a connection, both in Shaw's practice and in his dramatic theory. It is in the early histories that we find the first clear examples of deliberate pastiche: a posed Napoleon talking 'Buonapartiana', despite Shaw's attempt to remedy Sardou, in *The Man of Destiny*; Caesar apostrophising the Sphinx, and the God Ra talking at the 'modern audience with great contempt' full of Ye-es, Lo-s and archaic cadences in the first Prologue of *Caesar and Cleopatra*. The device recurs repeatedly in the third and final period of Shaw's work, in the extravaganzas, those incompletely achieved parables for the theatre. In these plays what Edmund Wilson called the 'music of moralities'[61] often compensates for the lack of a sense of power, even where, as in *The Apple Cart*, political power is the issue. Ironically, Shaw now exhibits more 'love of oratory' than 'effectiveness of assertion'. One may say that a dramatic world where a Powermistress General claims to govern England by mimicking the highfalutin' speeches of a rival politician, and where the subjects of Charles II debate whether a sample of Dryden is worse 'fustian' than the preachings of the Ranters, is a pageant of styles, enriched by pastiche.[62]

Saint Joan is complex, and it would take a long essay to develop an argument that can only be summarised here. The play should be approached as a chronicle or epic play,[63] exhibiting several

61 Edmund Wilson, *The Triple Thinkers* (1938), Harmondsworth, 1962, p. 206. The point about the diminished sense of political power is my own.

62 *The Apple Cart*, Penguin ed., 1956, p. 81, and *In Good King Charles's Golden Days*, London, 1939, pp. 69–72.

63 For context of form and theatre see:
(*a*) The subtitle.
(*b*) Before writing *Saint Joan* Shaw stated he wished to write a

styles: and the sequence of styles – within a sequence of scene-settings – is in keeping with Shaw's relativist or many-angled vision. For the borrowed legend we have romantic rhetoric (with 'debunking' devices); for the legend historicised we have the dialogue of dialectical voices (Cauchon–Warwick, Scene IV) and the farcical–tragical–ceremonial Epilogue for history as a masquerade. And the unity of the play depends on making one dramatic mode throw ironic light on another. It is a composite work with an interplay of perspectives. Attempts to approach it with criteria taken over from judging formal tragedy, with expectations of unity of tone, or inward complexity in any one speech, amount to distorting the context of reading. It may be recalled how many critics have singled out Joan's recantation speech and judged it, on close reading and from the same standpoint, in practically synonymous terms: it is said to be 'romantic pathos' or consciously 'poetic' or a 'cliché' in its presentation of an emotion. And so it is.[64] But it is in keeping with other elements taken over from earlier historic–heroic or melo-dramatic dramatisations of the Jeanne d'Arc legend – the language of a cult – something Shaw rejected in the Preface but which he ended by using in a new theatrical frame.[65] (The speech at the end of the Rheims cathedral scene – where she discovers her isolation – is, clearly, pathos used with deliberate theatricality: Joan begins 'with her eyes skyward', and the speech conveys both faith *and* self-deception by its tone and content.)

Further, the play exploits other modes of language and sets

chronicle play for a Shakespearean or open stage – 'this new old theatre'. (Article written for the Guild Theater, New York, *Shaw on Theatre*, pp. 177–83.)

(*c*) Shaw's definition in the Preface: 'the romance of Joan's rise, the tragedy of her execution, and the comedy of the attempts of posterity to make amends...' (Section on modern distortions of Joan's history.)

64 These terms are taken, respectively, from:

(1) Raymond Williams, *Drama from Ibsen to Eliot*, Harmondsworth, 1964, p. 169.

(2) T. R. Henn, *The Harvest of Tragedy* (1956), London, 1966, pp. 194–5.

(3) T. R. Barnes, 'Shaw and the London Theatre', in *The Pelican Guide to English Literature*, vol. 7, pp. 213–14.

65 For Shaw's debt to Tom Taylor's *Jeanne Darc* (1871) see Meisel, *Shaw and the Nineteenth-Century Theater*, pp. 367–70.

them *against* the romantic pathos: within the trial scene alone we have the dialogue based on documents – Joan's voice taken over or reconstructed from the Quicherat trial records[66] – and the language of ceremony. The latter may serve as an example of double use: as externalised ritual and as parody. The *form* of words in the act of excommunication is echoed by the litany of praise chanted at Joan in the Epilogue. Those who intone: 'Cast out from the unity of the Church. Sundered from her body. Infected with the leprosy of heresy...' are using a traditional word-formula to sanctify judicial murder; and those who indulge in a similar incantation to offer adoration posthumously to Joan – 'The girls in the field praise thee...' – are using words to conceal the futility of words. Or, to put it another way, the stage-managed repetition of bits of traditional rhetoric 'corroborates' the roles assumed by the clerics and by the lip-servers in turn. History is histrionic: 'no frontier can be marked between drama and history and religion, or between acting and conduct'.[67] Again, Shaw is on the threshold of working out a drama of role-enactment, fitting out each role with words which, at a particular time and only for that time, are sufficiently compelling to fake reality.

In sum, Shaw's dramatic language is inseparable from a relativist vision that works in several styles, mostly variants of the nineteenth-century rhetorical convention. Parody and pastiche can, as shown, both exploit and revitalise such an eclectic fossil-language for the theatre. When controlled, such devices put the old language into a new framework, using the rhetorical expressiveness for a wide range of voices or vocal impersonations: from comic pose to public or historic role; the dialogue can mock itself and the speech-flow can project the will to believe; the robust or crude energy of conventional rhetoric can be used parasitically, and reach towards a new relevance and tone. Yet, when these devices are not controlled they are not devices at all; then the melodramatic or romantic rhetoric loses the dramatic

66 See the discussion of Shaw's use of Quicherat in the article by Louis Martz, 'The Saint as Tragic Hero', in *G. B. Shaw, A Collection of Critical Essays*, pp. 151–2.

67 Preface to *Plays Pleasant* (Penguin ed., 1949, pp. 11–12; Standard ed. p. xi), where the wider argument is that 'public and private life become daily more theatrical'.

equivalent of quotation marks; the old is not made new; and the shift from style to style fails to carry a corresponding shift of sympathy or attention. Then the eclectic use of styles expresses not different voices but only the chameleon dramatist letting 'the play write itself and shape itself'[68] – a romantic principle of play-writing for a type of drama that requires either a classical or a modernist discipline.

There is irony in what James Joyce wrote as a young man reviewing the first Dublin production of *The Shewing-up of Blanco Posnet* for a Trieste paper: 'This lively and talkative spirit cannot be subjected to the noble and bare style appropriate to modern play-writing.'[69] For what Shaw needed was not 'the noble and bare style' – Joyce's own style in *Exiles* – but a certain dose of Joyce's later discipline in handling the multiple style, including parody and pastiche, as the expression of a multiple, dramatic standpoint. Perhaps the result would have been an extension of what Shaw had practised without full control: a dramatic language for roles fitted out with appropriate loan-words from the museum of rhetoric.

The absurd and the hyper-articulate

The direction opposed to the externalised rhetoric – that language for masks – is one where the pre-fabricated word-clusters are broken down and the attempt is made to let a new experience come through in words and rhythms dictated from within. Certain experiences – particularly the despair and the sense of waste voiced repeatedly in the plays written under the impact of the First World War – seemed to impel Shaw in that direction. There were signs of a corresponding impatience with the glib rationality that often went with the received language, signs of a desire to break it down. It was a direction glimpsed but not taken; and it is possible to demonstrate how Shaw used the old dramatic language to defend himself from the need to renew it.

Already in the confident pre-war plays, there were those

68 Shaw frequently boasted of this. This quotation comes from the late (1944) Postscript to *Back to Methuselah*, World's Classics ed., 1945, p. 283, where Shaw describes his part in the production of his plays as not greater than that of an 'amanuensis or organ-blower'.

69 See *The Critical Writings of James Joyce* (ed. E. Mason and R. Ellmann), London, 1951, p. 208.

settings for 'speech in the void', or speech against an object that mocks it. In the dream-dialogue in *Man and Superman* Act III it is out of the 'omnipresent nothing' that there emerges, to the sound of ghostly violins, 'a man in the void...seated, absurdly enough, on nothing'; but the speech of this man is reassuringly operatic, as is the Devil's recital of the evidence for man's destructiveness. Keegan, another of Shaw's personae for the visionary Talker, is heard to conduct, at the beginning of Act II of *John Bull's Other Island*, a solo dialogue: the Grasshopper's 'responses' mock his accent, his lyrical idealism, his questioning. But the framework is so explicit, and the parody so gentle, that only Patsy, the young Irish labourer, is terrified by what he takes to be a diabolical voice. Barbara's 'transfigured' speech (p. 69, example 2) is to be spoken on and against a stage dominated by the shell; and that is one reason why the rhetoric on the 'factory of death' weakens the effect by stressing the obvious. The Mayoress (see p. 51) speaks in a state of trance. In the last act of *Heartbreak House* silence is ordered by Shotover, an old man speaking out of frenzy and rum, and though the elegant chatter goes on, the conversationalists become conscious of their futility ('We sit here talking and leave everything to Mangan and to chance and to the Devil') and their talk breaks over the sound of the final explosion.

This is the act that owes most to the impact of the war; and in some of the post-war plays the figure of the Speech-maker, destroyed or isolated in his flow of words, recurs. The Elderly Gentleman in *Back to Methuselah* talks, on arrival on the ancestral shores at Galway Bay, with the superfluity of a dead language, in clichés and worn images: ranging from 'blood is thicker than water' to a long speech defending, 'to use an antiquated form of expression, the temple of the Holy Ghost', and another one defending a dying civilisation in the name of its 'ever-burning torch' and coral insects building islands, acorns growing into oaks, and so on.[70] His language is incomprehensible to the more advanced 'longlivers'; soon after landing he breaks down because he cannot communicate; and he is put under the care of a nurse by the uncomprehending Woman who calls out the identity-kit peculiarities of the visitor:

70 *Back to Methuselah*, Part IV, Act I. World's Classics ed. pp. 149, 168, 173.

[*speaking into space on one note, like a chorister intoning a psalm*] Burrin Pier Galway please send someone to take charge of a discouraged shortliver who has escaped from his nurse male harmless *babbles unintelligibly with moments of sense distressed hysterical foreign dress*...[71]

He recovers, only to be repeatedly mocked by his nurse companion, Zoo, who considers the Elderly Gentleman a remnant from the race that persists in escaping from 'contact with truth that hurts and frightens you' into an 'imaginary vacuum', sharing 'the slavery of the shortlived to images and metaphors'.[72] Finally, he comes face to face with the Oracle – the prescribed ritual of the antique Pythoness is re-enacted as a 'mummery' or as 'tomfoolery' only for the benefit of the 'shortlivers'. The Oracle has only this to say: 'Go home, poor fool.' He despairingly admits 'I cannot live among people to whom nothing is real'; he is allowed to stay, but when the Oracle offers him her hand and looks into his face he falls dead – with 'discouragement'.[73]

So the parable on an effete civilisation includes a parable on a dead language. The fifth play in this cycle, half swallowed up though it is in the almost incontinent stream of talk, is potentially one of the most vital things in Shaw's 'Metabiological Pentateuch'. It exhibits, among other things, the monstrous reflex-speech of the Automata, the synthetic couple created by the sculptor Pygmalion. The two mechanical homunculi, intended to represent 'those limited and absurd creatures', civilised man, can answer questions when linguistically stimulated or, as their creator explains, 'when the waves of sound started by your speaking enter their ears they respond accordingly'. First the Male Figure makes a set speech (too long to quote in full, though the length contributes to its vacuous energy):

We are part of a cosmic system. Free will is an illusion. We are the Children of Cause and Effect. We are the Unalterable, the Irresistible, the Irresponsible, the Inevitable: in a word the Determinist.

> 'My name is Ozymandias, king of kings;
> Look on my works, ye mighty, and despair.'

The Male Figure then introduces his female counterpart as Cleopatra–Semiramis and launches into a catechism-like definition

[71] *Ibid.* pp. 153–4 (my italics).
[72] *Ibid.* pp. 167, 177.
[73] End of Act III, *ibid.* pp. 215–16.

of the nature of his oneness with her, which is in turn disputed in mock-scholastic terms:

Such as the king is so is the queen, the king thought-out and hand-made, the queen thought-out and hand-made.... The king logical and predetermined and inevitable and the queen logical and predetermined and inevitable. And yet they are not two logical and predetermined and inevitable, but one logical and predetermined and inevitable. Therefore confound not the persons, nor divide the substance; but worship us twain as one: two in one and one in two, lest by error ye fall into irretrievable damnation.[74]

This has a local intensity that cannot be accidental. The expressionistic identification of mechanical gesture and speech – the Automata 'pose', dance 'pompously', and 'acknowledge applause' before they indulge in the postures of speech-making – is complete. The old rhetoric of heroic poses – the quotation from Shelley to establish bombast, the fossil-phrases of Pauline theology used to parody the tenets of Mechanism – gives, for once, a Swiftian violence to the verbal satire. (And the speech-exhibition ends in violent action: the Female Figure destroys her maker by biting a piece out of his hand.) These mechanical dolls have come a long way, in terms of Shaw's own sensibility and dramatic conception, from the speaking doll created by his first, more popular, Pygmalion figure; in Eliza's mechanical parroting of the clichés and noises of upper-class speech there was just a suggestion, within the comedy of manners, that social speech is synthetic, laboratory-induced. But now Shaw's Automata mimic the hollowness of a wide range of expression, mouthing words taken from 'the sacredest of scriptures and the noblest of utterances',[75] with bits of ill-digested jargon from a deterministic philosophy of science. (They are also dependent on the morning newspaper for knowing what to think.) Their speech points to language as an obstacle to thought and feeling.

In direction, if not in total effect, the speech of the Automata anticipates the final breakdown of noble utterance in Lucky's speech in *Waiting for Godot*: stimulus–response speech that can only be felt, or made dramatically expressive, when it mocks itself. And one may assume that the intensity that goes into

[74] *Ibid.* p. 254. The whole Automata play-within-the-play: pp. 252–61.
[75] *Ibid.* p. 265 (spoken by the She-Ancient).

this brief scene springs from Shaw's own despair. Explicitly, the Automata and their speech are identified with 'art' and the 'body' and 'images': the idols rejected by the Ancients;[76] and this identification in turn fits in with those sections in the Preface where Shaw takes himself seriously as that new kind of iconoclast who, dismissing much of his early work as merely a professional need ('potboilers' in the 1944 Postscript), can now become 'the iconographer of the religion of my time, fulfilling my natural function as an artist'.[77] Implicitly, Shaw is rejecting, through the mask-language of the Automata, the mechanical element in his own theatre.

Is there any sign of the desired 'new iconography' in the dramatic language of Shaw? The Automata play-within-the-play is itself followed by some curious pointers. The Ancients in their evolution towards disembodied being have lost the faculty of speech, we are informed by the two who have remained loquacious; and these two are beginning to have their own troubles ('I find it more and more difficult to keep up your language. Another century or two and it will be impossible');[78] they over-compensate by excessive talk, by expounding the Automata playlet in a long would-be Socratic dialogue. Added to Pygmalion's verbose introductory lecture, the 'explication' that surrounds the Automata is more than twice the length of the playlet. Then, as if set against the wearisome speech of the Ancients, we find The Newly Born questioning the meaning of words for the first time.[79] We note that she is first made to overhear a disillusioned youth 'Speaking like grammar', ironically conjugating the verb 'to swear', and that she is 'saddened' by such talk. Then come her questions ('What is tomorrow?' 'What is sleep?'), the last one spoken drowsily before she is carried screaming into the temple in the growing darkness. Shaw's deliberate attempt at allegorical drama once more takes in language. At the same time the texture of the dialogue itself conveys fatigue; a fatigue that has about it a groping quality, and the sense of a potentially creative breaking point. Then the voices of the Will take over; the monologue of Lilith, with which *Back to Methuselah* ends (cf. p. 69, example 5), is what it claims to be: a non-human voice asserting itself in the void.

[76] *Ibid.* p. 264. [77] *Ibid.* p. lxxxv and p. 289.
[78] *Ibid.* pp. 275–6. Exchange between the two Ancients.
[79] *Ibid.* pp. 277–8.

A year before *Methuselah* was published, André Gide, in an article on Dada, pointed to a connection between the experience of war, the death of others, the questioning of everything, and the refusal to 'pick up the thread of the old discourse that had been interrupted'. For language itself had become 'too undermined for anyone to recommend that thought continue to take refuge in it'.[80] But Shaw's dramatic language remained intact, a refuge from his own awareness of a breakdown in values. It remained a Faustian language (in the sense defined earlier, p. 47), unbroken, 'straight' and willed. The old rhetorical convention, to which Meisel ascribed 'superabundant energy' and 'superhuman expressiveness', becomes in many of the post-war plays an energy that runs counter to what Shaw is trying to say, and an expressiveness more 'super' than human.

This use of the old stage rhetoric as a defence, manic defence, can be seen clearly in the set speeches and in much of the dialogue of *Too True to be Good* (1931). At the beginning of the play the Monster-microbe in the sickroom, or in the patient's delirium, is heard lamenting its own infection ('Oh!! Oh!! Oh!!! I am so ill! so miserable. Oh, I wish I were dead.') in the soothing rhythms of traditional farce. We are instantly reassured by the 'nightmare', as intended. In Act II the pious Sergeant quotes the first page of the Pilgrim's Progress and then announces:

> Well, London and Paris and Berlin and Rome and the rest of them will be burned with fire from heaven all right in the next war: that's certain. They are all Cities of Destruction.[81]

The Sergeant's superficial colloquialism is no doubt intended to lighten the rhetoric and give a sense of reality. Yet, in the context of discursiveness and flirtation, the Sergeant's words

80 Cf. André Gide, 'Dada', *N.R.F.* (April 1920), reprinted in *Pretexts*, London, 1959, p. 291. The phrases from Meisel are taken from *Shaw and the Nineteenth-Century Theater*, p. 434. Cf. Roland Barthes on the 'euphemistic grace' of classical form and language, *Writing Degree Zero* (1953) (transl. A. Lavers and C. Smith), London, 1967, pp. 68ff.

81 *Too True to Be Good*, Standard ed. p. 81. For the destruction of cities contrast *The Waste Land* v, ll. 366–76; for the dramatic speech of another Bible-inspired Sergeant see Arden's *Serjeant Musgrave's Dance* (e.g. end of Act I, Scene iii).

hardly convey fear of a new apocalypse. In the next sequence the Elder 'declaims with fanatical intensity', concerning the unpredictable universe of Einstein:

> Nothing can save us from a perpetual headlong fall into a bottomless abyss but a solid footing of dogma; and we no sooner agree to that than we find that the only trustworthy dogma is that there is no dogma. As I stand here I am falling into that abyss, down, down, down.[82]

That 'perpetual headlong fall into a bottomless abyss' sounds familiar and reassuring; while in the speech on the end of reason:

> Its spread of enlightenment has been the spread of cancer: its counsels that were to have established the millennium have led straight to European suicide.[83]

the balanced syntax, the rhythms, the hyper-articulateness, fend off the intellectual despair. And if one supposes that this is once more intended as parody, that the Elder represents, like Settembrini in Thomas Mann's *The Magic Mountain*, the sorrows of the rationalist windbag, then we may consider that long final 'sermon' where Aubrey, the burglar–preacher, abandoned one by one by his listeners and fading into inaudibility, speaks of his despair over the post-war world and his refusal to despair (in conclusion invoking 'some pentecostal flame of revelation' and the closing words of the Lord's Prayer, as if seeking balm for what he himself has been saying):

> War has rent these veils. Our cathedral roofs are torn, our souls in rags. The young are spying through the holes. They exult: they've found us out: they expose their own souls. We try to patch...with scraps of the old stuff – they tear from us the rags left to us. Utterly naked ...The word NOT inserted into all our creeds....Is NO enough? Obsessed with a belief when denying...No: I must have affirmations. Preach:
>
> 'So that the pugnacious spirit of man
> Can reach out and strike deathblows...'
>
> Preach, preach, preach, – nothing to say. Glory for ever and ever. Amen.

[82] *Ibid.* p. 85.

[83] *Ibid.* p. 89.

It is not to be supposed that Shaw could have written that. What he did write, making the Preacher reflect on the characters who have just abandoned him, as 'unreal' or 'too absurd to be believed in', was this:

The iron lightning of war has burnt great rents in these angelic veils [idealisms], just as it has smashed great holes in our cathedral roofs and torn great gashes in our hillsides. Our souls go in rags now; and the young are spying through the holes and getting glimpses of the reality that was hidden. And they are not horrified: they exult in having found us out: they expose their own souls; and when we their elders desperately try to patch our torn clothes with scraps of the old material, the young lay violent hands on us and tear from us even the rags that were left to us. But when they have stripped themselves and us utterly naked, will they be able to bear the spectacle?

The Preacher then faces this world of lost values (in just under fifty lines):

The war has been a fiery forcing house in which we have grown with a rush like flowers in late spring following a terrible winter. And with what result? This: that we have outgrown our religion, outgrown our political system, outgrown our strength of mind and character. The fatal word NOT has been miraculously inserted into all our creeds: in the desecrated temples where we knelt murmuring 'I believe' we stand with stiff knees and stiffer necks shouting 'Up, all! the erect posture is the mark of the man: let lesser creatures kneel and crawl: we will not kneel and we do not believe'. But what next? Is NO enough? For a boy, yes: for a man, never. Are we any less obsessed with a belief when we are denying it than when we were affirming it? NO: I must have affirmations to preach. Without them the young will not listen to me; for even the young grow tired of denials. The negative-monger falls before the soldiers, the man of action, the fighters, strong in the old uncompromising affirmations which give them status, duties, certainty of consequences; so that the pugnacious spirit of man in them can reach out and strike deathblows with steadfastly closed minds.[84]

The core of feeling is in the Preacher's final words: 'I must preach and preach and preach no matter how late the hour and how short the day, no matter whether I have nothing to say',

[84] *Ibid.* pp. 105–7. (Cf. Note on the word 'absurd' in Shaw, below.) The last line of my elliptical version is taken from the next thirteen lines of the same speech.

and the structure of rhetoric is the barrage against that feeling. Shaw could not abandon the language that effectively anaesthetises the experience of loss or anguish. We might accept his twice-repeated dissociation from the Preacher;[85] we are still left with the willed movement of the language itself: the balanced syntax, the thumping rhythms, the over-emphatic words that work against the feeling ('they are *too* absurd'; 'the *fatal* word NOT has been *miraculously* inserted into all our creeds'). Here some principle of 'more is less' is at work. Once a dramatic language is used like this it not only evades certain experiences – inward doubt, for example – but it soon ceases to be dramatic altogether. For rhetoric as barrage can no longer even be used to 'dramatise' a particular attitude or voice; all voices sound the same. This should explain how Shaw has contrived to make Hitler/Battler in *Geneva* speak like everybody else in that and in many other plays, with amiable reasonableness on the subject of his 'mighty movement';[86] as if Shaw had never heard that particular voice, and could not understand its power. At the opposite pole, George Fox is made to refer to 'the inner light' in a political harangue;[87] it is as if Fox, like Shaw, had never experienced silence.

A language without power and silence, that seems to be the end of the convention of prose rhetoric in drama. No doubt there are circumstances peculiar to Shaw alone: the divided personality whose attitude to art we have briefly discussed; the rejection of anything less than the conscious and the fully articulated – something strongly suggested by an autobiographical article where he identifies art with ether (after an operation at the age of forty-two), since both liberate into anti-social states, enabling a man 'to plunge into the darkness that existed before (my) birth and be simply nothing'.[88] It is also true that the language

85 (1) In a note at the end of the play where Shaw distinguishes between the author – a professional talk-maker – and the preacher, Aubrey, a 'rascal who happens to be also a windbag'. Both windbag and professional talker are, however, bracketed by the author's belief 'that the world cannot be saved by talk alone'.

(2) At the end of an article Shaw wrote to defend his late plays from criticism by J. W. Krutch, *The Nation* (6 March 1935). *Shaw on Theatre*, pp. 236–41.

86 *Geneva* (1938), Act IV, Standard ed. p. 112, and other places.

87 *In Good King Charles's Golden Days* (1939), p. 75, and other places.

88 'G.B.S. Vivisected' (14 May 1898), *Our Theatres in the Nineties*, pp. 380–4.

of his comedy – which remained his predominant mode – depends 'on a cultivated and stable society' and on 'speaking the same language as his audience'.[89] Although he showed signs of an intensified search for a new dramatic form and language in the period between the two wars, he was getting old by then, and he did not have the power of self-renewal that occasionally comes to artists, like Titian and Yeats, in their old age.[90] Moreover, the despair of his later years, concealed by rationalising rhetoric and flippancy, seemed to go with a contempt for the old, and a fear of new, modes of language. The plays discussed in this section cumulatively point to this.

In Act II of *Too True to be Good* a character declares that 'speech belongs to the higher centres', and great literature and conversation – 'saying nothing or telling lies' – are equated; but 'Since the war the lower centres have become vocal. And the effect is that of an earthquake.'[91] Perhaps Shaw's hyper-articulate rhetoric came from the 'higher centres' to keep the 'lower centres' from becoming vocal. He is the last prominent dramatist in Europe of whom this can be said, and among the last to be creative within a moribund dramatic language.

Appendix: Notes on Shaw's use of the word 'absurd'

(The page numbers refer to this chapter, unless otherwise indicated.)

It would take a computer to work out the frequency of Shaw's use of this word. The following samples are offered because they appear to underline the argument of the final section of this chapter. The word 'absurd' is itself repeatedly used by Shaw as a defence – to indicate his dissociation from non-rational meaning *and* expression towards which he is nevertheless drawn. Of course, the word 'absurd' is used by Shaw in its traditional sense, and has not yet acquired its post-Camus and 'theatre of the absurd' connotation. But the word is still on the same side of the fence, both as concept and as a mode of expression.

89 Edmund Wilson, *The Triple Thinkers*, p. 219.

90 This may help to explain the curious absence of any sign of awareness in Shaw of developments in drama elsewhere in Europe.

91 See the whole exchange between Aubrey and the 'Countess', *Too True to be Good*, Act II, Standard ed. pp. 65–6.

1. 'The poet tries to make words serve his purpose by arranging them musically, but is hampered by the certainty of becoming absurd if he does not make his musically arranged words mean something to the intellect as well as to the feeling.' (Cf. p. 50 and n. 21 – full quote indicates a certain envy of the composer who may 'reduce the words to mere ejaculation'.)

The fear of the non-rational.

2. 'B.B.'s feeling, absurdly expressed as it is, is too sincere and humane to be ridiculed.' (A stage direction for a style shift involving the use of pastiche. *The Doctor's Dilemma*, Act IV, Penguin ed. p. 178; Standard ed. p. 167. Cf. p. 71.)

This is an attempt to counteract the loss of sympathy resulting from a particular stylistic effect (pastiche). It represents a fear of dehumanised utterance. Clearly Shaw wanted, from time to time, a language of feeling – aimed at empathy or audience participation – and then found himself pulled away into satire, felt as 'absurd expression'. He would have liked his plays to have more 'reality' or humanity; that is why he hoped to attempt naturalism in the Ibsen or Chekhov idiom. (Cf. pp. 56ff.) See also his contrast between a character in Ibsen who is 'in the old phrase, the temple of the Holy Ghost' and 'the Dickens–Thackeray spirit...that of a Punch and Judy showman'. (P. 57, n. 41: *M.C.E.*) In fact Shaw associates the mechanical and the farcical with the absurd, and wants to avoid it.

3. 'There really is some evidence that we are descended from creatures quite as limited and absurd as these.' (The explicit label applied to the Automata and to contemporary man. Spoken by Pygmalion in *Back to Methuselah*, p. 251; cf. p. 77.)

Direct rejection – fascination and horror.

4. 'They are too absurd...' (The Preacher on the characters in the play, *Too True to be Good*, cf. p. 82 above.)

and 5. 'seated, absurdly enough, on nothing.' Don Juan in *Man and Superman*, III. (Penguin ed. p. 131; cf. p. 76 above.)

Defensive use of 'absurd' from rational standpoint.

6. 'Had Swift seen men as creatures evolving towards godhead he would not have been discouraged into *the absurdity of describing them as*

irredeemable Yahoos...' (*Back to Methuselah*, World's Classics ed. p. 300 – conclusion of the 1945 Postscript; my italics.)

Shaw dissociates himself from the 'absurdity' of Swift's vision, and, by implication, from a radical, or non-euphemistic, language of satire.

7. 'Just when I am really rising to the height of my power that I may become really tragic and great, *some absurd joke occurs* and the anti-climax is irresistible. I cannot deny that I have got the tragedian and I have got the clown in me; and the clown trips me up in the most dreadful way.' (Henderson, *Bernard Shaw, Playboy and Prophet*, p. 608, quoted by Eric Bentley, *Shaw*, p. 16; my italics.)

In this direct apology 'absurd' is equated with the flippant; it reveals a longing for a theatre of priests instead of a theatre of clowns. Contrast the interesting apology for the *Tomfooleries*:

'tomfoolery is as classic as tragedy. High comedy seldom achieves a whole act without revealing traces of its origin in the altercations and topical discussions of the circus clown with the ringmaster: what else indeed are the passages between Monsieur Jourdain and his philosophers and fencing masters in Molière's most famous comedy?...The following plays are tomfooleries pure and simple.' (*Translations and Tomfooleries*, Standard ed. p. 81.)

One can spend a few days reading the *Tomfooleries* and be tempted to see in them precursors of the Theatre of the Absurd. But they are not that. They are farce *à outrance*; even here the dialogue is explicit, there is no threat, no sub-text. For example, in *The Music Cure* we come upon the comic sado-masochistic situation where Reginald is 'transported' by the prospect of being 'beaten to a jelly' by the aggressive lady pianist. It remains a gentle joke, despite the superficial resemblance to an Ionesco piece (*ibid.* pp. 234–5.)

2: Eliot

One of Eliot's earliest essays on drama – 'The Possibility of a Poetic Drama' (1920) – expresses a role as much as a critical theory: a voice crying in the wilderness of English drama, drawn towards the 'mirage' of poetic drama though conscious that 'it was impossible to believe in a dramatic "tradition"' in England, that the poets of the nineteenth century wasted their energy in blank verse within merely personal forms, and that there was no satisfactory dramatic form and language to choose from. On the one hand, there are the poeticising dramatists who 'will continue to write poetic pastiches of Euripides and Shakespeare', on the other hand, among the impressive achievements of other art forms, the insufficiently stylised Shavian comedy of ideas.

A mute theatre is a possibility (I do not mean the cinema); the ballet is an actuality (though under-nourished); opera is an institution; but where you have 'imitations of life' on the stage, with speech, the only standard that we can allow is the standard of the work of art, aiming at the same intensity at which poetry and the other forms of art aim. From that point of view the Shavian drama is a hybrid as the Maeterlinckian drama is, and we need express no surprise at their belonging to the same epoch...

The essential is not, of course, that drama should be written in verse...The essential is to get upon the stage this precise statement of life which is at the same time a point of view, a world – a world which the author's mind has subjected to a complete process of simplification.[1]

To envisage the re-creation of a dramatic tradition where there is none, aiming at the intensity of poetry while rejecting the aestheticist cult of poetic drama, seeking to 'get upon the stage ...a point of view, a world' while rejecting the comic–didactic theatre of Shaw, is to take up a very radical position (much more radical than the programme for Shaw's 'New Drama' a generation earlier). And it is characteristic that from the start Eliot should place the question of dramatic form and language at the centre, as a conscious search, a choice to be made from many 'possibilities'. It is also characteristic that these 'possibilities' should include the extreme pole of a mute theatre; while almost at the same time, in '"Rhetoric" and Poetic Drama' (1919)[2] Eliot is discussing the value of 'rhetorical' as against 'conversational' speech, defending the rhetoric of self-dramatisation in Shakespeare, and even the tirades of a Rostand (Cyrano on the Noses) as the articulate expression of emotion, preferable to, for example, the Maeterlinckian literary drama. Later, in the succession of major essays on drama where the question of language is always central, the 'possibilities' can be seen to include the music hall and/or liturgy conceived as an aesthetic device to concentrate expression (less sacred than the Mass, approaching the ballet);[3] then, after twenty years of

1 *The Sacred Wood*, 7th ed., London, 1950, pp. 67–8. The casual statement: 'The essential is not...that drama should be written in verse', is really quite a central position. Thirty years later, in 'Poetry and Drama', Eliot again stressed what poetry and prose have *in common* as dramatic speech: 'the prose in which the characters speak is as remote, for the best part, from the vocabulary, syntax and rhythm of our ordinary speech – with its fumbling for words, its constant recourse to approximation, its disorder and its unfinished sentences – as verse is. Like verse, it has been written and re-written.' And he goes on to instance as the greatest prose stylists Congreve and Shaw. *On Poetry and Poets*, London, 1957, pp. 72–3. Also *Selected Prose*, Harmondsworth, 1953, p. 68.

2 This essay should be read side by side with the discussion of rhetoric in Marlowe and Jonson, written in the same year (*Selected Essays*, London, 1951, pp. 119 and 155), which prepares the way for Eliot's periodic use of open, even florid, rhetoric for local effects.

3 In 'A Dialogue on Dramatic Poetry' (1928). The distinction between dramatic and religious liturgy is repeated in 'Religious Drama: Mediaeval and Modern', *University of Edinburgh Journal*, Autumn 1937.

hostility to naturalistic drama,[4] Eliot turns to the possibility of conversational verse 'in overt competition with prose drama'.[5] So, each play in succession is, among other things, a conscious choice from consciously stored 'possibilities': for *Sweeney Agonistes* the speech heard in the streets and pubs of London, but assimilated through the rhythms of jazz, the music hall, and the 'archaeologically' reconstructed phallic–Aristophanic chorus; for *Murder in the Cathedral*, the versification of *Everyman* and some doggerel, in a framework of the inwardly conceived and Christianised Dionysiac chorus, with a prose sermon to explain a moment of illumination, and prose parody to implicate and 'alienate' the audience; and in the four plays that followed we see the struggle to find the point of intersection between liturgy and approximate naturalism, between speech out-of-time ('the musical order' and the unsayable) and the speech of our time ('the dialect of the tribe'). In his entire critical and creative work in drama, this least naive of writers, in Schiller's sense of the naive, is preoccupied with the act of choosing, from among the simultaneously present or else evolving 'possibilities', an at once communal and inward language.

Thus Eliot is the first dramatist to write from within a *musée*

4 In the essay intended to mark a revolution in drama, 'Four Elizabethan Dramatists' (1924), with its attack on William Archer's criteria of realism in *The Old Drama and the New* (1923). See *Selected Essays*, p. 111 especially.

Cf. 'the juggling of Rastelli [is] more cathartic than a performance of *A Doll's House*. 'The Beating of a Drum', *The Nation and the Athenaeum*, 6 Oct. 1923, p. 12.

Cf. more than a decade later: realism in the theatre 'has tended to depart so far from poetry as to depart from prose too; and to give us people on the stage who are so extremely lifelike that *they do not even talk prose, but merely make human noises*.' 'The Need for Poetic Drama', *The Listener* (25 Nov. 1936), p. 995 (my italics).

5 'Poetry and Drama' (1950), *Selected Prose*, p. 79. Cf. 'The Aims of Poetic Drama' (*Adam*, Nov. 1949) and 'The Three Voices of Poetry' (1953) – the former an early variant, the latter a development of 'Poetry and Drama'. All three essays are concerned with how 'it was in 1938, then, that the third voice began to force itself upon my ear'. The watershed is thus given with exemplary precision; between the group of essays in notes 3 and 4 and those in note 5, Eliot wrote nothing specifically on the subject of dramatic language. *The Family Reunion* (1939) embodies the unsatisfactory complexities of the transition.

imaginaire of speech with full consciousness. It is as if, to adapt a well-known dictum, Eliot had come to drama 'not merely with his own generation in his bones, but with a feeling that the whole of the drama from Aeschylus and within it the whole of the drama of his own country has a simultaneous order'.[6] But in searching for a viable dramatic language the 'possibilities' found in 'the drama of his own country' (or in his own country *tout court*) are the ones that matter; there is no fully universal 'imaginary museum' for language, though there may be for form. The 'Aeschylean' chorus will make use of the Anglican liturgy; and – perhaps an ironic development – the Euripidean plot model for *The Confidential Clerk* will be combined with the 'possibilities' offered by the language of Edwardian comedy. What does stand out is Eliot's constant backward look when struggling to create new possibilities of expression in drama.[7]

Eliot's intense language-consciousness includes a feeling for language as organic – passing through all the phases of the life cycle, and threatened, again and again, with exhaustion. To some extent such a view was 'in the air' when Eliot turned to drama – it found its culmination in Spengler's cyclic view of culture (which Eliot did not acknowledge, though there is at least a certain affinity between them); Joyce came under the spell of Vico, the first thinker to plot, in his *Scienza Nuova* (1725), the primitive sources and the gradual desiccation of language; and T. E. Hulme, who did influence Eliot, held that a particular convention in art was strictly analogous to organic life: 'All the best tunes get played on it and then it is exhausted.'[8] The influence is not important, but the critical and creative result

6 'Tradition and the Individual Talent' (1919), *Selected Essays*, p. 14.
Cf. the rich catalogue of dramatic forms (starting with Noh plays, Bhasa and Kalidasa, the Greeks, and so on to mediaeval, Spanish and French drama) which, ideally, could constitute our imaginary museum: 'Seneca in Elizabethan Translation' (1927), *Selected Essays*, p. 75.

7 I think the ideal language for Eliot would be one that 'gathers into itself all the voices of the past, and projects them into the future', in the words of the final chorus in *The Family Reunion* (II, I). Eliot developed a kind of double hearing: 'the timeless and the temporal together', echoes from the past heard under contemporary speech.

8 T. E. Hulme, *Speculations*, London, 1924, p. 121, quoted and discussed, in a different context, in Sean Lucy, *T. S. Eliot and the Idea of Tradition*, London, 1960, pp. 33–5.

is: when it comes to choosing a 'possibility' in dramatic language, Eliot's first choice is what he takes to be the primitive, and therefore most vital source: the Ur-ritual as unearthed by anthropologically minded classical scholarship (for *Sweeney Agonistes*); Aeschylus rather than Euripides, *Everyman* and the medieval Mysteries rather than Shakespeare, for Euripides and Shakespeare represent stages of decay.[9] In his later search for the right secular and contemporary drama Eliot still echoes Greek proto-myths while trying to base his 'self-education', his search for a more conversational verse, on a study of 'the evolution of Shakespeare'.[10] It is not too much to say that an inward mimesis of other dramatists' 'evolution', and of the organic evolution of a dramatic language, is an essential part of Eliot's critical thinking and creative practice. But can the organic growth of language be 'mimed' without too great a loss in spontaneity? It is a question to keep at the back of one's mind when examining Eliot's struggle for a viable dramatic language.

In theory, such a conception of language offers a dramatist the bold innovatory potentialities of modern, or Modernist, art; he should be able to use language as he uses myth, 'manipulating a continuous parallel between contemporaneity and antiquity'.[11] And something like that Eliot hoped to achieve in poetic drama. In practice – perhaps through an American's over-intense concern with the wholeness of the culture of Europe – Eliot experienced a powerful pull towards the past. It is not for nothing that he once said that the desired 'orthodoxy of sensibility' and 'sense of tradition' can be measured by 'our degree of approaching "that region where dwell the vast hosts of the dead"'.[12] On the one hand, approaching 'the dead' may refertilise the resources of the dramatist's language. On the other hand, there is the 'burden

[9] Eliot states these preferences, in such antithetical and evolutionary terms, repeatedly. See 'Euripides and Professor Murray' (1920); 'Four Elizabethan Dramatists' (1924); 'Religious Drama: Mediaeval and Modern' (1937) (for details see Bibliography).

[10] 'Poetry and Drama'. The phrase is taken from that essay, *Selected Prose*, p. 84.

[11] 'Ulysses, Order and Myth', *The Dial*, LXXV (1923). The essay contains a specific rejection of the antiquarian kind of classicism, of 'turning away from nine tenths of the material which lies at hand, and *selecting only mummified stuff from the museum*' (my italics).

[12] *After Strange Gods*, London, 1934, p. 38. Eliot quotes from the conclusion of Joyce's *The Dead*.

of the past' and the conscious struggle with the exhaustion of language. Or, as Eliot stated in 'What is a Classic?' (1944), the great and classic poet 'exhausts the language'. 'It is only after the language – its cadence, still more than vocabulary and syntax – has, with time and social change, sufficiently altered, that another poet as great as Shakespeare . . . can become possible.'[13] Such a view can be a creative prop; certainly, Eliot's radical reaction against Shakespearean blank verse – an exhausted language – helped to make 'possible' Eliot's own non-Shakespearean 'cadences'. But the idea of the exhaustible language can also be inhibitive. What if the dramatist feels that the language he has just revitalised is, in turn, exhausted or about to be exhausted? Or if he feels that the greater part of the speech he hears every day is exhausted speech, like Celia listening to Edward's voice

> What I heard was only the noise of an insect,
> Dry, endless, meaningless, inhuman –[14]

then the dramatist – and here Eliot anticipates Beckett – has to carry, in addition to all his other technical difficulties, the burden of dead languages: the discarded language of his previous play; the vast number of unusable exhibits from the museum; as well as large areas in the language, written and spoken, in his time.

In this context Eliot's predilection for such poetic devices as borrowing, quotation, allusion and pastiche takes on a new interest. One recalls certain statements from his criticism, as this one on Massinger's indebtedness to others in his dramatic verse:

> One of the surest of tests is the way in which a poet borrows. Immature poets imitate; mature poets steal; bad poets deface what they take . . . The good poet welds his theft into a whole of feeling which is unique, utterly different from that from which it was torn . . . A good poet

[13] *On Poetry and Poets*, London, 1957, pp. 64–5.

[14] *Collected Plays*, p. 154 (*The Cocktail Party*, I, ii). Cf. Molloy: 'the words I heard, and heard distinctly, having quite a sensitive ear, were heard for the first time, then a second, and often even a third, as pure sounds, free of all meaning, and this is probably one of the reasons why conversation was unspeakably painful to me. And the words I uttered myself, and which must nearly always have gone with an effort of the intelligence, were often to me as the buzzing of an insect.' Beckett, *Molloy, etc.*, London, 1959, p. 50.

will usually borrow from authors remote in time, or alien in language, or diverse in interest.[15]

The use Eliot makes of such a principle in his non-dramatic poetry is well-known. It is enough to point to, say, the Ariadne stanza in *Sweeney Erect* ('Display me Aeolus above') with its deliberate pastiche of Jacobean dramatic verse, a borrowing from *The Maid's Tragedy*; or, to take a less recondite example, the distracted voice of Ophelia in the London pub:

> Goonight Bill. Goonight Lou. Goonight May. Goonight.
> Ta ta. Goonight. Goonight.
> Good night, ladies, good night, sweet ladies, good night, good night. (*The Waste Land*, 170–3)

which is, as it stands, a dramatic juxtaposition. Are there such devices in Eliot's dramatic poetry? There are; but we find that those allusions and borrowings that are merely 'remote in time' or 'alien in language' hardly matter. They may have been an aid to composition but they do not work as dramatic speech for a crudely simple reason: the borrowed language is not public enough. (And in drama the borrowed language must not only be used, but seen and heard to be used.) For example, one really cannot claim to get a sharper or richer response to the exchange between Thomas and the Second Tempter in *Murder in the Cathedral*

> Thomas: Who shall have it?
> Tempter: He who will come.
> Thomas: What shall be the month?
> Tempter: The last from the first...

when one discovers, with the help of Professor Grover Smith,[16] that it is taken almost verbatim from Conan Doyle's 'The Musgrave Ritual'?– 'diverse in interest'. Again, one might

15 *Selected Essays*, p. 206. Cf. in praise of Jonson's idea of verbal Imitation: 'His [Jonson's] third requisite in a poet pleases me especially: "The third requisite in our poet, or maker is Imitation, to be able to convert the substances or riches of another poet, to his own use."' *The Use of Poetry and the Use of Criticism*, London, 1964 (new edition, with new preface), pp. 54–5. There are also several examples of praise for individual poets, for example in the essay on Dryden, for a 'method...very near to parody' and for 'a fine passage plagiarized from Cowley'. *Selected Essays*, pp. 307–8.

16 *T. S. Eliot's Poetry and Plays*, Phoenix Edition, Chicago and London, 1960, p. 194, note 16.

connect, in a scholarly diversion, the First Knight's dark threat to the Priests in the same play:

> Business before dinner. We will roast your pork
> First, and dine upon it after.

with the kind of primitive ritual, the sacrificial feast, Cornford had rediscovered in Aristophanes and Eliot imported into Sweeney's 'cannibal isle' and 'missionary stew'. Yet the ritual of Christian martyrdom must be, and is, established by a much broader 'borrowing': through the public language of Christian liturgy, hymns and the sermon. And then it hardly matters whether the audience recognises the individual phrases from the psalms, and other places in the Bible, in the Introit, for the allusions are made public, the fragments linked, through liturgy; and one can respond to 'Numb the hand and dry the eyelid' without recognising the specific rhythms of the *Dies Irae*. But when, after *Murder in the Cathedral*, Eliot found that formal liturgy was, for him, an exhausted language, he moved towards various compromise languages with a peculiar form of allusiveness: echoes of the former language in a residual liturgy.

One way of looking at the evolution of Eliot's dramatic language – impelled as it is by the idea of the language cycle as much as by specifically new requirements – is to see in it a series of sacrifices. To achieve a broadly based convention – such as liturgy – he abandoned the subtle allusiveness, the Jacobean–Symbolist complexity of his quasi-dramatic poetry; there is no successful equivalent to *Prufrock* or *Gerontion* in the plays. The 'floating feelings'[17] Eliot once held up as an ideal of dramatic verse were pruned and fixed in broad liturgical or incantatory patterns in *Murder in the Cathedral*. No sooner had this been

17 See Eliot's early comment in 'Tradition and the Individual Talent' on a passage from *The Revenger's Tragedy* (given by him as one of those 'unseen' critical tests): 'the whole effect, the dominant tone, is due to the fact that a number of *floating feelings* having affinity to this [the structural] emotion by no means superficially evident, have combined with it to give us a new art emotion.' There seems to be a link between this idea of a complex dramatic language and the idea of poetic language based on the Metaphysical poets: 'The poet must become more and more comprehensive, more allusive, more indirect, in order to force, *to dislocate if necessary, language into his meaning*.' *Selected Essays*, p. 20 and p. 289 respectively (my italics).

achieved than Eliot began to move, with great transitional strain, towards 'speech within the limits of one imaginary character addressing another'. So 'liturgy' was sacrificed for approximately 'naturalistic' verse – using these terms here as shorthand, marking opposed poles.

We find nearly all we need to know about Eliot's movement from liturgy to approximate naturalism – from such ideals as 'intensity' and 'abstraction from actual life'[18] to writing 'for other voices', for character – in his own self-critical surveys in 'Poetry and Drama' (1951) and 'The Three Voices of Poetry' (1953). But one recognition we can now add: in 'disciplining his poetry' in a quasi-naturalistic direction Eliot has created a need for 'spoken action' and 'subtext' which he does not often satisfy. (See also: Introduction, pp. 19–21.) 'Subtext', in the language of modern prose drama, aims at patterns of speech, pause, gestures, all working together throughout a play to create a meaning larger than the verbal text. Some of Eliot's key conceptions are superficially similar: the idea of an 'under-pattern, less manifest than the theatrical one'[19] for the early plays; and for the late plays the ideal ('the unattainable ideal') to express in words, emotions *beyond the namable*:

> It seems to me that beyond the namable, classifiable emotions and motives of our conscious life when directed towards action – the part of life which prose drama is wholly adequate to express – there is a fringe of indefinite extent, of feeling which we can only detect, so to speak, out of the corner of the eye and can never completely focus...[20]

Both these concepts have great potentiality for drama; but they go with limitations in Eliot's practice, which he may not have fully perceived. The *under-pattern*, bound up as it is with the idea of 'doubleness' in action and with two, often separate, levels of language, goes with a linguistic dualism: a gulf between

18 Key ideas from 'A Dialogue on Dramatic Poetry' (1928) and 'Four Elizabethan Dramatists' (1924) respectively. *Selected Essays*, p. 58 and p. 111.

19 See the whole paragraph beginning 'It is possible that what distinguishes poetic drama from prosaic drama is a kind of doubleness in the action', in 'John Marston' (1934), *Selected Essays*, p. 229. This should be read against the longer passage on levels – including two levels of speech – in the Conclusion to *The Use of Poetry and the Use of Criticism* (2nd ed.), London, 1964, pp. 153–5.

20 'Poetry and Drama', *On Poetry and Poets*, pp. 86–7.

sacred/profane, hieratic/demotic, real/make-believe, between the Word and words. Eliot's plays are shot through with the palpable effects of his feeling for 'the fall of language'. And this almost Manichean vision of two languages does not have the flexibility and naturalness of different levels of action and speech in Shakespeare (invoked by Eliot in *The Use of Poetry* in this context).

The later aim, the expression of emotions *beyond the namable,* is linked with Eliot's hope that dramatic poetry 'at its moments of greatest intensity...can touch the border of those feelings which only music can express.' (The humility and the tentativeness is characteristic, as is the post-Symbolist tension: 'we can never emulate music...nevertheless...') The ultimate aim is a harmonious fusion of what Eliot calls the dramatic and the musical 'order'. Yet in practice, in the last three plays Eliot seems to rely increasingly on the 'music' (the colloquial rhythms with the triple accentual stress:

I 'thought that I could 'help him | I took him to 'concerts[21])

to work on us, to take us 'beyond the namable'. Against these often 'subliminal' rhythmic effects, the other aspects of Eliot's dramatic language – the syntax, the words and images, even the placing, the length, and the interlinking of speeches in dialogue – tend to become over-explicit and thin in undertones. So, paradoxically, what was intended to reach beyond the namable, tends to name more often than it suggests; the verse becomes 'transparent' (as Eliot wanted it to be) in neo-classical window-frames.

In the late plays the 'fringe effect' is often sacrificed to broader, explicit devices, including stage rhetoric drawn from melodrama and farce – a territory shared with Shaw – in the attempt to make poetic drama communal again, that is socially useful, popular. The last 'possibility' was a *return* to the conventions of speech in the comedy of manners and naturalistic drama – a return in the precise sense of going back to something once judged unfit and then found usable again. One may assume that Eliot saw in that theatrical convention – in its interaction with the social world – a world-of-appearance and a profane

21 Northrop Frye gaily disagrees with Eliot's own definition of his verse-line, but seems to overlook the distinction between primary and secondary stress, in *T. S. Eliot*, Edinburgh and London, 1963, pp. 37ff.

ritual; and though he did go back to a dramatic language which he knew has been often 'played' before, he saw in it the 'possibility' of re-creation – it was for him, almost certainly, an impoverished but not yet exhausted language.

All these considerations prompt a question – which can only be answered implicitly, through the detailed discussion that follows. Did not Eliot's pursuit of a new poetic–dramatic language 'consume vast energy...which could never lead to a wholly satisfying result'? (The words are those Eliot applied to all the nineteenth-century poets who turned to drama, in the essay with which we began.)[22] The stress here is on a new and supreme degree of language-consciousness that goes with the bold experimentation – the movement from possibility to possibility – and the way each stage is prepared through manifesto, and retrospectively tested in self-critical essays. It is as if – probably for the first time – a dramatist's involvement with language has itself become dramatised: a conflict enacted in public, with an intense feeling for specific limitations and waste:

> 'Trying to use words, and every attempt
> Is a wholly new start, and a different kind of failure
> Because one has only learnt to get the better of words
> For the thing one no longer has to say, or the way in which
> One is no longer disposed to say it.
>
> (*Four Quartets*, 'East Coker', V)

Ritual and Liturgy

> And whether in Argos or England
> There are certain inflexible laws
> Unalterable, in the nature of music.
>
> (*The Family Reunion*, Part Two, scene I, Chorus)

Eliot's sustained attempt to revitalise the poetic language of drama by going back to the origins – Aristophanes, Aeschylus and the medieval drama – is certainly important in his own work; and it gains an additional interest once we realise that Eliot's work does not stand alone but at the centre of the larger movement to re-mythologise language, to achieve intensified meaning – or feeling – through primordial images and rhythm. The first wave, the Romantic one, culminated in the gigantic

[22] *The Sacred Wood*, p. 67. (See n. 1.)

attempt to re-create the Dionysiac for modern man: Wagner's entire work, and the dramatic theory of the young Nietzsche. That the imaginative link between the origins of Greek tragedy and the new total language of music, words and movement was largely an imaginary link,[23] is less important than the will to re-create myth and ritual, and its language, conceived as the superlative anti-naturalist mode. A sentence from Nietzsche may serve to point to the essential link between the return to ritual and the language of drama: 'The introduction of the Chorus is the decisive step whereby we declare war, openly and honestly, on all Naturalism in art.'[24] But it is a significant negative fact that the imagined return to the spirit of Greek tragedy should have issued not in verbal but in music drama. Anyone who has studied the *words* of *Tristan und Isolde* – or rather listened to the words emerging – will have understood that here language itself is taken through the stages of ecstasy, the words are beside themselves, in the supreme effort to suggest an all-consuming passion or Nothingness. The ultimate direction of such a language is submergence, in music or silence. But the concreteness of the English language has not been hospitable to this extreme pole of language; the chief, if indirect, outcome in drama written in English – mediated by the international Symbolist–aestheticist ideal of a language approximating music – is the early drama of Yeats. Eliot, who was from the start hostile to the drama represented by Maeterlinck,[25] had little use for any dramatic language

23 See Francis Fergusson, *The Idea of a Theater* (1949), New York, 1953, pp. 80–100. The belief that European drama had its origins in ritual has itself been questioned by A. W. Pickard-Cambridge (in *Dithyramb, Tragedy and Comedy*, Oxford, 1927) and by G. F. Else (in *The Origin and Early Form of Greek Tragedy*, Harvard, 1965).

24 Friedrich Nietzsche, 'Die Geburt der Tragödie aus dem Geiste der Musik' (1872), *Werke*, vol. 1, München (no date), p. 46 (my translation). Eliot in 'The Need for Poetic Drama' (1936, *loc. cit.*) justifies the revival of the chorus as an element that fulfils the need to 'emphasise, not to minimise' that a play is in verse; the chorus supports the '*musical pattern*, as well as the dramatic pattern of the play' (Eliot's italics).

25 See p. 87. Cf. the repeated attempts made by Eliot to define the relationship of poetry and music in contradistinction from the principles of Mallarmé (not to mention Shelley and Swinburne), e.g. in 'Ezra Pound: His Metric and Poetry' (1917) and 'The Music of Poetry' (1942) (cf. also pp. 108–9).

generated by etiolated myth; as late as 1950 he characterises the language of Yeats' *early* plays as 'not really a form of speech quite suitable for anybody except mythical kings and queens'.[26]

There is ritual and ritual, and Eliot would have no truck with the Romantic tribe of myth-makers and their language: the hypnotic Wagnerian mode, or language as music, and 'speech of soul'. His aloof critical temperament – using the rationally based works of Frazer, Cornford and others, and not Nietzsche, on the sources of the Dionysiac – *at first* brought him into affinity with that modern movement where ritual is only one 'possibility', liturgy *a* language. Yet, after *Sweeney*, Eliot's experience of the Christian pattern of atonement through the perennial myth of the dying god made him the only modern dramatist to use liturgy as *the* language of ritual. The high point is the use of the incantatory chorus in *Murder in the Cathedral*, not as a vehicle of commentary or even illumination, but as a medium of participation, drawing the audience into the inner movement of the ritual of sacrifice. (Francis Fergusson found a place for Eliot side by side with the sophisticated Parisian dramatists of the inter-war period in the post-Wagnerian use of myth and ritual.[27] But, clearly, Eliot has moved very far both in conception and, for our purposes, from the *playful* way with myth-based language. Here is a simple contrast: the Eumenides of Giraudoux, three little girls, begin their 'recital' with 'Queen Clytemnestra has a bad colour. She uses rouge';[28] in *The Family Reunion* the Eumenides stand silent in the window embrasure, causing Harry to interpret, at length, the meaning of this unspeakable experience.) Eliot's early idea of liturgy, already referred to, makes a clear-cut distinction between the Mass, and liturgy in drama:

We cannot be aware solely of divine realities. We must be aware also of human realities. And we crave some liturgy less divine, something in respect of which we shall be more spectators and less participants.

[26] 'Poetry and Drama' (*Selected Prose*, p. 75). See also the attack on Yeats in *After Strange Gods*, p. 46: 'a highly sophisticated lower mythology summoned, like a physician, to supply the fading pulse of poetry with some transient stimulant so that the dying patient may utter his last words'. [27] *The Idea of a Theater*, Ch. 7 (Introduction).

[28] Giraudoux, *Electra* (1937), Act I (*The Modern Theater*, vol. I, New York, 1955, p. 199). The next metamorphosis of the Eumenides is the chorus of flies in Sartre. (See in particular the longer chorus in *The Flies* (1943), Act III, Scene i.)

Hence we want the human drama, related to the divine drama, but not the same, as well as the Mass.[29]

It is a classic distinction between participatory and spectatorial language. But the way Eliot used liturgy – the way he developed – is more complex.

To read *Sweeney Agonistes, Fragments of an Aristophanic Melodrama* – taking up Eliot on the words of the subtitle – alongside Cornford's *The Origin of Attic Comedy* (1914) is to gain insight into Eliot's rediscovery of the 'Ur'-ritual. For Cornford 'the tragic Myth and the comic Logos', the highly organised structure of Greek drama and the broken-down folk drama of puppets and mummers – with parallels in Punch and Judy, and St George and the Dragon – have the same underlying pattern. Such a discovery opened the way back to what Eliot took to be the primitive sources of drama: offering the hope of a revitalised dramatic language through 'imitation by means of rhythm – rhythm which admits of being applied to words, sounds, and the movement of the body'.[30] While Shakespeare's Plutarch gives us a direct understanding of how the actual words of the text were transmuted (how the description of Cleopatra's barge, for example, became dramatic speech), Eliot's Cornford gives us only the conception behind the dramatic language. It was nevertheless a generative conception. It led to the 'possibility' of ritual and liturgy. And it led to Eliot hearing, as it were simultaneously, the antique drum and the beat of the jazz drum under vulgar, contemporary, metropolitan speech: the fallen liturgy of *Sweeney*. 'This invention of language' – to apply what Eliot said of Baudelaire's intense imagery of damnation taken from the sordid life of the metropolis – 'is the nearest thing to a complete renovation that we have experienced.'[31]

29 *Selected Essays*, p. 49. The date is 1928, the year Eliot made public his conversion to Christianity in the Preface to *For Lancelot Andrewes*. While this cannot be simply equated with a break with the Modernist aesthetic, the 'possibilities' of poetic drama are, for the next ten years, restricted to open or concealed ritual on a Christian ground.

30 'The Beating of a Drum.' The article opens with Darwin and ends with the view that through various rationalisations 'we have lost the drum'. Cornford too is invoked; and the two titles, 'The Origin of Species' and 'The Origin of Attic Comedy', meet the eye on the same page. The words quoted are Eliot's quotation from Aristotle: Butcher, p. 139.

31 'Baudelaire', *Selected Essays*, p. 426.

Sweeney is, then, most successful as an experiment in speech, or more precisely, in turning speech into rhythmic sound effects. We know that Eliot intended the whole work to be accompanied by 'light drum taps to accentuate the beats (esp. the chorus which ought to have a noise like a street drill)';[32] and that emphatic modern rhythm was associated by him with the internal combustion engine. We are meant to experience the play upon our pulses. We shall see later how colloquial cross-talk is itself turned into near-abstract orchestration. Here we should recall how many of the elements in the short play are language-as-sound: the constant repetition of names, questions and greetings, for phonic play ('Good bye. Goooood bye'); the telephone bell's 'Ting a ling' and the 'knock, knock' woven into the texture of the dialogue (spelt out as fourteen lines); Sweeney's speech, about *his* unutterable experience, merging into crooning ('We're gona sit here and have a tune'); the six visitors, with the unnecessary names, forming a broken chorus even before they burst into jazz song and into the final nightmare-chorus. The spirit of the Hoo-ha's pervades this work; the toys of Dionysus, top, rattle, dice-bones,[33] have been rediscovered. But one can see why Eliot excluded *Sweeney* from the *Collected Plays*; from his point of view it was the first dead end; the experiment with popular forms drawing on the music hall and the street were left to others. The return to the 'origins' of drama resulted in a small-scale work best *heard* on record or radio – the original radio play.

Sweeney remained a fragment probably through a creative breakdown; and from it Eliot turned to a theatre of priests: from the Aristophanic to the Aeschylean chorus, from the demotic to the hieratic liturgy. This inward progression, doubtless compelled by an overwhelming human and aesthetic need, corre-

[32] See letter to Hallie Flanigan, the producer of the play-fragment at Vassar (1933) quoted in Carol H. Smith, *T. S. Eliot's Dramatic Theory and Practice*, Princeton, 1963, p. 52. Cf. the well-known reference to the 'internal combustion engine' (Introduction to Charlotte Eliot's *Savonarola*..., London, 1926) with Eliot's appreciation of Stravinsky's *Sacre du printemps*: 'it did seem to transform the rhythm of the steppes into the scream of the motor horn, the rattle of machinery, the grind of wheels...and the other barbaric cries of modern life'. 'London Letter', *Dial*, LXXI (Oct. 1921).

[33] As in Orphic Fragment 23, K. Freeman, *Ancilla to the Pre-Socratic Philosophers*, Oxford, 1962.

sponded with that hypothetical evolution of drama and dramatic language which Eliot had come to accept as the true pattern: the primitive ritual developed into the highly organised rhythm of sacrifice.[34] If much of *Sweeney* was incantatory in the sense of a primitive spell, in *The Rock* (1934) we can trace both the idea and the stylistic method whereby the incantatory becomes an attempt to reach out towards 'a perfect order of speech', a form of redeemed speech. In the third chorus the Word of the Lord utters a reproach:

> I have given you hands, which you turn from worship
> I have given you speech, for endless palaver;

the ninth chorus – as if responding, in its praise of artistic creation, itself a metonymy for building the church – intones:

> Out of the sea of sound like music
> Out of the slimy mud of words, out of the sleet and hail of verbal imprecisions...
> There spring the perfect order of speech, and the beauty of incantation.[35]

We cannot equate liturgy with the use of chorus: it can be more direct, as in the formal chant of the priests in Part II of *Murder in the Cathedral*, and more indirect, as in the gradually fading liturgical echoes in much of the dialogue in the later plays, from the intense exchanges between Harry and Agatha in *The Family Reunion* (Part II, Scene 2) to the quiet litany at the end of *The Elder Statesman*. Nevertheless, it is Eliot's handling of the chorus that shows us in a most concentrated form this meta-personal language. The following four extracts, taken from three plays, may serve to illustrate both Eliot's development of the chorus, and the intrinsic values and problems of incantatory

34 Cornford observes – in the somewhat different context of ritual developing into comedy – that the Medicine-man's 'hocus-pocus lives on in the ceremonials of the priest; his incantations and *carmina* make him the ancestor of the oracle-monger and the poet'. *The Origin of Attic Comedy*, London, 1914, p. 202 (Section 100).

35 *Collected Poems*, pp. 165 and 180. For a good example of liturgy pushed to a formal extreme see the section in Chorus VII beginning 'Then came at a predetermined moment, a moment in time, and of time...'; in the six lines that follow the word 'time' is repeated nine times, six times in conjunction with 'moment'; it is a litany.

language. For convenience of comparison, they have an affinity in theme, expressing that psychic fear which is, for Eliot, the central obstacle to, and the condition of, growth:

(1) When you're alone in the middle of the night and
  you wake in a sweat and a hell of a fright
When you're alone in the middle of the bed and
  you wake like someone hit you on the head
You've had a cream of a nightmare dream and
  you've got the hoo-ha's coming to you.
(Final Chorus, *Sweeney Agonistes*)

(2) But now a great fear is upon us, a fear not of one but of many,
A fear like birth and death, when we see birth and death alone
In a void apart. We
Are afraid in a fear which we cannot know, which we
  cannot face, which none understands,
And our hearts are torn from us, our brains unskinned
  like the layers of an onion, our selves are lost lost
In a final fear which none understands.
(Second Chorus, *Murder in the Cathedral*, Part I)

(3) (...) I have felt
The heaving of earth at nightfall, restless, absurd. I have heard
Laughter in the noises of beasts that make strange
  noises: jackal, jackass, jackdaw; the scurrying
  noise of mouse and jerboa; the laugh of the loon,
  the lunatic bird. I have seen
Grey necks twisting, rat tails twining, in the thick
  light of dawn. (...)
(Second Chorus, *Murder in the Cathedral*, Part II)

(4) I am afraid of all that has happened, and of all that is to come;
Of the things to come that sit at the door, as if they had been
  there always.
And the past is about to happen, and the future was long
  since settled.
And the wings of the future darken the past, the beak and
  claws have desecrated
History. Shamed.
The first cry in the bedroom, the noise in the nursery, mutilated
The family album, rendered ludicrous
The tenants' dinner, the family picnic on the moors. Have torn
The roof from the house, or perhaps it was never there.
And the bird sits on the broken chimney. I am afraid.

Ivy: This is a most undignified terror, and I must struggle against it.
Gerald: I am used to tangible danger, but only to what I can understand.
Violet: It is the obtuseness of Gerald and Charles and that doctor, that gets on my nerves.
Charles: If the matter were left in my hands, I think I could manage the situation. (*The Family Reunion*, Part I, Scene iii)

The context of the first passage is simple: Sweeney's friends line up to 'comment' on the death-in-life experience the protagonist has been struggling to express in his 'gotta use words' speech. Technically, the Aristophanic[36] and the music-hall chorus are fused in a melodrama that is also melo-drama; the four-beat line stimulates and hypnotises at one and the same time; the imagery has the satirical explicitness of a song from Brecht (who also drew on Aristophanes). The effect, with an extra folksy 'creepiness', is parody, which neutralises any intended participatory understanding, 'by the most sensitive and intelligent members of the audience',[37] of Sweeney's supposedly numinous experience.

The context of the passages from *Murder in the Cathedral* is inseparable from Eliot's boldest invention in drama: a chorus that gives voice to two kinds of experience 'normally' unspoken or inexpressible: the stages of dumb mass suffering, and the inward agony of the chief 'agonist' placed, deliberately, beyond communication. The chorus starts by representing the passive consciousness yet ends as the chief agent of participation – drawing the audience into the action with its own reluctant passion; it speaks 'out of' the inarticulate with formalised articulateness, attempting to move from the almost subhuman towards the superhuman. The chorus itself turns, as the play

[36] It has been frequently pointed out that the nightmare chorus owes a lot to the Lord Chancellor's patter in *Iolanthe*, Act II. But it is also possible that Eliot was familiar with the distinctly Gilbertian tone of the translations of Aristophanes then current; for example, Peisthetaerus on the terrors of bird-death:

'And the customers, buying, come poking and prying
  And twitching and trying
To feel if your bodies are tender and plump.
And if they decide on your flesh to sup...'

The Birds (transl. B. B. Rogers), London, 1906, p. 69.

[37] Cf. n. 19 on the two planes in *Sweeney Agonistes*.

progresses, on the wheel of suffering and action, which is not only a key metaphysical image but also a paradigm for the play's movement. Moreover, with this progression the language of the chorus itself undergoes a change: a gradual intensification, an orchestral *crescendo*[38] from the half-rationalised forebodings (most of Part I) to the near-hysteria of the two choruses before and after the murder of Beckett ('the death-bringers', and 'Clean the air!'). The contrary movement, to the still point of the work – comparable to Chorale 8 in Bach's *Matthew Passion* ('Wenn ich einmal soll scheiden') – is marked by the verses based on the *Dies Irae* which frames a litany on the Void, recognisably 'Eliotic', which comes out most strongly when spoken by a single voice. There is also the final *Te Deum* which, alone among the choruses, makes direct use of the Anglican liturgy.[39]

The two passages chosen (2 and 3) may illustrate the use of liturgy for intensification in the sense defined. The first passage shows the stage of passivity growing into anxious incomprehension. The language changes correspondingly: from the monotonous three-beat lines of the 'living and partly living' sequence which precedes it, to an at once irregular and emphatic rhythm; from lulling abstractions of the human condition ('We have seen births, deaths, and marriages') to the immediate threat to mind and body; the image-clusters or parallelisms (our hearts/our brains/our selves) are like the obsessive repetitions of an anxiety state, not a mere litany. The violent image ('your brains unskinned like the layers of an onion') is universal: it expresses a personal *and* communal fear.

This is not intended to be an unqualified defence of the choruses in *Murder in the Cathedral*. The final chorus, in particular, bears the mark of strain, of too many levels within the formal – ecclesiastical – liturgy: the psalm-like simplicity of 'the darkness declares the glory of light' is all but lost, can barely move, in the over-extended formula of affirmation, where we are given the

38 The phrase used by John Peter, 'Murder in the Cathedral', reprinted (from *The Sewanee Review*, Summer 1953) in *T. S. Eliot, A Collection of Critical Essays* (ed. Hugh Kenner), Englewood Cliffs, N.J., 1962. (This reference to p. 164.)

39 For the use of the *Te Deum* in histrionic ritual, see the epilogue of *St Joan*, discussed on p. 74. Contrast the text of the *Te Deum* in the Book of Common Prayer.

theological rationale of praising (down to a formal q.e.d.: 'Therefore man, [relative clause], must praise Thee'), followed by the women, as the charwomen of Canterbury, liturgising 'the hand to the broom'; and the prophetic modernism – 'sight-seers come with guide-books' – only adds to the sense that the movement here is willed.[40]

But it needs to be stressed that most objections to the choruses amount to a symptom of impatience against the liturgical mode in drama as such. Ezra Pound turned off his radio set in Rapallo when listening to the play, with a despairing 'Oh them cawkney voices'; and Hugh Kenner, who repeats the story, caps this action-judgement with his impatience: 'The language of the Chorus: their ululating logorrhea, doubling and tripling the image'.[41] Dull would he be of soul...who has never turned off the radio, or stopped the recording of the 1953 Old Vic production. (In the latter the frequent 'awfulness' does make one realise the extreme difficulty modern actors experience in speaking the lines of a chorus. The same is true of most English-language performances of Greek tragedy; yet other languages, or theatrical traditions – French, Italian, modern Greek – have preserved a much more 'natural' link with formal recitation.) But the particular objection of Hugh Kenner – the repetitiousness so different from Eliot's early poetry – is misplaced; or rather it amounts to saying: the chorus is liturgy, liturgy includes litany, and litany is – for Dr Kenner – logorrhea as sense, and ululation as sound.

Perhaps modern man suffers from an auditory allergy. And if enough people feel 'allergic' to liturgy, then the latter will be felt as an *exhausted* language in drama, comparable to blank verse. It is possible to be successful in a dramatic language – as Eliot is in most of the choruses of *Murder in the Cathedral* – and yet be successful only within the limits of resuscitating an archaic mode of speech. That is the cultural condition of language Eliot himself recognised (part of the crisis of dramatic language).

40 In production – as at the Old Vic, 1953 – the 'theological' lines may be assigned to the priests, and not to the women. Antiphon is better here than unison, but the strain remains.

41 Hugh Kenner, *The Invisible Poet*, London, 1960, p. 242. The passage quoted by Kenner in support of his judgement is the litany on the void referred to above.

Thus it was possible for him to revitalise liturgy with great resourcefulness – all other examples from Péguy's *Le mystère de la charité de Jeanne d'Arc* to contemporary attempts at secular ritual drama, appear amateurish in comparison – and yet see the necessity of rejecting it as only a dead end.[42]

As it is, Eliot rejected the chorus too late to avoid the unsuccessful compromise of *The Family Reunion*. The passage quoted (4) should show what kind of compromise it is. The first four lines, ending with 'the beak and claws have desecrated History', present a sympathetic chorus and we are to participate in their heightened awareness, respond to the awe-ful dimension of time and history. But in the lines that follow not only is their particular experience 'rendered ludicrous' – 'the family picnic on the moors' *sub specie aeternitatis* – but the speakers are beginning to exhibit their own feebleness, parody themselves. Within a few lines the chorus splits up, and the parody becomes broad: each aunt and uncle is given a line, generalising some form of moral obtuseness in Eliot's idiom; they hardly have a speech of their own. The rhythm and the syntax of the verse are strained unnaturally by this transition from participation to parody. Helen Gardner has justly observed that in *The Family Reunion* the hero experiences the change and the chorus is static; the exact reversal of *Murder in the Cathedral*. It is also true that the members of the chorus are

> conspicuous for their lack of comprehension. They are not interpreters to the audience of a story which without them might seem too remote from common experience. They seem partly to warn us against certain misunderstandings by presenting them in an obviously absurd form and partly as comic relief.[43]

Unfortunately, their not being 'interpreters' makes them superfluous as a chorus – they do not deepen the meaning of action; and 'the obviously absurd form' is thrust upon them with inappropriate solemnity. From the point of view of our larger argument the treatment of the chorus in *The Family Reunion* demonstrates that it is probably impossible for the language of liturgy to be sacred and profane, participatory and parodistic, at one and the same time. Liturgy can approximate the mass (as in *Murder*

42 'Poetry and Drama', *Selected Prose*, pp. 76–8.

43 Helen Gardner, *The Art of T. S. Eliot*, London, 1949, pp. 140–1.

in the Cathedral) and it can suggest a black mass (as in *Sweeney*); it cannot do both without exhausting that 'possibility' altogether.

Eliot abandoned the chorus after *The Family Reunion*, as the first step in his decision to 'minimise' – rather than emphasise – that a play is written in verse. The only time we have a kind of chorus is the well-known libation scene at the end of Act II of *The Cocktail Party*. Here the context alone gives the litany a histrionic ambiguity: the Guardians are enacting a ritual which we have seen to grow out of the social ritual of pouring out drinks. (The exchange between Edward and Reilly: 'Whiskey?/Gin./Anything in it?/Nothing but water.' is three times repeated in Act I to establish the pattern.) The audience can take its choice: the words of the libation are the pleasing hocus-pocus of a secret society, or else a formal rite of passage which is also a fitting requiem for Celia:

Alex: The words for those who go upon a journey.

. . . . . .

Julia: Protect her from the Voices
Protect her from the Visions
Protect her in the tumult
Protect her in the silence. [*They drink*]

Eliot did not end the play here, and never again used explicit liturgy. But in the next act, as so often in the three last plays, the social routine continues to be felt as a profane ritual; and the dialogue remains shot through with liturgical echoes.

The Dialect of the Tribe

Since our concern was speech, and speech impelled us
To purify the dialect of the tribe...

(*Four Quartets*, 'Little Gidding', II)

They don't understand what it is to be awake,
To be living on several planes at once
Though one cannot speak with several voices at once.

(Harry in *The Family Reunion*, Part II, scene i)

The Eliot of *Sweeney* approached 'common speech' in London as it were anthropologically, coming to it from a distance, assimilating the dialect of a tribe. Yet there was no detachment in this approach, but fascination and horror – fascination with the rhythmic pattern, horror at the lack of meaning. And both these attitudes are important, because they underlie what can only be called Eliot's linguistic dualism.

Eliot is the first modern dramatist to make the rhythmic life of everyday speech something primary: he starts with the idea of rhythm, 'so utterly absent from modern drama, whether prose or verse';[44] and he hopes to alter expression in drama through it. Eliot's early hopes for drama were based on the 'probability' that a 'new form will be devised out of colloquial speech',[45] and on the 'possibility' offered by the decaying music hall, 'the expressive figure of the lower classes', for example the exact tone of voice in which the middle-aged charwoman impersonated by Marie Lloyd would enumerate the objects she found in her bag.[46] Eliot's early approach to everyday language is almost as opposed to the Symbolist emphasis on 'music' at the expense of living speech, as it is to the naturalist drama expressing only – or failing to express – 'the morally corrupt' middle classes, giving us people who 'do not even talk prose, but merely make human noises'.[47] Perhaps this approach can be termed semi-abstract (sufficiently abstract to anticipate Beckett being drawn to a sentence by its *shape*, and Pinter making rhythmic patterns out of material supposedly heard by a 'tape-recording' ear). Liturgy, itself a move towards abstraction – with the emphasis on the rhythmic or musical pattern – largely by-passes the problems of everyday speech in poetic drama; as we saw, it either parodies or sanctifies speech. But the main development of Eliot after *Murder in the Cathedral* was towards increasing exploitation of everyday speech, in a quasi-naturalistic way – complicated by a residual liturgical tone, and by giving the verse, even where it is conversational, a ground bass of rhythm that is often more insistent than the sense.

Eliot's horror at the meaninglessness of ordinary speech is inseparable from hearing 'endless palaver' against a potentially 'perfect order of speech', or 'human noises' against the 'musical pattern'. Such a dualism can be regarded as a linguistic con-

[44] 'The Beating of a Drum', see n. 30.

[45] 'at any rate, the recognised forms of speech verse are not as efficient as they should be; probably a new form will be devised out of colloquial speech.' (Introduction to *Savonarola*, *loc. cit.*)

[46] 'Marie Lloyd' (1923), *Selected Essays*, pp. 457–8.

[47] *Ibid.*; and 'The Need for Poetic Drama', context given in n. 4. For Eliot and Symbolism, see also n. 25.

sequence of a 'double-decker' view of the universe. It is as if the split between Appearance and Reality – crystallised in the young Eliot by his study of F. H. Bradley[48] – had to express itself in dramatic and linguistic parallels: a doubleness of action and two levels of language where one level is speech-of-appearance which mocks or falsifies 'real' speech. We may reflect that the appearance/reality dualism is eminently dramatic, even theatrical, and that there is much in the greatest drama – from *Hamlet* to *Ghosts* and *Six Characters in Search of an Author* – that works through the enactment of this vision. But no one before Eliot has come to drama with such a dualistic approach to language itself. And perhaps no one before has had to devote so much energy to converting an initial non-dramatic or even anti-dramatic impulse – the impulse to purify the dialect of the tribe out of existence – into finding ways to dramatise speech-of-appearance.

We may consider Eliot's parody of everyday speech first – a deliberate exaggeration of the trivial clichés, mannerisms, evasions of speech, the tendency to say nothing. The cross-talk of the bored prostitutes and their clients in *Sweeney* – against the pressure of mechanical noises – is an early example; the vapid ritual of courtesies and introductions – Wauchope's Captain Horsfall, Mr Klipstein, Mr Krumpacker, the last two following up with thirty-nine lines of 'tribal' dialect, U.S. version; while the repetition of phrases, as well as marking a fascination with shifts in stress and intonation over the same words, are so much 'Wind in and out of unwholesome lungs', as in Dusty's telephone 'conversation':

> Oh I'm *so* sorry. I *am* so sorry.
> But Doris came home with a terrible chill
> No, just a chill

48 See Hugh Kenner, *The Invisible Poet*, pp. 35–59 (Bradley and the poetry) and pp. 279–83 (Bradley and Eliot's theatre as make-believe). Cf. the passage Eliot himself quotes in his essay on Bradley (1927), *Selected Essays*, p. 447, also my suggestion that Eliot's linguistic dualism is connected with the idea of the fall of language (p. 96). For a different emphasis see Denis Donoghue, 'The Holy Language of Modernism', *Literary English since Shakespeare* (ed. G. Watson), New York, 1970, pp. 394–407. The essay – published since this was written – points to the inner connection between the all-inclusive (F. H. Bradley–Idealist) experience and the all-inclusive or 'Holy' (Symbolist) language in Eliot's early poetry. By contrast, 'the effort of the plays is to allow people, now, to live and act by a Holy Language'.

Oh I *think* it's only a chill
Yes indeed I hope so too –
Well I *hope* we shan't have to call a doctor
Doris just hates having a doctor
She says she will ring you up on Monday
She hopes to be all right on Monday (...)[49]

(*Collected Poems 1909–1935*, p. 120)

Eliot returns to the exploitation of the farcical surface of empty conversation in the later plays, in a higher social milieu. (Here the dialogue is strongly coloured by recognisable theatrical conventions: near-Coward in the party scenes of *The Cocktail Party*, near-Wilde in the recognition scene in *The Confidential Clerk*, and melodrama in *The Elder Statesman*. This is an example of Eliot going back to a worn-out 'possibility' – borrowing speech from the museum – including the nineteenth-century conventions Shaw had used.) What we notice is the pervasiveness of empty talk, the time it takes up. In *The Cocktail Party*, where such talk is essential to the opening of the play – to establishing the first level of action and tone, as well as the 'subliminal' verse – human noises proliferate until they minimise the speakers. Eliot is one of the first deliberate exploiters of the minimum content in 'ordinary' talk, stylised so as to draw attention to itself. There is the banal social patter of the Guardians pretending to be ordinary, for example Julia in the manner of a lady tycoon, her worldly role, demanding that 'serious' conversation be made with the vapid circumlocution that kills it:

Edward do sit down for a moment. (...)
  There are so many questions
I want to ask you. It's a golden opportunity
Now Lavinia's away. I've always said:
'If I could only get Edward alone
And have a really *serious* conversation!'
I said so to Lavinia. She agreed with me.
She said: 'I wish you'd try'.

49 Eliot is possibly the first dramatist to stylise the telephone as an instrument of noise, trivial talk, and anti-communication. Cf. Reilly: 'you can't tell the truth on the telephone' (*The Cocktail Party*, I, i); and Martin Browne says that the telephone was part of a series of planned 'interruptions of the most intimate conversations by apparently extraneous trivialities'. *The Making of a Play*, Cambridge, 1966, pp. 11–12.

and so on for fifty lines of seemingly profitless exchange, until Julia makes Edward promise to dine with her on Friday and talk to her about 'everything', then:

Edward: Everything?
Julia: Oh, you know what I mean
The next election. And the secrets of your cases.[50]

There is more to this than the comedy of verbal evasion. In the scheme of the play such an exchange – like the patter of the whole group – demonstrates the gap between talk and communication; and it links up with any number of points in the play where evasion marks the fear of talking to a person, about things that matter to the speakers. Such speech-of-appearance serves as the rhythmic foreground noise to the 'real' speech – the 'poetry' as distinct from 'verse' – which is released only in the privileged moments of communication which will be examined later.

Colloquially based verse is also used by Eliot for another form of speech-of-appearance: a language for the hypocrite – in the Greek sense of one who plays a part on the stage – speaking through the public persona that buries the true self. A long scene in the second act of *The Cocktail Party* is given over to stripping the Chamberlaynes of their illusory selves – a theatrically valid form of healing – which includes Reilly's demonstration that Edward is using false language. Edward offers to explain his condition in words that only conceal and exculpate: he talks of being 'on the edge of a nervous breakdown', of being 'a very unusual case'; he volunteers to talk of his childhood, and offers seeming self-criticism: 'I am obsessed by the thought of my own insignificance.' Reilly throws back Edward's language at him:

Reilly: 'Nervous breakdown' is a term I never use:
It can mean almost anything.
Edward: And since then, I have realised
That mine is a very unusual case.
Reilly: All cases are unique, and very similar to others.[51]

Such epigrammatic snubs turn Edward's condition – the way he *talks* about it – into a miniature comedy of a modern *malade imaginaire*. But, as the scene develops, it all becomes a little too obvious, too dependent on the ironic interlocutor 'showing up'

50 *The Cocktail Party*, Act I, Scene i. *Collected Plays*, pp. 128–30.
51 *The Cocktail Party*, Act II, Scene i. *Collected Plays*, pp. 174ff.

false speech. He does not, in fact, practise the method he claims for himself: 'letting you talk as you please, And taking note of what you do not say'. Eliot – through Reilly – manipulates the dialogue all too explicitly, so that the audience may take note of each false word.

In the last two plays Eliot uses, and appears to take delight in using, broad conventions from the comedy of manners to show a character in the act of creating a false impression through carefully mimed speech-of-appearance. A good example is Lucasta, first introduced in *The Confidential Clerk* chirping away:

> Then just by bad luck, the boss did want a letter
> And I couldn't find it. And then he got suspicious
> And asked for things I'm sure he didn't want –
> Just to make trouble! And I couldn't find one of them.
> But they're all filed somewhere, I'm sure, so why bother?[52]

How this mode of speech is shed by Lucasta at the beginning of the next Act – the borrowed dialect giving way to speech authentically hers – we shall see presently. The progression from one to the other – the dramatised doubleness – is one of Eliot's most successful inventions. But we recall that the same play is weighed down by an excessive use of the same kind of dramatic speech: B. Kaghan, Lady Elizabeth and Eggerson, all speak in that carefully wrought verse of the surface which is, if one needs a label, stage naturalism. It is as if Eliot, in learning to write words *for* characters – in learning to exploit a new-old 'possibility' – felt compelled to over-compensate for earlier neglect by allowing too large a share of stage-time to the newly accepted 'dialect'.

In *The Elder Statesman* speech-of-appearance is the antagonist, the clearly dramatised distraction from authentic speech. The greater part of the dialogue is woven of 'stage words', presented as a mere prelude to the attempt at authentic communication and the final epiphany. Lord Claverton's struggle to shed his public and false persona is inseparable from his recognition of himself as a 'broken-down-actor', now desiring a deeper communion with his daughter,

> ...off the stage, without his costume and makeup
> And without his stage words.[53]

[52] *The Confidential Clerk*, Act I. *Collected Plays*, p. 224. [53] *Ibid.* p. 341.

And the visitation of the two 'ghosts' from the past brings to Lord Claverton the torment of guilty memories in the language of the past, at once over-familiar and deadly: Gomez with his knowing clichés

> My dear chap, you are obtuse!
> I said: 'Your secret is safe with me',[54]

and Mrs Carghill, the old flame, drawing on the music hall – Eliot's almost forgotten 'possibility' (perhaps revived by the Osborne plays published, by Eliot's firm, in the years before the last play).

> Don't you remember what a hit I made
> With a number called *It's Not Too Late For You to Love Me*?
> I couldn't have put the feeling into it I did
> But for what I'd gone through.[55]

Here speech is pathetic in both the theatrical and in the current sense. In the same play, we have the successful parody of talk as a deliberate distraction. Act II opens in the quiet convalescent home where Mrs Piggott – the matron who refuses to be called matron – interrupts a deepening duologue between Lord Claverton and his daughter with a torrent of words:

> Good morning, Lord Claverton! Good morning, Miss Claverton!
> Isn't this a glorious morning!
> I'm afraid you'll think I've been neglecting you...
>
> But I hope you're happy?
> Is there anything you need that hasn't been provided?
> All you have to do is to make your wants known.
> Just ring through to my office...[56]

It is a pointed scene, with two persons attempting to escape from the twittering insubstantiality of public speech, and it ends with Mrs Piggott's reassuring remarks to her guests:

> And remember when you want to be *very* quiet
> There's the Silence Room. With a television set.[57]

We know from the dedicatory poem that Eliot's last play has many personal references. One of these might be to the elder

[54] *Ibid.* p. 313.
[55] *Ibid.* p. 324.
[56] *Ibid.* p. 317.
[57] *Ibid.* p. 319.

dramatist who has learnt to use the dialect – the 'palaver' – that now takes in the voice from the holiday camp, and television in the silence room. But the dialect remains a distraction, a rhythmic mockery. It is made up of 'stage words' pressing in on a private room where the 'real' dialogue between two characters is given its precarious opportunity.

Note on lower-class speech

Occasionally Eliot uses quasi-naturalistic speech for sympathetically drawn lower-class characters. The prototype appears to be Downing, the chauffeur in *The Family Reunion*, who has many of the attributes of the stage butler. His speech exhibits all the desired idiomatic formulas:

> Sir,
> If I may make so bold, Sir,
> I always thought that a very few cocktails
> Went a very long way with her Ladyship. (...)
>
> But you know, it is just my opinion, Sir
> That his Lordship is rather psychic, as they say.
>
> *The Family Reunion*, Part I, scene i (*Collected Plays*, pp. 71–2)

In his retrospective criticism of *The Family Reunion* (in 'The Three Voices of Poetry') Eliot said that the chauffeur was 'perhaps' a 'complete human being' in contrast to Harry, whom he had come to consider 'an insufferable prig'. This moral judgement casts an interesting side-light on Eliot's desire to 'humanise' character and language in the late plays – one motive for the approximate naturalism. However, a character like Downing is 'human' only in terms of the conventional stage colloquialism just quoted. Extended examples of such 'humble speech' can be found in the many lines given to Eggerson, the original confidential clerk in the play of that title:

> Well, to tell the truth, Sir Claude, I only touched on these matters,
> They're much too deep for me. And I thought, Mr Simpkins,
> He's highly educated. He'll soon begin to grasp them.
>
> *The Confidential Clerk*, Act I (*Collected Plays*, p. 220)

Throughout the play Eggerson speaks with such over-carefully wrought idiomatic phrasing. He is conceived as God's humble servant, who knows his place and speaks like himself. Speech-in-character is here intended to establish common humanity and the higher common sense. A certain aristocratic social tradition – perhaps a variant of the self-placing humility expressed by the chorus in *Murder in the Cathedral*:

'the small folk who live among small things' – is here allied to a neo-classically correct idea of *decorum* in speech, where the true character speaks always like himself.

Confessional duologues

I feel an overwhelming need for explanation
But perhaps I only dream that I am talking...
(Harry in *The Family Reunion*, Part II, scene i)

If a man has one person, just one in his life,
To whom he is willing to confess everything – ...
Then he loves that person and his love will save him.
(Lord Claverton in *The Elder Statesman*, Act III)

the reaching out towards something which cannot be had *in*, but which may be had partly *through*, personal relations.
(Eliot on Baudelaire, *Selected Essays*, p. 428)

Much of the public, the theatrically mimed, speech in Eliot's drama is, then, an evasion; the words go with poses and make-believe. But the plays are so constructed that there is a constant pressure towards scenes of 'real' communication: the point where two characters lead one another to make a discovery – to understand the past, to clarify identity – *through* talk. At such points there is a struggle to find not only the right but the essential words. It is probable that such duologues were the creative kernels in each play, the given experience Eliot started from; and they are certainly the 'points of intersection' where we must test his success in moving from the structural 'verse' to the 'poetry'. The ideal implicit in the duologues is to find expression for a personal experience in a conversational dialogue that is poetic without strain – through inward movement. Eliot himself defined this ideal in his analysis of a famous love duet, the balcony scene of *Romeo and Juliet*:

The stiffness, the artificiality, the poetic decoration, of his early verse has finally given place to a simplification, to *a language of natural speech*, and this language of conversation again raised to great poetry which is essentially dramatic: for the scene has a structure of which each line is an essential part.[58]

58 Note to 'Poetry and Drama', *On Poetry and Poets*, pp. 87–8 (my italics). The balcony scene in *Romeo and Juliet* is at first sight a

The duologues most often take the form of an intimate exchange between a *confessor*, or *confidant*, and the protagonist who needs to question or be questioned: to lessen the burden of past experience and to discover what he or she *is* or has to do (Harry and Mary, Harry and Agatha, Celia in Reilly's consulting room, can be considered as paradigms). It is easy to see that such a formula is dramatic, and also one that is *given* to Eliot for extra-dramatic reasons, connected with the significance of the confessional in religious experience. On the approximately naturalistic plane there is here, further, an affinity with Ibsen's recurrent duologues – where a character discovers 'real' experience through confrontation with voices from the illusory past; and even though we do not know whether Eliot was aware of such an affinity from *The Family Reunion* onwards, we are entitled to suppose that Eliot's need to dramatise the psychological and retrospective facts of a given experience was a factor, an impetus, in his gradual move towards 'a language of natural speech'.

Eliot did attain, after all, mastery in presenting a confessional duologue 'expressionistically' early on in his work, in the confrontation between Thomas Becket and the four Tempters; what Thomas himself calls 'the strife with shadows' is, clearly, a projection of inner voices, stylised through rhythms and rhymes imitating *Everyman*. But this was the direction in which Eliot did not want to move.

We may take our first example of the other direction from *The Family Reunion* (Part I, Scene ii) where Harry and Mary attempt to find the meaning of their shared childhood. This is the first stage in Harry's confrontation with his past; it is also the place where Eliot attempts to modulate from ordinary conversational dialogue into communication at a deep level. The opening sequence, with its discussion of the repressive lack of change at Wishwood in their childhood, is natural both in itself

surprising choice for Eliot, until we remember the theme of love in the duologues – *eros* frustrated pointing to *agape* – and that the play has become a kind of test-piece for the fusion of words and music: Shaw found Romeo more limited than Tristan; and Peter Brook recently used the verse of the wedding night scene to demonstrate the difference between colloquial and stylised speech. (Cf. Chapter 1, p. 50, n. 21, and Peter Brook, *The Empty Space*, London, 1968, pp. 120–2.)

and as one of those transitions – a conceivable ideal for all talk – where the casual exchange becomes significant:

Harry: But do you remember
Mary: The hollow tree in what we called the wilderness
Harry: Down by the river. That was the stockade
From which we fought the Indians, Arthur and John.[59]

The images work at once and yet are naturally extended, carried forward by the ensuing dialogue (the hollow tree as the children's place of freedom, becomes, when cut down, the image of repression); the conversational rhythms and the mutual completion of sentences quicken our attention as readers or listeners; and we are ready for the stage of intensification, the conceptual insight in formal verse:

Mary: You hoped for something, in coming back to Wishwood,
Or you would not have come.
Harry: Whatever I hoped for
Now that I am here I know I shall not find it.
The instinct to return to the point of departure
And start again as if nothing had happened
Isn't that folly? It's like the hollow tree,
Not there.[60]

With hindsight one can see that in such a duologue Eliot had already held the key to a mode of dramatic speech which, as we know from the later plays and the critical essays, he was to spend twenty years in trying to perfect: a gradual intensification, a layer-by-layer movement from the periphery to the centre, colloquial speech converted into dramatic poetry. But, as yet, he could not trust this method; indeed it was not a method, only a 'possibility'. In the scene under discussion alone we can see him resorting to three other ways of intensifying speech: first, Harry is made to communicate his experience of *nada* to Mary in recognisably Eliotic diction in the passage ending with the arresting lines:

And the eye adjusts itself to a twilight
Where the dead stone is seen to be batrachian,
The aphyllous branch ophidian.

59 *Collected Plays*, pp. 78–9.
60 *Ibid.* p. 80.

secondly, the duologue moves into the dithyrambic or trance-state duets on the sacrificial Spring – powerful, but severing the carefully building-up links between the speakers and the words spoken; finally, at the end of the scene, enter the Eumenides, fortunately dumb, but provoking Harry into addressing them (as though at a first visit to the seance):

> I tell you, it is not me you are looking at,
> Not me you are grinning at, not me your confidential looks
> Incriminate...

This scene can serve as a central example of how difficult Eliot found the transition from the formal juxtaposition of styles of speech in *Murder in the Cathedral* to writing verse dialogue not 'beyond' the two characters speaking. As for the Eumenides, one may perhaps add to the volume of criticism they have already attracted that they make Harry say nothing to or about them that his own confessional duologues – with Harry, or the quasi-priestess Agatha – might not sufficiently communicate.[61]

Before turning to *The Cocktail Party* for another key example, we should note that a full discussion of the confessional duologue would give more space to Eliot's two last plays than is possible here. For *The Confidential Clerk* and *The Elder Statesman* are both examples of what we might term confessional drama: the elaborate farcical and melodramatic elements – the speech-of-appearance, discussed earlier – are organised *towards* confessional exchanges: those of Colby and Sir Claude, and Colby and Lucasta in *The Confidential Clerk* are mutual and initiatory, while Lord Claverton's formal confession at the end of the last play is one-sided and valedictory. In practice, there are serious objections to the way these duologues are placed in the structure of the plays even when the new conversationally inward dialogue is perfectly

61 Cf. Eliot's self-criticism on *The Family Reunion* in 'Poetry and Drama', where the lyrical duets are condemned as being 'beyond character'. By contrast, in an earlier part of the same essay, some lines of Horatio are praised for lifting us 'for a moment "beyond character" but with no sense of unfitness of the words coming, and at this moment, from Horatio'. *On Poetry and Poets*, pp. 82–3. Concerning Eliot's unclearly enacted purpose in passing from Harry and Mary to the Eumenides, see his letter to Martin Browne, discussed by F. O. Matthiessen, *The Achievement of T. S. Eliot* (2nd ed.), New York and London, 1947, pp. 167–8.

achieved. And Lord Claverton's confession has to carry not only the burden of 'the sin no one believes in' but also the change from slick moral rhetoric to the still litany of love, from a jejune self-approach into a deep act of contrition that is to transfigure the speaker. And under that burden the language sinks. Only one duologue seems to achieve all it sets out to do, the Colby–Lucasta scene at the beginning of the second act of *The Confidential Clerk*. (The scene has an affinity with the Harry–Mary one: in both scenes two potential but self-obstructed lovers reveal themselves in a moment of insight.) This dialogue has a movement that is groping yet well-defined; the colloquial speech rhythms and the repeated key words, become, quite unobtrusively, incantatory. J. L. Styan has shown how this is achieved in his perceptive close reading of a passage in *The Elements of Drama*.[62] To this we may add that Eliot has even managed to be 'Eliotic' here without going 'beyond' the speakers:

Colby: Are you sure that you haven't your own secret garden
Somewhere if you could find it?
Lucasta: If I could find it!
No, my only garden is...a dirty public square
In a shabby part of London – like the one where I lived
For a time, with my mother. I've no garden.
I hardly feel that I'm even a person:
Nothing but a bit of living matter
Floating on the surface of the Regent's Canal.
Floating, that's it.
Colby: You're very much a person...[63]

This is both formal and colloquially based; Lucasta's intenser language of despair appears to 'rebel' against the somewhat etiolated 'secret garden' image – a key image for the inner world – first introduced by herself; there is explicit conflict and understanding, and yet more is suggested than said. The syntax itself is dramatic.

The duologue between Celia and Reilly – after Reilly, as confessor or Heracles in Harley Street, has had time to lie on his couch – is probably the central event in *The Cocktail Party* and Eliot's most sustained attempt at modulating from smooth *vers*

62 Cambridge (paperback ed.), 1967, pp. 97–8.
63 *Collected Plays*, p. 245.

de société to the poetry of mystical illumination (part of what we find in *Four Quartets*). Celia enters with fragments of genteel U-speech, but there is a quick move from:

> However,
> I don't want to waste your time. And I'm awfully afraid
> That you'll think that I was wasting it anyway.

to the stark directness of 'I just came in desperation', still in the same apologetic speech. Then come the stages of gradual intensification – from 'the natural surface appearance' to 'the sanctified being'[64] – through changes in the 'key' of language. First, the details of personal experience – a degree of isolation so intense that 'It no longer seems worth while to *speak* to anyone';

> They make noises, and think they are talking to each other;
> They make faces, and think they understand each other –

a revulsion that leads her to examine herself. (The confessional formula is exactly suited for someone who has developed a horror of 'normal' speech.) Celia's attempt to define her experience is a groping for words and meanings:

> It's not the feeling of anything I've ever *done*
> Which I might get away from, or anything in me
> I could get rid of – but of emptiness, of failure
> Towards someone, or something, outside of myself;
> And I feel I must... *atone* – is that the word?

as if stumbling on a word that until then had a neutral tone or archaic sense for her, and using it for the first time in a personal way. The hesitations, the pauses, the questions, the indefinite pronouns, are the language of agnostic faith or implicit love (to use Simone Weil's expression).[65] When Eliot moves to the next stage of intensification – to incantation arising out of the formal

64 These phrases are borrowed from a slightly different context. In his Introduction to *Shakespeare and the Popular Dramatic Tradition* by S. L. Bethell, London, 1944, p. 13, Eliot says that a verse play 'should remove the surface of things, expose the underneath, or the inside, of the natural surface appearance'. He then lists the things a verse play should expose or reveal, and includes the 'doomed or sanctified being'.

65 *Waiting on God* (1950), Fontana ed. p. 160.

colloquy – to render Celia's experience of a 'quintessential something', the transition seems natural:

> what happened is remembered like a dream
> In which one is exalted by intensity of loving
> In the spirit, a vibration of delight
> Without desire, for desire is fulfilled
> In the delight of loving. A state one does not know
> When awake. But what, or whom I loved,
> Or what in me was loving, I do not know.

Given the personality of Celia, the very abstraction of the speech – 'what happened is remembered'; 'one is exalted'; the chain of substantives – seems right at that moment. When heard in the theatre the whole confession-sequence has an immediacy; and yet it is likely to remain in the permanent memory. Even those easy naturalistic questions of motivation – is this a case of 'sublimation', is not the language itself an escape from 'sordid particulars'? – tend to confirm its value as *dramatic* speech. (Just as a passage in the autobiography of St Teresa, say, becomes dramatic – mysticism in juxtaposition – when one perceives that the mystic's voice is speaking over and against other modes of expression.) There remain the objections that have by now become familiar – Eliot's Manichean split between 'the common routine' and Celia's way, and the anti-humanist implications;[66] and Eliot has failed to work out Celia's salvation with the diligence recommended by Reilly – hence the failure of the last Act. But these objections – largely to structure, and partly to values – are really outside our present scope; it is the flexibility and the achieved range within the confessional formula that has to be stressed.

At the end of the duologue just discussed Reilly says to Celia that the way chosen by her – the sacrificial journey – means loneliness *and* communion like the other way, the common routine.

> Both ways avoid the final desolation
> Of solitude in the phantasmal world
> Of imagination, shuffling memories and desires.

[66] Denis Donoghue surveys and discusses the chief objections in *The Third Voice*, Ch. 7. It is also interesting to contrast Raymond Williams praising this play – largely for the language – in *Drama from Ibsen to Eliot* (1952) and objecting to its set of values, with passionate irony, in *Modern Tragedy* (1966), pp. 163–6.

The solitary and phantasmal world, and the language that goes with it – the potential Beckett world – was a permanent pull and dimension in Eliot's dramatic language. His sustained search for a language working through dialogue, in the larger sense, can be seen as an attempt to *avoid* solipsistic language – that powerful temptation which we shall briefly examine. Seen in this light, these duologues gain further significance for modern drama. In a recently rediscovered essay, written as early as 1909, Lukács wrote: 'The new drama has no confidantes, and this is a symptom that life has robbed man of his faith that he can understand another man.'[67] As it is, Eliot was a dramatist who did attempt to make good use of the confidant(e). We may take it as a symptom of his belief that language in the theatre can be used to show at least two persons trying to communicate, against all the odds.

Illumination and the unsayable

Speech without word and
Word of no speech

(*Ash-Wednesday*, II, verses to the Lady of silences)

Anyone who comes to Eliot's plays from the non-dramatic poetry is already tuned in to the recurrent fear of, or withdrawal from, human speech; and the attempt to create conditions for 'the unspoken word' and 'the still point'. In the early poetry we find the dramatised evasions – Prufrock's 'Oh do not ask "What is it?"', and the narrator withholding any reply to the lady's monologue of friendship in *The Portrait of a Lady*, merely instructing himself that he 'must borrow every changing shape:

To find expression...dance, dance
Like a dancing bear,
Cry like a parrot, chatter like an ape.'[68]

So, in the early dramatic criticism we get the references to the uses of a drum, to ballet and, once, to the 'possibility' of a mute theatre. The world of *Sweeney Agonistes* has a close affinity

67 Georg Lukács, 'The Sociology of Drama', reprinted in *The Theory of the Modern Stage*, p. 442.

68 *Collected Poems, 1909–35*, p. 20.

with the early poetry; and the protagonist's central speech codes the desire to evade verbal communication:

> I gotta use words when I talk to you
> But if you understand or if you don't
> That's nothing to me and nothing to you.[69]

After about 1927, even more important is the particular form of mysticism – the negative way of St John of the Cross – which is implicit in the recurrent scenes in Eliot's drama where the speaker claims an incommunicable illumination. The well-known quotation from St John of the Cross – which first appeared as the epigraph to *Sweeney* – urged the soul 'to divest itself of the love of created beings'; and the characters who come nearest to this divestment seem also to be compelled to divest themselves of created language. There is either silence, or an abundance of words followed by a rationalised, explicit statement that such experience is 'unsayable'. Thomas Becket states that his final decision to face martyrdom is taken 'out of time'; there is a hiatus between what he knows about action and suffering and what he is willing to communicate; instead, other modes of speech – the incantation of the chorus, the prose sermon – offer hints at what is Thomas' inward and silent moment of illumination. Harry, in *The Family Reunion*, is given not hints but explicit and repeated declarations that language does and must fail him, his insights are *unspeakable*; as when, in the first scene, after a series of hallucinatory images – which do succeed in presenting a hyper-normal state of unrelatedness – he says:

> This is what matters, but it is unspeakable,
> Untranslatable: I talk in general terms
> Because the particular has no language.[70]

In the last three plays there is a struggle to pass beyond the isolated – and incommunicable – illumination; but there are silences amounting to suppression (as distinct from that ideal relationship between words and silence which Eliot expressed in the magnificent fifth movement of 'Burnt Norton': 'Words,

69 *Ibid.* p. 131.

70 *The Family Reunion*, Part I, Scene i. *Collected Plays*, p. 66.

after speech, reach into the silence'). In *The Cocktail Party* (Act I, Scene ii) Edward discovers under the make-believe

> the obstinate, the tougher self; who does not speak,
> Who never talks, who cannot argue;[71]

and this insight is woven into the texture of the play. Celia – who also says 'I cannot argue' – is forced into silence after the confessional duologue we have studied; what makes the last Act appear an epilogue – as Eliot himself said, with some evasiveness, in 'Poetry and Drama' – is that the essential words have been spoken, and there is only a dirge for Celia and the Chamberlaynes' polite clichés clustering around the earlier cliché of making 'the best of a bad job'. It has been noticed before[72] that in *The Confidential Clerk* Colby 'goes numb' towards the end of the second Act; his lines at the end have the quality of soft padding; yet Colby is the shadowy successor of Eliot's earlier elect beings with a central insight. The carefully subdued litany of love at the end of *The Elder Statesman* appears to find its emotional centre in the lines where Charles, the lover, understandably in this instance, laments the inadequacy of love's speech:

> Yet, like the asthmatic struggling for breath,
> So the lover must struggle for words.[73]

In this last scene, an epiphany rather than the working out of love in a relationship, the serene dialogue emulates the conclusion of *Oedipus at Colonus* and, almost certainly, the final reconciliation scenes in Shakespeare's late plays. This is significant because it exactly accords with the aspiration with which 'Poetry and Drama' ends. There, in the context of that 'mirage of perfection' where the musical and dramatic order are one, Eliot says:

> it is ultimately the function of art...to bring us to a condition of serenity, stillness, and reconciliation; and then leave us, as Virgil left Dante, to proceed toward a region where that guide can avail us no farther.

71 *Ibid.* p. 153.

72 D. E. Jones, *The Plays of T. S. Eliot*, London, 1960, p. 178.

73 Contrast in Eliot's dedication to his second wife, the lines on the lovers:

> 'Who think the same thoughts without need of speech
> And babble the same speech without need of meaning.'

The unspeakable experience of the isolated self (Sweeney, Harry), the incommunicable illumination (Thomas), the final epiphany (*The Elder Statesman*), are some of the points where Eliot *attempts* to achieve what he once defined in this way: 'What poetry should do in the theatre is a kind of humble shadow or analogy of the Incarnation, whereby the human is taken up into the divine.'[74] But all words are only 'shadow' in relation to the Word, to recall the linguistic dualism Eliot shares with many forms of mystical intuition. Only approximations are possible – a language of 'hints and guesses'; 'the condition of serenity, stillness and reconciliation'; points where language begins to annihilate itself.

But the language of illumination in Eliot's drama is not like that, it is hardly there at all – at least not as a language of experience, immediate and urgent, nor yet as an authentic if tentative language of contemplation, as in *Four Quartets* (which has a musical, not a dramatic order). At the points where words seem to fail, what we find is not a crisis of speech, but an all too explicit and highly rationalised formula: a refusal to tell. This is a difficult judgement, but it would appear that the 'particular has no language' because Eliot will not have it so. The *agon*, the agony – a key word for Eliot who conceived his *agonistes* with both the Greek drama and the Christian and modern meaning in mind – is evaded. The insight of a suffering character is not traced back to the original response that might have compelled words very different from the backward-looking formulation, approved by the moral or theological censor. The confessional duologues, we argued, represent the exception; there the framework allows a leap of language to that point of abstraction which still reveals the personal voice, as in Celia's anxious catechism. But after Celia's exit, Julia, the Guardian, takes over:

> You and I don't know the process whereby the human is
> Transhumanised: what do we know
> Of the kind of suffering they must undergo
> On the way to illumination?[75]

[74] 'The Aims of Poetic Drama', *Adam* (Nov. 1949), p. 12. This passage is omitted from an otherwise almost identical passage in 'Poetry and Drama'.

[75] *Collected Plays*, p. 193.

The strained phrase 'the human is transhumanised' tells us a good deal about how illumination is proclaimed and then evaded in Eliot's drama. There is an eagerness for the short cut: the quickest way out of the realm of the human, including the language of particular experience. The aim is 'the humble shadow or analogy of Incarnation'; the recurrent practice is dis-incarnated speech.

Eliot once remarked, commending the practice of conversation to those who wish to attain a *living* style: 'anyone who would write must let himself go, in one way or the other, for there are only four ways of thinking: to talk to others, or to one other, or to talk to oneself, or to talk to God'.[76] The context happened to be journalism at its best, but it is in drama that we expect to find these four kinds of talking embodied. Yet, is any character in Eliot overheard 'talking to God'? A character 'on the way to illumination' is allowed to say only that which might be pleasing to the God of the theologians.[77] No one improvises, no one is prompted to use words outside the orthodox style register. (No one even invokes the name of God in vain, as does Yeats' pedlar at the end of *Purgatory* (1939) or Estragon, calling out at the top of his voice 'God have pity on me!'[78]) It is as if Eliot had been unable to shed certain early doctrines which are, to say the least, inhospitable to drama: in particular the 'impersonal theory of poetry'; and the pronouncements against the 'inner voice, which breathes the eternal message of vanity, fear, and lust',[79] and against that uncertain 'divine illumination' from

[76] 'Charles Whibley', *Selected Essays*, pp. 500–1.

[77] Cleanth Brooks has argued that the Christian content in Eliot's poetic language is a 'Discourse to the Gentiles' – in *The Hidden God*, New Haven and London, 1963, pp. 68–97. The argument was itself addressed to theologians; further it is more convincing when dealing with *Four Quartets* than with the plays. The examples taken from the plays – Thomas attempting to involve the audience in guilt by 'shock tactics', Harry haranguing his family on 'Some monstrous mistake and aberration of all men', and Celia on being 'taught to disbelieve in sin' – are all examples of a particular rhetoric of persuasion; they turn on the trick – as in Shaw – o making the audience the villain of the piece. They proselytise, somewhat indirectly. But they do not communicate a religious experience; their language is willed, without inward pressure.

[78] *Waiting for Godot*, London, 1956, p. 77.

[79] 'The Function of Criticism', *Selected Essays*, p. 27.

which 'the daily man' may draw the wrong conclusions, abandoned to 'the Inner Light, the most untrustworthy and deceitful guide that ever offered itself to wandering humanity'.[80]

All this amounts to a refusal of experimental openness – in the very area where Eliot had the greatest potential contribution to make in modern drama: in finding the authentic language of the 'inner self' in search of communion.

Trying to see Eliot's dramatic work as a whole is like looking at one of those optical diagrams where, according to the way we look, we see first one then another figure stand out in relief. There is Eliot the ceaseless experimenter, moving from one 'possibility' to another, learning from each, and refusing easy solutions. And there is Eliot the preserver, who refused extreme solutions – such as Yeats' withdrawal from the public theatre, and Beckett's struggle to re-create language from its ruins. The experimenter started with a radical modernist approach to dramatic language; the preserver went back, ironically, to the 'tradition' of naturalism, elements of which served his desire to 'humanise' dramatic language. Whichever way we look, we find much of that 'sustained, heroic and indefatigably resourceful quest'[81] which Dr Leavis finds in the poetry alone. If there is less resourcefulness – or more fatigue – in the growth of Eliot's dramatic language, it is because Eliot withheld from it much of the pressure that went into his poetry. In part this springs from his quest for a 'social usefulness' for poetry in the theatre – something increasingly conceived as the need to come to terms with the established conventions of the theatre: even at the cost of taking over a certain load of conventionality, which went against the grain of his creativity (the pull of an inward language).

The conservative impulse in Eliot's dramatic language is, clearly, inseparable from his increasingly conservative conception of the viable theatre and, beyond it, of the Christian–Classical culture under extreme attack. The language itself had to be preserved. We may apply to his dramatic language what he said

80 *After Strange Gods*, p. 59. The immediate context is an attack on D. H. Lawrence.

81 In 'Eliot's Classical Standing', *Lectures in America*, London, 1969, p. 30.

of poetry: 'it should help, not only to refine the language of the time, but to prevent it from changing too rapidly: a development of the language at too great a speed would be a development in the sense of progressive deterioration, and that is our danger today.'[82] Eliot recognised that the stuff of dramatic language, human speech, was unique – it was not for him, after *Sweeney Agonistes*, to speed up its development (or subject it to abstract pattern-making) on the moving platform of modern art, as though it were music, or only human noise.

82 'Milton II', *On Poetry and Poets*, p. 160.

3: Beckett

Gli atti suoi pigri e le corte parole
(His lazy actions and grudging speech)
Purgatorio, IV, 121

When *Waiting for Godot* first appeared it was at once clear that Beckett had taken a direction diametrically opposed to the direction Eliot had taken in *The Cocktail Party*: while Eliot was teaching himself the discipline of writing verse dialogue in and for character in a quasi-naturalist convention, Beckett created a new form of poetic drama which drew, among other sources, on the radical aims of modernist art Eliot had once shared. There is a certain insight to be gained from briefly considering where Eliot and Beckett potentially converge, seeing that their actual work is so significantly divergent.

It was Eliot who in his early criticism had stressed the importance of 'abstraction from actual life', of a dramatic language that concentrates or compresses expression; it was Eliot who wanted to create a verbal rhythm that would have the power of primitive – pre-rational – drama. (*Sweeney Agonistes* came perhaps nearest to embodying these aesthetic aims.)[1] It is Beckett who seems to have written all his plays, with all their differences, from a primary expressive urge tending to abstraction, to compression, and to the rhythms of a primitive – not just pre-rational but seemingly counter-rational – dramatic language. It is, further, Beckett who has pushed his dramatic language back to that 'still point' – the world of perpetual solitude – which Eliot

[1] This view is also expressed by Roy Walker, in 'Love, Chess and Death', *Twentieth Century* (Dec. 1958), p. 538.

expressed only in his non-dramatic poetry. Eliot took pains to avoid, or to counterbalance, the pull towards subjectivity; his whole development as a dramatist might be seen as a conscious and progressive effort to 'objectify' his dramatic language, in terms of situation and character; he was prepared to sacrifice expressive power for the sake of deliverance from a private language and the attendant danger of *stasis*. (The formal development corresponds to Reilly's directing his 'patients' away from:

> the final desolation
> Of solitude in the fantasmal world
> Of imagination, shuffling memories and desires.
> *The Cocktail Party*, II)

By contrast, Beckett starts from an acceptance of that solipsistic condition. For him language is irredeemably private: words germinate in the skull of the speaker, at an inestimable distance from things and other persons, motive and argument, local time and place. 'Art is the apotheosis of solitude'[2] wrote Beckett in his early work on Proust; and this 'creed' was not abandoned when he came to drama. From the start Beckett accepts the paradox of dramatic *stasis*; movement in his plays is nearly always a succession of still points or a cyclic recurrence of verbal occasions. His dialogue – as will be seen – is a quasi-dialogue, composed of counterpointed or subtly doubled monologues.

As a single example we may contrast Eliot's verbal duel for a squabbling couple (the wife just back from Hades) in *The Cocktail Party* with Beckett's triangle of perennially contending voices in the limbo of *Play*. In the Eliot passage, husband and wife confront one another's isolation with lines that have the rational continuity and transparency of Racine (though the argument itself has a bearing on Sartre's *Huis Clos*).

[2] *Proust* (1931), London, 1965, p. 64. The context has clear affinities with Eliot's early criticism. 'The artistic tendency is not expansive, but a contraction. And art is the apotheosis of solitude. Even on the rare occasions when word and gesture happen to be valid expressions of personality, they lose their significance on their passage through the cataract of the personality that is opposed to them.'

Cf. T. S. Eliot, 'Four Elizabethan Dramatists', *Selected Essays*, pp. 109ff.

Edward: What is Hell? Hell is oneself,
Hell is alone, the other figures in it
Merely projections. There is nothing to escape from
And nothing to escape to. One is always alone.

Lavinia: Edward, what *are* you talking about?
Talking to yourself. Could you bear, for a moment,
To think about *me*?

Edward: It was only yesterday
That damnation took place. And now I must live with it
Day by day, hour by hour, for ever and ever.
(*The Cocktail Party*, I, iii)

Set against this the opening of the second sequence from the Beckett play, with the warning that the effect can barely be judged apart from the whole choral sequence, the sound of those low voices responding with para-normal rapidity to the flickering spotlight:

Spot on M

M: When first this change I actually thanked God. I thought, It is done, it is said, now all is going out –

Spot from M to W1

W1: Mercy, mercy, tongue still hanging out for mercy. It will come. You haven't seen me. But you will. Then it will come.

Spot from M to W2

W2: To say I am not disappointed, no, I am. I had anticipated something better. More restful. (*Play*, p. 15)

This is not *about* a psychic limbo. The language is made to sound *as if* it came from limbo – at least it creates the verbal equivalent of a 'final desolation of solitude' somewhere beyond the tangible world. The total lack of interaction between the speakers is not stated but expressed through the fast-flowing fragments of speech that never interlock. And the rhythm, the tonal pattern, which is heard before the meaning is caught, evokes a liturgy, perhaps a hellish half-liturgy, to go with the 'hellish half-light' (p. 16).

In a speculative study of dramatic form, written before Beckett's work was known, Northrop Frye defines what he calls the 'archetypal masque' which 'tends to detach its settings from time and space' and where 'we find ourselves frequently in a sinister limbo, like the threshold of death in *Everyman*, the sealed underworld crypts of Maeterlinck, or the nightmares of the future in expressionist plays...The action of the archetypal masque takes place in a world of human types, which at its most concentrated becomes the interior of the human mind.'[3] If this definition fits Beckett's theatre – and it is at least a useful pointer – we can regard Beckett's dramatic language as a sustained attempt to create the words for such an archetypal action, in a setting of limbo or skull.

Beckett himself has deliberately refrained from theorising about drama or dramatic language, and we need only the minimum of theory – a brief look at some of Beckett's known critical positions – to sidelight the close study of the language of the plays. We need to understand, first of all, the extent of Beckett's dependence on words as a primary element in drama, despite his undisputed mastery of gesture, movement and setting – the art of visual counterpoint. (The dustbins, the sand-mound and the urns are containers for human voices – visual equivalents for Krapp's tapes.) In asserting the primacy of language Beckett equates language and 'content' and, ultimately, language and 'reality'. This amounts to something that might be called Beckett's *verbalism* – though one is not eager to add to the world's glut of 'isms'. Beckett's early position is this:

> For Proust, as for the painter, style is more a question of vision than of technique. Proust does not share the superstition that form is nothing and content everything...For Proust *the quality of language is more important than any system of ethics or aesthetics*. Indeed he makes no attempt to dissociate form from content. The one is a concretion of the other, the revelation of the world.[4]

The essay on Proust is written from the standpoint of approval and expresses an explicit enough creed – the familiar (by now hackneyed) anti-naturalist trust in language as vision. Later in the same essay, Beckett praises Proust for the 'radiographical quality of his observation' and for 'being less interested in what is said than in the way in which it is said'.[5] Clearly this is still

3 'A Conspectus of Dramatic Genres', *The Kenyon Review* (Autumn 1951), p. 559. Cf. also Northrop Frye, *Anatomy of Criticism* (1957), New York, 1965, pp. 290–1.

4 *Proust*, pp. 19–20 (my italics).

5 *Ibid.* p. 83.

the aesthetic behind Beckett's often-quoted remark declaring his interest in the *shape* of ideas, in the *shape* of a sentence. Thus Beckett praises the beauty of St Augustine's statement on the two thieves (which found its way into *Waiting for Godot*): 'Do not despair: one of the thieves was saved. Do not presume: one of the thieves was damned', and adds: 'That sentence has a wonderful shape. It is the shape that matters.'[6]

By the time Beckett came to drama he seems to have shifted to a more extreme point[7] where language is perhaps the only reality, but words cannot be trusted – they can neither communicate *nor* express, they can only fail. Verbal expression may be a compulsive need, but it is self-defeating – in saying anything the potentially sayable becomes unsayable. We find an epitome of this despairing yet creative paradox in the *Three Dialogues* (1949), for example in the first dialogue on the painter Tal Coat where B. speaks of an art that runs away in disgust even from the attempts of the 'revolutionaries', preferring to the pretence of 'being able, of doing a little better the same old thing, of going a little further along a dreary road...',

> the expression that there is nothing to express, nothing with which to express, nothing from which to express, no power to express, no desire to express, together with the obligation to express.[8]

And we find both in the novels and in the plays a kindred paradox – the self 'consisting' of words trying to keep silent – in many places, for instance in the Unnamable's

> it has not yet been our good fortune to establish with any degree of accuracy what I am, where I am, whether I am words among words, or silence in the midst of silence, to recall only two of the hypotheses launched in this connection, though the silence to tell the truth does not appear to have been very conspicuous up to now, but appearances are sometimes deceptive.[9]

6 Quoted in Harold Hobson, 'Samuel Beckett, Dramatist of the Year', *International Theatre Journal*, no. 1, London, 1956; quoted: Martin Esslin, *The Theatre of the Absurd*, Harmondsworth, 1968, p. 52.

7 Cf. John Fletcher, 'Samuel Beckett as Critic', *The Listener* (25 Nov. 1965), pp. 862–3, and *Samuel Beckett's Art*, London, 1967, Ch. 2.

8 *Proust and Three Dialogues with Georges Duthuit*, p. 103. Also in *Samuel Beckett, A Collection of Critical Essays* (ed. Martin Esslin), Englewood Cliffs, N.J., 1965, p. 17.

9 *Molloy; Malone Dies; The Unnamable*, London, 1959, p. 392.

or in Winnie's playful antithesis:

> Say no more. (*Pause.*) But I must say more. (*Pause.*) Problem here.[10]

We need to respond here to the tentative and playful element within a crisis of verbal expressiveness. It is a mistake to translate Beckett's creative paradox into something like a fixed doctrine. For example, in his exegesis of the third dialogue, Richard Coe writes:

> Beckett's own art likewise is an art of failure: it is by definition trying to do something that it cannot conceivably do – to create and to define that which, created and defined, ceases to be what it must be if it is to reveal the truth of the human situation: Man as a Nothing in relation to all things which themselves are Nothing.[11]

By contrast, the sceptical or non-Beckettian critic points to the seeming inconsistency of paying tribute both to Beckett's achieved expressiveness, and to 'anti-art': failing form and language. With this in mind, J. R. Harvey writes: 'One cannot have it both ways: although we may feel that it is not so much his critics, as Mr Beckett himself, who tries to have it both ways.'[12]

Yet both these critical attitudes – ideological enthusiasm and commonsense logic – seem to miss an essential point which is, I think, this: the idea of the failure of language has served Beckett as a myth *for* creation. It is a 'negative' myth which, as a source of creative energy, is comparable to the familiar power of certain negative emotions as motives to action, and to 'the negative way' as a source of spiritual life.[13] (To deny is to affirm implicitly.) The whole texture of Beckett's language is created out of his ever-renewed sense of the failure of language. Going beyond Eliot's 'intolerable wrestle with words' and his relatively non-central notion that a language can be exhausted, for Beckett

10 *Happy Days*, p. 44.

11 Richard N. Coe, *Beckett*, Edinburgh and London, 1964, pp. 4–5.

12 J. R. Harvey, 'La Vieille Voix Faible: Writers on Beckett', *The Cambridge Quarterly* (Autumn 1966), p. 393.

13 The *via negationis* in theology is best approached through the writings of mystics who have stressed the 'nothingness' of God, particularly Eckhart and *The Cloud of Unknowing*; modern existential theology has clear affinities with this mystical tradition – and with Beckett. An attempt to study the peculiarly linguistic resources of the negative is made by Kenneth Burke in *Language as Symbolic Action*, Berkeley, 1966, Part III, Ch. 7, pp. 419–36.

the creation of words *against* the wreck of words becomes the central act. The ideas implicit in Beckett's language myth are barely tenable *as* ideas; the progressive deterioration of language – as if language were an organism – is at best an ambiguous hypothesis; and there can be no such thing as a language of the inner self cut off from the community, from at least implicit communication: a 'private language' is parasitical on a 'public language'.[14] But the myth of a failing language springs from one of the central myths of modern art: the writer is present at Genesis, creating words out of inert matter and chaos. The myth serves to intensify Beckett's own need to recreate words out of a struggle with a 'dead language'.[15]

When a linguistic tension as extreme as Beckett's is 'dramatised', at least two things happen. What is irreducibly public in drama gives a concreteness to the words: when they are as it were moored to the situation, spoken by the speaker(s), they create an actual or implicit dialogue; against the novels and the stories the stage offers Beckett a partial therapy for endlessly spiralling interior monologue. The contrary effect is that the language of drama moves away from everyday speech, towards an internal and abstract purity that never was. (Even the failure of language just discussed is hardly ever related to socially observable empti-

[14] This point clearly goes beyond the particular conditions of a *dramatic* language. Wittgenstein – whose late work has affinities with Beckett's equation of 'reality' and language – denied the possibility of a 'private language'. See *Philosophical Investigations*, Oxford, 1953, paragraphs 256, 257 and 259. Cf. also D. F. Pears, 'The Development of Wittgenstein's Philosophy', *New York Review of Books*, 16 Jan. 1969, p. 28, and A. J. Ayer, 'Can there be a Private Language?' in *Wittgenstein, The Philosophical Investigations* (ed. G. Pitcher), London, 1968, pp. 251ff.

At the time of writing, I have before me Beckett's last published work, the story *Lessness*, which opens with a sentence (every phrase of which is to be permuted): 'Ruins true refuge long last towards which so many false time out of mind'. This is parasitical on a 'public' language in several ways: (*a*) we eke out the syntax; we can read literary telegraphese; (*b*) we sort out the semantic and rhythmic groups from our knowledge of everyday English; (*c*) each word (excepting 'which') carries a load of literary connotations; (*d*) if we have read Beckett the sentence at once tells an archetypal Beckett story. (*Lessness*, London, 1970, p. 7.)

[15] Cf. my Introduction, particularly Section 6, for a discussion on the origin of this aesthetic.

ness or idiocy of speech, as in several plays of Pinter.[16]) This gives Beckett a unique place among modern dramatists: over and above the intrinsic value of his work, he marks the limits of verbal expressiveness in one direction.

Each play is a cyclic rundown, and the plays taken together can be seen to move towards a minimal language. The language of drama is itself taken by Beckett to an extreme point, towards the zero point which – as in the third law of thermodynamics – can only be approached asymptotically: getting ever closer to it without ever reaching it.[17]

Seen against the impasse of naturalism, the conventions of stage rhetoric, and verse drama, Beckett's plays – first performed perhaps ten or more years later than what might have been their ideal date from the standpoint of development in drama – were at once seen to be fertile and liberating. Yet by or after 1963 the aesthetic extremism of his dramatic language had tended to inhibit creativity: 'No more stories, no more words.'[18] Above all, Beckett's work has deepened the split in certain quite fundamental uses of language in modern drama (inwardness/externality; reduction/extension); and the cultural price to be paid for Beckett's unique achievement in 'making it new' may be an arrest of growth towards convergence or wholeness. It is probable, further, that Beckett's own intense consciousness of 'the burden of the past' – the museum of styles as a mausoleum – will intensify the stylistic self-consciousness of other dramatists in search of new ways of expression. The burden of Beckett is that in a little more than a decade he has pre-empted so many modes of expression in drama – including the art about to be examined, the re-creation of language through seeming decomposition, and the creation of dialogue through seeming monologue. For Beckett has all but exhausted what he has perfected.

[16] See Ch. 4, pp. 169ff. (for Pinter contrasted with Beckett), also nn. 4 and 5.

[17] This analogy was first made, in a different context, by Darko Suvin in 'Beckett's Purgatory of the Individual', *Tulane Drama Review* (Summer 1967), p. 25.

[18] The Voice in *Cascando*. See '*Play*' *and Two Short Pieces for Radio*, London, 1964, pp. 39ff. Cf. Beckett himself on the increasing difficulties of writing, at an earlier stage: 'For me the area of possibilities gets smaller and smaller.' Quoted by Israel Shenker, 'Moody Man of Letters', *New York Times* (6 May 1956, sec. 2, p. 1).

The living and the dead language

Estragon: All the dead voices.
Vladimir: To have lived is not enough for them.
Estragon: They have to talk about it.

English is a language 'abstracted to death', wrote Beckett in his early advocacy of Joyce's *Finnegans Wake* (then still called *Work in Progress*).[19] In a curious development of this point later in the same essay Beckett says that the relation of modern English to 'other European languages is to a great extent that of medieval Latin to the Italian dialects', and he draws a parallel between the linguistic situation of Dante and Joyce: 'both saw how worn out and threadbare was the conventional language of literary artificers, both rejected a universal language'. The inheritance of the writer in English is, then, something like a dead language. The context is familiar: we have reached the final 'Philosophical' stage in Vico's language-cycle, the stage of rational oversaturation. Beckett praises Joyce for going back to the springtime of the cycle, to a

> quintessential extraction of language and painting and gesture, with all the inevitable clarity of the old inarticulation. Here is the savage economy of hieroglyphics. Here words are not the polite contortions of 20th century printer's ink. They are alive.

With the capacity for renewal goes the gift that re-creates the language cycle: 'There is an endless verbal germination, maturation, putrefaction, the cyclic dynamism of the intermediate.'[20]

These ideas or metaphors may be seen as a hypothesis on language or another myth for verbal creativity, where (as argued earlier concerning 'the failure of language') it is not the validity of the ideas in themselves, but their creative use that we need to question. How does Beckett dramatise what amounts to a drama *of* language: decay and 'abstraction to death'? And how does he, nevertheless, achieve a 'quintessential extraction of language' where the words are 'alive'? Such questions offer at least one point of entry into Beckett's dramatic language.

19 'Dante...Bruno...Vico...Joyce', *Our Exagmination round his Factification for Incamination of Work in Progress* (1929), London, 1961, p. 15. The quotations in the next sentence are from *ibid.* pp. 17–18.
20 *Ibid.* pp. 15–16.

In the texture of each play a particular literary language is isolated or parodied: set in a dramatic frame wherein the process of decay may be perceived. (The words decay with their speakers, through deadly over-use or habit,[21] the linguistic portion of human decrepitude.) From Lucky in *Waiting for Godot* to Winnie in *Happy Days* (and the disembodied voices of the later plays) the decay of words – words from an 'old style' – becomes part of the action; yet, in the play as a whole the used language is made new. The 'language cycle' – which Beckett invokes in the passage quoted – is enacted in a paradoxical direction: out of 'putrefaction' comes 'endless verbal germination'. Or, to put it another way, the rundown of language towards a dead end, in a seemingly mechanical replay of the once-living-now-dead verbal formulae, is so controlled that the language gains 'new life' within the context of the play.[22]

We may start at an extreme point, with the violent movement from rationalist articulateness to final aphasia in Lucky's speech. Here the rundown in the cycle of language is clearly irreversible. But even here there emerges, from the wreckage of syntax, the lost or potential beauty of human utterance. The speech is placed and organised in such a way that the pathological breakdown in language – the agony of lost meaning – becomes a source of creative energy in the play.

It is necessary to affirm that this paradoxical experience is given as an immediate response in performance (it was what one experienced when the play was first performed in Paris and London) so as to underline that the dramatic 'sense' of Lucky's speech does not depend on subsequent close reading. Even a first reading or hearing should yield at least two perceptions: the decay of rational language expresses the decay of one kind of order – that constructed by theology and other 'logy' systems

21 Beckett sets against deadening habit 'The suffering being: that is the free play of every faculty'. *Proust*, p. 19. Cf. the conflict 'between the old "beautiful formulae" of our cultural tradition...and the latent new values of the human psyche': Eva Metman, 'Reflections on Samuel Beckett's Plays', in *Samuel Beckett, A Collection of Critical Essays*, p. 135.

22 One may think of the plays as a 'purgatory for words' bearing in mind the recurrent purgatory metaphor in Beckett, and the sense of purifying 'the dialect of the tribe'. (Beckett considered Joyce's *Finnegans Wake* 'purgatorial', *op. cit.* in n. 19.)

which turn man's hunger for *logos* into formulae; and, as the speech runs on and down – as Lucky accelerates and shouts before the final silence – the deteriorating syntax releases, as through fission, isolated word-clusters which sound like the lost 'true voice' in the speech.

Close reading – such as the line-by-line layout and commentary by Anselm Atkins[23] – confirms that 'Lucky's speech is as carefully constructed as the play itself, and its meanings reinforce the themes of the play.' The whole speech is an accurate rendering of the process whereby the aphasiac Lucky goes silent: the movement from the formal syntax of a hypothetical proposition (intercalated with 'other matter'):

> Given the existence...of a personal God...who...loves us dearly... and suffers...with those who are plunged in torment, plunged in fire

through the increasing repetition of contentless syntax-phrases which prevent the completion of any one sentence (like the three intermediate 'that'-clauses culminating in the violently parodic 'that, in view of the labours of Fartov and Belcher...') to the final eruption of isolated 'poetic' words:

> fading, fading, fading...on, on...
> alas alas on on
> the skull the skull the skull the skull...

And so the cycle runs down to exhaustion until – in keeping with 'the entropy of the play', as Atkins calls it – the repetition of such significant words is cut down, 'the skull' from four to two, then to one, with only one 'alas' to follow.

In Lucky's speech we witness the final movement in a language cycle: from the hyper-articulate (and atrophied) stage to that relapse into primal babble. Though Lucky is destructively silenced his language works creatively within the play. Against this is set Pozzo's old rhetoric and around it the dialogue of Estragon and Vladimir, seemingly ever-new and yet also running down.

23 Anselm Atkins, 'Lucky's Speech in Beckett's *Waiting for Godot*: A Punctuated Sense-Line Arrangement', *Educational Theatre Journal* (Dec. 1967), pp. 426–32. Cf. by the same author: 'A Note on the Structure of Lucky's Speech', *Modern Drama* (Dec. 1966), p. 309.

Pozzo's first and last word on the stage is 'On!'[24] to the cracking of the whip in Act I, to the jerking of the rope in Act II: Lucky's relentless 'on, on' externalised, unaccompanied by 'alas'. With appropriate irony, Pozzo's fine speechmaking – the comforts of theatrical grandiloquence and platitudes – proves more robust than the language of Lucky's subtler schools of thought. In Act I Pozzo is still the confident user of a 'dead language'; for him the 'old style' is still a possession, to be displayed histrionically as in the 'Ah, yes! The night' speech:

(*They stop looking at the sky.*) What is there so extraordinary about it? Qua sky. It is pale and luminous like any sky at this hour of the day. (*Pause.*) In these latitudes. (*Pause.*) When the weather is fine. (*Lyrical.*) An hour ago (*he looks at his watch, prosaic*) roughly (*lyrical*) after having poured forth ever since (*he hesitates, prosaic*) say ten o'clock in the morning (*lyrical*) tirelessly torrents of red and white light it begins to lose its effulgence, to grow pale (*gesture of the two hands lapsing by stages*) pale, ever a little paler, a little paler until (*dramatic pause, ample gesture of the two hands flung wide apart*) pppfff! finished! it comes to rest.

(Faber ed., 1956, p. 37)

Here the stage directions alone amount to parody: the 'prosaic' and the 'lyrical' modes mock one another in the framework of a bravura speech delivered to a captive stage audience. ('How did you find me? Good? Fair? Passable? Mediocre? Positively bad?...') The naturalistic 'say ten o'clock in the morning', and the poetic prose of 'it began to lose its effulgence, to grow pale' are two styles which are shown to be dead 'qua' styles. It is Beckett's counterpoint that lives.

The lyrical mode itself is a recurrent 'old style' in Beckett – part of his Symbolist and Irish heritage – which he clearly feels is 'less abstracted to death' than either conversational or discursive language. He falls back on lyricism to create a consciously poetic intensity. It has not, I think, been seen that Beckett's lyricism works best when it is playful or parodistic; and that in itself it is an ornate 'old style', and can be an indulgence (as later in the mental voice of *Embers*). There is, for example, the return of Pozzo in Act II, blind, dispossessed, crying out for

[24] A significantly placed syllable in Beckett. *On* is also the opening syllable of *Embers*; the last syllable of *The Unnamable*, and of the Voice in *Cascando*.

help, in vain, fifteen times in eight pages of dialogue. But he has one possession left: the faculty of speech-making, and his exit is marked by the now famous lament on time, ending with these lyrical cadences:

> They give birth astride of a grave, the light gleams an instant, then it's night once more. (*He jerks the rope.*) On![25]

Here parody of lyricism seems to have given way to pathos. The speech is usually taken to be an expression of Beckett's vision – 'poetic' and moving. Certainly part of our response is that we are moved; and those cadences work on us emotively in a way that a rational statement – say Pope's 'Born but to die, and reasoning but to err' – could not work. At the same time the pathos is qualified or bracketed by that relentless 'On!', by our conception of Pozzo, whose figurative functions include the tethering of thought and language, and by that earlier, explicit parody of the lyrical mode. With the pathos we sense the false pathos; there is a double tone in the dying fall of old-style lyricism.

The double tone is made more complex when, a little later, Vladimir echoes Pozzo's lyrical phrase and 'embroiders' it in a kindred style:

> Astride of a grave and a difficult birth. Down in the hole, lingeringly, the grave-digger puts on the forceps. We have time to grow old. The air is full of our cries. (*He listens.*)

In itself this is, it seems to me, a fair sample of indulgent poeticism. What makes it work dramatically – what moves us – is the total context: Vladimir is speaking on the threshold of sleep (or waking), and this borrowed fragment of speech, woven into his reverie, intensifies his own sense of unreality. The end of the speech – 'I can't go on! (*Pause.*) What have I said?' – quietly questions the speech, its content, and perhaps its style. At all events Vladimir has gone a long way from Pozzo's still confident, proprietary use of poetic words.

The seeming improvisation in the Gogo–Didi dialogue is a method by now well understood. The playful interaction of

25 Faber ed. p. 89. Raymond Williams invites us to compare the image of the grave with Synge's *Deirdre of the Sorrows*: *Drama from Ibsen to Brecht*, London, 1968, p. 305.

formal and conversational exchanges is immediately clear; and enough has been said of Beckett's debt to the music hall and to the *commedia dell'arte* in this connection.[26] But two points still need to be stressed: the seeming improvisation draws on this or that 'old style' repeatedly; and the revitalised language is itself running down.

Vladimir and Estragon – the ex-intellectual and the ex-poet – gather into their casual-seeming talk all kinds of literary reminders and remainders: quotes, half-quotes, recognisable tones. For example, Vladimir half-quotes the biblical proverb 'Hope deferred maketh the something sick', thereby giving the comic cross-talk on his physical affliction a relevance to the whole play; and Estragon weaves Shelley's 'pale for weariness' lines into a would-be conversation on boots. Vladimir assumes a high rhetoric of self-exhortation instead of helping the fallen Pozzo ('Let us represent worthily for once the foul brood to which a cruel fate consigned us!'); and Estragon evokes the old tragic tone (God have pity on me!...On me! On me! Pity! On me!). There is parody in all these exchanges; but the traditional overtones are also resuscitated – an overworked literary 'sample' is made to work dramatically.[27] This ambivalent device can also be seen in Beckett's way with traditional Christian images. 'It was two thieves crucified at the same time as our Saviour' is placed in a dialogue sequence which is tentative and open: it begins with a question on the Bible, takes in the question of Gogo's swelling feet, and ends with a curse (pp. 11–13). Even

[26] For Beckett's dialogue and music hall cross-talk see Peter Davison, 'Contemporary Drama and Popular Dramatic Forms', in *Aspects of Drama and the Theatre*, Sydney, 1965 (particularly pp. 188–90). For the relevance of the *commedia* see Edith Kern, 'Beckett and the Spirit of the *Commedia dell'arte*', *Modern Drama* (Dec. 1966), pp. 260–7.

[27] The four quotations are taken respectively from Act I, p. 10; p. 52; and Act II, pp. 79–80; p. 77. It is interesting to see that the French version is less literary. Instead of the Proverb there is a saying Beckett is reputed to have heard in the street ('*c'est long, mais ce sera bon*'); and in place of the split-up Shelley lines Estragon says '*Je regarde la blafarde.*' See Colin Duckworth (ed.), *En attendant Godot*, London, 1966, p. 4 and p. 46 with notes. English is for Beckett more allusive, more insistently 'old style'. One may add that Shelley's 'Pale for weariness' is an unmistakable style-marker for poeticising, as in Joyce's *A Portrait...*, Cape ed. p. 109. Cf. Pozzo on the sky: it grows 'pale, pale, ever paler, a little paler'.

words like 'Saviour', 'saved', 'hell', damned' are used as if newly released. For such a dialogue can exploit the aesthetics of the fragment – the altar-piece approached through the surviving wing of the broken triptych – and can re-create the power of a religious vocabulary, no longer held within the syntax of habit.

Yet the method is precarious, for the revitalised language is itself running down. In Act II, the playfully poetic sequence on the dead voices – with the swapping of synonyms and similes 'like leaves/like sand/like leaves' – is followed by the two tramps' most self-conscious and self-defeating attempts at keeping the dialogue going – to evade silence (pp. 66–77). They offer one another a series of ironic boosters ('let's contradict one another'; 'let's ask each other questions'; 'we always find something, eh, Didi, to give us the impression that we exist?') but invention is beginning to fail, bringing the fear of repetition, of 'talking about nothing in particular': the way half a century was spent, according to Gogo. The subsequent action and language games – playing Pozzo and Lucky, and the ritual of courtesies, curses and pardons – cannot prevent exhaustion. Estragon is tired, Vladimir says they are not in form; they stop, and the return of Pozzo and Lucky is greeted as 'reinforcements at last'. So we may add to the physical symptoms of degeneration in the second act of *Godot*[28] this decline in the improvisatory vigour of the Gogo–Didi dialogue. 'Verbal germination' is caught up in a downward-moving cycle.

In *Endgame* a traditional dramatic language is given a new life while it too is running down, in consonance with the man-centred universe. The slow-moving apocalypse of *Endgame* is embodied, tentatively, in the formal catastrophe of an old-style tragedy. It is as if we were given the final sequence of a play whose preceding acts do not survive; and the language of this torso-play appropriately draws on the tragic tone of final acts in a great tradition of drama, particularly in Shakespeare. Hamm – who is at once the protagonist trying to die in the 'old style' and the exhausted actor and writer – collects words towards his 'last soliloquy', with its gestures of recognition (*anagnorisis*) and violent

[28] For a discussion of degeneration in *Godot* see Duckworth, p. xci, drawing on L. Harvey's study 'Art and the Existential in *En Attendant Godot*', *P.M.L.A.* LXXV (March 1960).

vociferation, suffering and renunciation. This style survives the absence of action – of outer and inner pressure or reference; it is full of moving resonances which have ceased to move, since, in the play's terms, the tragic sense of life has no meaning.

The old 'tragic tone' runs through the play as a recurrent style-marker, as can be seen from a few brief extracts from Hamm's speeches, moving from the opening to the end:

(A) (*He clears his throat, joins the tips of his fingers.*) Can there be misery – (*he yawns*) – loftier than mine?
No doubt. Formerly. But now? (Faber ed., 1958, p. 12)

(B) (*With sudden fury.*) Will this never finish?...(*Frenziedly.*)
My kingdom for a nightman! (p. 22)

(C) (*With prophetic relish.*) One day you'll be blind, like me.
You'll be sitting there, a speck in the void, in the dark, for ever, like me. (p. 28)

(D) Our revels now are ended. (p. 39)

(E) Breath held and then...(*he breathes out*). Then babble, babble, words, like the solitary child who turns himself into children, two, three, so as to be together, and whisper together, in the dark. (*Pause.*) Moment upon moment, pattering down, like the millet grains of...(*he hesitates*)...that old Greek, and all life long you wait for that to mount up to a life. (*Pause. He opens his mouth to continue, renounces.*) Ah, let's get it over! (p. 45)

Such passages (and there are many others)[29] simultaneously exploit and parody the kind of phrases that might form part of a final soliloquy. (A) is part of a formal lamentation, the 'misery' bracketed by the yawn and by the detached question-and-answer, in keeping with the context which tells us that Hamm is 'to play'; (B) evokes the final – and futile – outburst of a defeated king, with its allusion to Richard III; (C) draws on the rhetoric of anguish, turned into 'relish' through the comfort of fine cadences that go with self-pity, whose ambivalent pathos is carried, in the full speech, by a hypnotic piling up of the future

[29] 'Quiet, quiet, you're keeping me awake' (p. 19); the evocation of classical–mythological hope: 'But beyond the hills? Eh? Perhaps it's still green. Eh? (*Pause.*) Flora! Pomona! (*Ecstatically.*) Ceres!' (p. 30). There are also isolated elegiac notes: 'We too were bonny – once' (p. 31); 'Yesterday! What does that mean? Yesterday!' (p. 32).

tense suggesting nostalgia for an old-style apocalypse; (D) establishes a formal parallel with Prospero's speech (*The Tempest*, Act IV, Scene i) and marks the place where a ceremony of ending – a formal parting and renunciation – begins; (E) finally appropriates the tragic tone in such a way that it is felt as a central statement in and about the play. Hamm's words lament their own slow accumulation and impotence as once the fallen tyrant – say Macbeth, in his 'Tomorrow and tomorrow' speech – came to recognise the meaningless accumulation of days 'to the last syllable of recorded time', at the end of a cycle of action. Here we respond to the words-without-action, to the left-over tone or overtones.[30] But this style too is, like Hamm's story-telling, only 'Technique, you know' (p. 40), and the tragic tone and its parody are formally brought together in the concluding sequence:

Hamm: Then let it end!...With a bang!...Of darkness! And me? Did anyone ever have pity on me?
Clov: What? (*Pause.*) Is it me you're referring to?
Hamm: (*angrily*). An aside, ape! Did you never hear an aside before? (*Pause.*) I'm warming up for my last soliloquy. (p. 49)

That last soliloquy combines a ritual of disvestment – Hamm discarding his gaff and toy dog – with a parody of the desired quietus ('Peace to our...arses'). It goes on to suggest the end of literary language, both lyric and narrative (Hamm composes a line of poetry – taken from Baudelaire in the French original; and a sequence for his story, chanting in pain, complacent in exhaustion) and the end of dramatic language itself. The two loud cries which echo the Passion ('Father! *Pause. Louder.* Father!') are followed by the gestures that remain: a whistle thrown into the auditorium with ironic compliments; a self-apostrophe – 'speak no more'; and a return to motionlessness by the principal player.

To reach this point the play generates its own cycle of run-down, more elaborate, slow-moving, and at times deliberately tedious than in any other Beckett play. The most obvious device

30 See the general conclusion of Antony Easthope, 'Hamm, Clov, and Dramatic Method in *Endgame*', *Modern Drama* (May 1968), reprinted in *Twentieth Century Interpretations of 'Endgame'*, Englewood Cliffs, N.J., 1969.

– Beckett's own alienation-device – is the verbal equivalent of a yawn which keeps recurring:

Hamm: This is slow work (p. 16).
Nell: Why this farce, day after day? (p. 18).
Hamm: This is deadly (p. 25). Do you not think this has gone on long enough? (p. 33).
Clov: What is there to keep me here?
Hamm: The dialogue (p. 39).
Hamm: I feel rather drained. (*Pause.*) The prolonged creative effort (p. 41).
Hamm: You haven't much conversation all of a sudden. Do you not feel well? Clov: I'm cold (p. 43).
Clov: I'm tired of our goings on, very tired (p. 48).

Of course these are only the most overt signals to the audience; the feel of rundown is ultimately created by the whole texture of the dialogue, so finely wrought that it is over-wrought. In performance, that pace slows down the faculty of response in the audience. In reading, the one-act structure – Beckett's ultimate solution for an original two-act design[31] – seems disproportionately long, and the sequences in the dialogue seem more arbitrary – in their placing and interrelation, in their 'dynamics' – than in either *Godot* or the later plays. Yet possibly no other structure and overall rhythm could have succeeded in creating the feel of that 'prolonged creative effort' Hamm spoke of. For the whole play bears witness to the relation between verbal creativity and effort ('germination' out of 'putrefaction') when, as Clov laments, 'the words you taught me...don't mean anything any more, teach me others' (p. 32).

Three later plays can be seen as ruthlessly exhibiting specimens of a 'dead language', and yet, as the words are replayed by the tape recorder or the compulsive voices of memory, they come to life within each play. *Krapp's Last Tape* shows how a man's own words become archaic to him through the pathetic comedy of keeping private sound archives; and to double the parody

[31] Cf. Ruby Cohn, 'The Beginning of *Endgame*', *Modern Drama*, Dec. 1966, pp. 319–34. I formed the view that there is something wrong with the structure of *Endgame* before reading Professor Cohn's account of the original MS and her praise of the final single-act compression. This praise rings true; but I still think the structure of the dialogue is strained.

Krapp is a would-be writer whose youthful style – as recorded – reaches out towards literary perfection, towards the *magnum opus.* In *Happy Days* Winnie finds solace in reciting, over and over again, fragments of an 'old style' which equates – in its decay as well as in its comforts – a line from Milton with the writing on a toothbrush. In *Play* the words intoned at the bidding of spotlights are not only a dramatic device relating the dead speakers to the community of ghosts from *The Persians* to *The Ghost Sonata,* but they speak in a worn-out convention, the 'old-play' dialogue of melodrama and farce. So each of these plays enacts, as part of its total meaning, a particular drama *of* words, the decay and renewal of a style.

When Krapp's *old* tape has run nearly half its length, the voice of young Krapp is heard condemning the still earlier records he has just been listening to ('those old P.M.s are gruesome'); and he criticises his youthful literary style in a manner which is in turn over-literary:

> 'Sneers at what he calls his youth and thanks to God that it's over. (*Pause.*) False ring there. (*Pause.*) Shadows of the opus...magnum. Closing with – (*brief laugh*) – yelp to Providence.'
>
> (Faber ed., pp. 12–13)

The record goes on – interrupted by the backstage popping of corks and by Krapp finding solace in the old-style Victorian hymn 'Now the day is over' – to offer, instead of the desired record of essential experience, the self-conscious writer 'warming up' with the help of ornate, archaic diction:

> back on the year that is gone, with what I hope is perhaps a glint of the old eye to come, there is of course the house on the canal where mother lay a-dying, in the late autumn, after her long viduity (*Krapp gives a start*)...

At that point, in a comic–pathetic counterpoint, old Krapp breaks in to repeat the lost words 'a-dying' and 'viduity', and savours the curious definitions of the latter. Not only is the meaning of a lost word then recovered and made dramatic – in Krapp's relish of archaeological discovery – but the brief word-drama serves to purify Krapp's style, free it from its stuttering archaisms. The play is now free to move on – through the record of 'moments' and of a 'vision', which Krapp impatiently switches off – to the one authentic-sounding experience among all those fossilised memories: the moment in the punt with the girl (pp. 15–16). Here Krapp is released from the false ring in his style (presumably an overflow from his *magnum opus*). The syntax and the rhythm, the 'purity of diction' and the slow-paced speaking voice, combine in re-creating the stillness of the experience. And the structural placing of this 'still point' – as counterpoint to the parody of the mechanical language of memory – saves it from being a mere 'idyll' in the lyrical mode. And though old Krapp offers a brief slangy counterblast even to that authentic experience and speech ('Just been listening to that stupid bastard...', so begins the *last* tape), he comes to accept it provisionally ('Ah well, may be he was right') and ends by replaying the sequence – and that sequence alone – until the tape runs out. In the economy of the play young Krapp has found the language that – for one moment – frees him from the pained decadence of his own style, just as old Krapp has been enabled to release the 'living moment' from the mechanical rotation of his defunct memories.

In *Happy Days* Winnie's endless stream of talk dramatises the condition of a person who finds solace in the verbal remnants of an old culture; she might claim 'These fragments I have shored against my ruins.' The 'classics' help her through the day; through the two acts of the play she quotes – or strives to quote – lines called 'wonderful' (in Act I) and 'unforgettable' or 'exquisite' or 'immortal' (in the deteriorating extreme state of Act II).[32] These broken classical lines are held in the frame of the opening prayer – the Lesser Doxology 'world without end, Amen' – and the duet from *The Merry Widow* sung by Winnie as a solo at the end of the play. The Christian liturgy and the pre-1914 nostalgic *schlager* of Lehár give the outer range of the 'old style'. The lines themselves are all evocative, but only a few are likely to be recognised and so become a doubly dramatic quote – one ironically intensified by *our* memory of the source. Such lines are: Milton's 'Hail, holy light', which – seemingly lost in Act I – re-emerges with dramatic irony at the opening of Act II, and the moving use of 'Fear no more the heat of the sun' as a hearing test for Willie in Act I. Other quotes are

[32] Faber ed., 1963, Act I, p. 11; p. 13; p. 25; Act II, p. 37; p. 43; p. 45.

fragmented and blurred beyond immediate recognition, like the eloquent phrases – with 'woe' as their key-word[33] – whereby the old tragic tone is woven into Winnie's random flow of 'happy' talk, for example:

Oh well, what does it matter, that is what I always say, so long as one...you know...what is that wonderful line...laughing wild... something something laughing wild amid severest woe. (Act I, p. 25)

Although the source has been established[34] (Gray's 'Ode on a Distant Prospect of Eton College': 'And Moody Madness laughing wild/Amid severest woe') it is too recondite to work as an allusion; it is the dramatic use that matters: the life of old words in Winnie's decaying memory.[35]

The comforting clichés and fine but empty phrases that Winnie herself keeps calling 'old style' – to the accompaniment of her automatic smile – run through the play like a part in counterpoint. The overall effect of these phrases is to bring back to mind a once-living-now-dead order: the old-fashioned instructions on the medicine bottle ('Loss of spirits...'); the elegant literacy of 'not a day goes by' or 'It is perhaps a little soon – to make ready – for the night.'[36] For good measure, Winnie keeps using outworn poetic words: 'tis, beseech, enow, God grant, dire need. With this in mind, Ruby Cohn states that 'Winnie's "old style" is implicitly contrasted with Dante's *dolce stil nuovo*; she even utters the phrase "sweet old style"'. We thus get a contrast between the 'vigorous literature of the Renaissance' and 'the weary decadence' of the present time: like her toothpaste Winnie's words are running out.[37] Yet the 'old style' phrases – like the

33 Act I, p. 1; p. 13; p. 25.

34 Ruby Cohn, *Samuel Beckett: the Comic Gamut*, New Brunswick, N.J., 1962, p. 254. Cohn establishes the source of all the 'woe' lines, and even traces back such isolated phrases as 'ensign crimson' and 'Pale flag' to Romeo's speech over the mock-dead Juliet. Thus are two lines of Shakespeare transmuted into the names of lipstick.

35 Cf. my discussion on the dramatic use of quotation and allusion in Eliot: Ch. 2, pp. 92–4.

36 Pp. 16 and 20; p. 18; p. 33. Other examples of the 'old style' can be found on pp. 25, 26, 32, 37 and 40.

37 Ruby Cohn, *op. cit.* p. 253 (non-continuous extracts). The list of poetic words also comes from the same study; all other points and examples come from my study of the play made before reading Ruby Cohn's work.

'immortal' lines – also succeed in invoking a double condition; the condition of a memory and a language that refuses to die. The fragments add up; the 'dead language' is, once again, given dramatic life. The whole play has the incongruous power of a broken classic, with a 'fall-out' of words, unstable yet still generative, ultimately felt as 'classical'.[38]

In *Play* the language of the dead is partly suggested by the clichés of the genre, a banal old play. The first section – which is a compressed exposition of the sexual triangle as if played out 'on earth' – is shot through with samples of a style that could be called a defunct literary naturalism. The dialogue that lies buried in the chorus-like incantation of voices in the first sequence is something like this:

W.1: (to W.2) I know what torture you must be going through, [so] I have dropped in to say I bear you no ill-feeling.
W.2: I am ringing for Erskine. [the butler]
[later in the evening]
M.: [Darling, I might as well] make a clean breast of it.[39]

In the rapid concentration of the play, the appropriate clichés get telescoped into parody:

M.: At home, all heart to heart, new leaf and bygones bygones. I ran into your ex-doxy, she said, one night, on the pillow, you're well out of that.[40]

Such compression is the first stage in giving even that style new dramatic life. But the total pattern goes far beyond parody to create a spectral liturgy heard for the first time. *Play* takes Beckett to a more extreme aesthetic than any of the earlier plays[41] – to the primacy of rhythmic and tonal effects. The early impulse to counteract a 'language abstracted to death' then ends by pointing to another kind of abstraction, to the composition of

38 The text should be performed in the manner of a classic; Madelaine Renaud's performance suggested Racine in the *Comédie Française* manner. This seems to have been an intended effect. See Jean-Louis Barrault's B.B.C. interview (1 May 1965), quoted in Duckworth, pp. xxxii–xxxiii.

39 Based on a sequence in *Play*, Faber ed., 1964, p. 13.

40 *Ibid*. p. 14.

41 Cf. in *Play* 'Mallarmé's aesthetic quest assumed metaphysical dimensions.' Renee Riese Hubert, 'Beckett's *Play* between Poetry and Performance', *Modern Drama* (Dec. 1966), p. 346.

words for disembodied voices which marks the dead end of dialogue as interaction.

Impelled by the desire for further innovation, Beckett moved on to attempt the expression of the process of verbal expression itself. His late radio plays could be seen as allegories on the tiring genesis of tired words: *Words and Music* exhibits Words as the mechanical slave of the effete master, Croak; *Cascando* presents the low, panting, syntax-torn Voice expressing, as its chief concern, the desire for its own extinction: 'no more stories ...no more words...'[42] The texture of each of these radio plays – dissimilar as they are – uses words primarily as tonal rhythmic elements in 'radiophonic' composition. In *Words and Music* Words is capable only of two kinds of utterance: the recitation by rote of prefabricated formulas, and a poeticising collage made up of lyrical fragments. The formulas for Sloth and Love turn out to be identical:

> [Sloth/Love] – is of all the passions the most powerful passion and indeed no passion is more powerful than the passion of [Sloth/Love], this is the mode in which the mind is most strongly affected and indeed – [43]

There follows the weaving of lyrical lines – interwoven with music and the groans of Croak, whom Words cannot comfort – suggesting the composition of a poem; the broken prose lines add up to a completed stanza, with the kind of emendation one expects to find between two drafts. ('Waiting for the hag' becomes 'Shivering for the hag'; 'That old moonlight' becomes 'That old starlight'.) These strike one as crystallisations of two essential elements in Beckett's dramatic language. The verbal automatism first seen in Lucky has now been severed from the aphasiac's still human speech, it has become total abstraction; Words even suggests Vice in a modern morality. And the lyricism re-appears as the last, creative 'antidote' to dead verbal formulas:

Words: (*trying to sing softly*)
All dark no begging
No giving no words
No sense no need.

42 *'Play' and Two Short Pieces for Radio*, London, 1964, p. 39.

43 *Ibid.* pp. 27 and 28 – there is a minor variation in punctuation, and the second repetition of the formula (on love) completes the sentence.

Dialogue in and out of monologue

Then babble, babble, words, like the solitary child who turns himself into children, two, three... (Hamm in *Endgame*, p. 45)

I used to think that I would learn to talk alone. (*Pause.*) By that I mean to myself, the wilderness. (*Smile.*) But no. (*Smile broader.*) No no. (*Smile off.*) Ergo you are there. (Winnie in *Happy Days*, Act II)

European drama as we know it began when Aeschylus showed what could be done with poetry spoken in character by moving from declamatory or narrative monologue to the exhibition of dramatic conflict in dialogue between two characters. But the rich potentialities of triangular dialogue were first exploited by Sophocles when he – in Aristotle's words – increased the number of actors to three. In discussing this development, E. F. Watling, a modern translator of Sophocles, lists the advantages of a three-personed dialogue, and concludes that

in the hands of Sophocles, drama became not only triangular but three-dimensional; to the length and breadth of mythical narrative he added the depth of human character as he observed it in his fellow mortals. What had hitherto been a frieze of more or less static figures confronting one another in profile became a perspective of living human beings reacting one on another and shaping their own destinies by the interplay of their contrasted characters.[44]

When the National Theatre coupled its first production of Beckett's *Play* with the *Philoctetes* of Sophocles[45] we were able to witness the extent to which Beckett had abandoned, in his own triangular play, the 'three-dimensional' Sophoclean dialogue, going back instead – or advancing through regression[46] – to a broken chorus of 'more or less static figures confronting one

[44] E. F. Watling, Introduction to *Electra and Other Plays*, Harmondsworth, 1953, p. 14. See also H. D. F. Kitto, *Greek Tragedy, a Literary Study* (1939), London, 1961, pp. 149ff. Cf. Aristotle, *Poetics*, 1449a, 13 (Butcher, p. 19).

[45] 7 April 1964, and following season.

[46] The cultural–psychological parallel has been drawn by Eva Metman – from a Jungian point of view: 'Beckett leads us into a deep regression from all civilized tradition, in which consciousness sinks back into an earlier state of its development into an *abaissement de niveau mental*, where neglected and rejected contents become activated.' *Loc. cit.* (n. 21), p. 129.

another in profile'. One suddenly realised the extent to which Beckett's drama had put into question all previous conceptions of dialogue; and the insights of that contrast may serve to suggest an outer scale for the question now before us: is Beckett's 'dialogue' dialogue?

The inner scale for discussing this question is given by Beckett's own progression: *Waiting for Godot*, above all, but also *Endgame* and *All that Fall* create a richly 'polyphonic' dramatic language, a formal dialogue; *Krapp's Last Tape*, *Embers* and *Happy Days* are subtle transformations of an interior monologue into the semblance of dialogue; while *Play* and the later radio plays – *Words and Music*, *Cascando* – explore the rhythm of voices and then return to the univocal monologue. This pattern of development – somewhat simplified here for the sake of initial clarity – becomes even more interesting when we consider that Beckett may have turned to the theatre from the novel partly because 'dramatic projection offered relief from monologue'.[47] And within the cycle of novels themselves there is a movement from patches of quasi-naturalistic dialogue to a purely self-mirroring or self-quoting monologue. For example, in the opening pages of *Watt* (written 1942–4) – while still in the tangible and Irish-sounding world that precedes Mr Knott's house and its tormented linguistic investigations – we have this on the birth of a son to Goff and Tetty:

> I went up those stairs, Mr Hackett, said Tetty, on my hands and knees, wringing the carpet-rods as though they were made of raffia.
>
> You were in such anguish, said Mr Hackett.
>
> Three minutes later I was a mother.
>
> Unassisted, said Goff.
>
> I did everything with my own hands, said Tetty, everything.
>
> She severed the cord with her teeth, said Goff, not having scissors to her hand. What do you think of that?
>
> I would have snapped it across my knee, if necessary, said Tetty.[48]

47 W. York Tindall, *Samuel Beckett*, p. 41.

48 *Watt*, London, 1963, p. 12. (Cf. also the railway-station dialogue at the end of this novel.)

Contrast this with one of the opening sequences of *The Unnamable*, where the nameless narrator is beginning to offer permutations on his need to go on speaking about things of which he cannot speak, inside his 'distant skull':

> I speak, speak because I must, but I do not listen, I seek my lesson, my life I used to know and would not confess, hence possibly an occasional lack of limpidity. And perhaps now again I shall do no more than seek my lesson, to the self-accompaniment of a tongue that is not mine. But instead of saying what I should not have said, and what I shall say no more, if I can, and what I shall say perhaps, if I can, should I not rather say some other thing, even though it be not yet the right thing? I'll try, try in another present, even though it be not yet mine, without pauses, without tears, without eyes, without reasons.[49]

The comic patter of the exchange from *Watt* has its counterpart in the early plays: in the Gogo–Didi and Nagg–Nell dialogue (as when Nagg begs Nell to scratch his back), and it contributes to the bright surface of *All that Fall*. It is the simplest element in Beckett's 'natural' gift for dialogue, which needs stressing. (Roger Blin was mainly impressed by the immediacy and naturalness of the dialogue in *Godot*, while the play's deeper significance escaped him.[50]) By contrast, the *Unnameable*'s endlessly spiralling monologue – with such barely 'dramatisable' expressions as 'a tongue that is not mine', and with its hypothetical statements on what should not have been said and what should, perhaps, be said[51] – anticipates the later monodramas, in particular *Cascando*. More important still, the solipsistic monologue in search of its own extinction in silence creates a permanent pull in Beckett's drama. The tension between the monologue-possessed writer, and drama as a dialogue-directed art, runs through all the plays.

What, then, is the specifically dramatic gift that has gone into resolving this tension – whether through stage figures brought to personal encounter or through the shadowy impersonations of the isolated self in monodrama?

Waiting for Godot and *Endgame* need only brief discussion here

49 *Molloy; Malone Dies; The Unnamable*, p. 308.

50 Reported by John Fletcher, *Samuel Beckett's Art*, London, 1967, p. 43.

51 Paralleled by the Unnamable's search for 'future and conditional participle' (p. 302), perhaps the least likely tenses for sustained dialogue.

to stress the implicit argument in the previous section. In each of these plays Beckett has stylised the dialogue for and through two pairs of couples, adding to the richness of these plays the counterpoint of sharply contrasted styles of dramatic speech. In *Godot* this counterpoint has the clarity of great art, and the voices of Lucky and Pozzo are triumphantly individualised for all time, while the quasi-monologues of these two stage figures *interact* with the otherwise so separate world and language of the two tramps. Since the texture of the whole play is both varied and clear, it does not matter that the tramps themselves are *not* clearly differentiated in their style of speech, that their lines can be swapped around or re-arranged in different sequences,[52] and that their 'idiom' is not individual.[53] Listening to Vladimir and Estragon we respond to the words *in dialogue*, and we do not ask: are these split-off segments of an ultimate monologue?

Yet this is just what we do ask about the quasi-dialogue of Hamm and Clov in *Endgame*. We remember these figures through what they say *about* their putative father–son, tyrant–slave relationship – and, of course, through the unique violence of contrast in their physical state, the visual impact of permanent sitting against ceaseless running – but we cannot differentiate their way of speaking. For example, Clov's opening speech not only uses one of Hamm's key images – Zeno's paradox of the infinite heap of millet – but speaks in Hamm's rhythms;[54] and Clov's last soliloquy sounds like something split off from Hamm's last soliloquy:

> I ask the words that remain – sleeping, waking, morning, evening. They have nothing to say.

In their style of speech Hamm and Clov lack the dramatic counterpoint we experience when Pozzo confronts Lucky (or Lear the Fool). And even if the two figures are intended to be psychic projections – in Martin Esslin's words, 'different aspects of a single personality'[55] – we may object that Hamm and Clov

52 See Niklaus Gessner's amusing variations in *Die Unzulänglichkeit der Sprache*, Zürich, 1957, pp. 48–9.

53 Differentiation in terms of gesture and life-style is much clearer (see John Fletcher, pp. 50–1) than is differentiation in styles of speech.

54 Cf. p. 145, (E) above.

55 Esslin, *The Theatre of the Absurd*, p. 65.

are not autonomous enough, while, at the same time, there is nothing in the structure of the dialogue that would make us experience their exchanges as split monologue. Despite the frequent internal variations of Hamm's tone[56] there is danger of monotony. The counterpoint comes from the comic–pathetic exchanges of Nagg and Nell, which retain – in painful reduction – something of the verbal vivacity of the tramps' dialogue in *Godot*.

All that Fall is unique in Beckett's dramatic work both as a structure *for* and in its texture *of* voices. On her groping way to the station – that is for two-thirds of the play – Maddy Rooney, a would-be monologuist, gets entangled in a series of frustrating dialogues with recognisably Anglo-Irish voices (Beckett's human equivalent for those sound effects from Arcadia, sheep, bird, cow, cock). The rest of the play, until the entry of the boy Jerry as messenger (pp. 24–36), is a sustained duologue between Maddy and Don Rooney, beautifully dovetailed despite the self-distorting and linguistically self-conscious speech-failures of both interlocutors.[57] The play is, then, organised around a series of points where monologue and dialogue intersect or clash in comic–pathetic incongruity. (The conception is thus quite different from Dylan Thomas' *Under Milk Wood*, despite the surface resemblance of these two radio plays in creating an action solely by voices, out of seemingly authentic local speech – an aural tapestry.)

We can see from the opening sequence how this lively monologue–dialogue counterpoint works. After a very brief exchange of words with Christy, Mrs Rooney questions the carter about her way of speaking ('Do you find anything...bizarre about my way of speaking?') and then goes on to reject Christy's offer of a small load of dung, with such vehemence that her interlocutor is frightened away. There follows Mrs Rooney's first formal

56 Cf. pp. 145–7. See also 'voice of rational being' and 'normal voice' (p. 27); constant variation of tone in Hamm's story-telling (pp. 35–7); the 'senile quaver' that he puts on (p. 42). At the same time, the stylistic differentiation between Nagg and Nell as against Hamm and Clov is itself reduced. At least one critic (Theodor W. Adorno in 'Towards an Understanding of *Endgame*') has attributed Nagg's joke about the tailor's trousers compared to God's creation to Hamm – presumably because it sounds like one of Hamm's stories. See *Twentieth Century Interpretations of 'Endgame'*, p. 97.

57 It is in this sequence that Mr and Mrs Rooney agree that they are 'struggling with a dead language'. Cf. Introduction, p. 27.

soliloquy – against the sound of her dragging feet – with its sequence of self-lamenting apostrophes ('Oh let me just flop down flat on the road like a big fat jelly out of a bowl and never move again!') and the broken-voiced invocation of Minnie, the dead girl, and of love. We are then taken into the present moment, the foreground: one sentence conjures up laburnum; there is the sound of Mr Tyler's bicycle bell; and the interior monologue is converted into 'bizarre' but lively interpersonal duologue (p. 10):

Mrs Rooney: That was a narrow squeak.
Mr Tyler: I alit in the nick of time.
Mrs Rooney: It is suicide to be abroad. But what is it to be at home, Mr Tyler, what is it to be at home? A lingering dissolution.

This dialogue tone is flexible enough to move from a discourse on bicycle parts to an exchange of bids on Mrs Rooney's degree of being alive ('Alive?/Well, half alive shall we say/Speak for yourself, Mr Tyler, I am not half alive nor anything approaching it.') and so on to another cycle of grief, a call for sympathy, a rejection of sympathy. Inevitably, Mrs Rooney is left alone to soliloquise – in a comic–pathetic lament – over her condition: 'Oh cursed corset!...Oh, to be in atoms, in atoms. ATOMS. (*Silence. Cooing. Faintly.*) Jesus! (*Pause.*) Jesus!' Then the sound of a car is heard, and Mr Slocum's appearance initiates another duologue. These transitions from duologue into monologue and back into duologue do not merely establish a pleasing counterpoint of speech; they intensify the listener's awareness of Maddy Rooney's isolation by making all her attempts at dialogue seem aborted attempts, verbal responses which 'fit' so badly that they must be superseded by monologue.

To vary the pattern, later in the play Beckett first makes Mrs Rooney clamour for inclusion in the chorus of voices at the station ('Do not imagine, because I am silent, that I am not present...' p. 21) and then insist on soliloquising in a dialogue sequence with her husband. ('Do not mind me, dear, I am just talking to myself' p. 34.) The former is a form-conscious device, calling attention to the radio as a medium[58] where silence puts

[58] Cf. Hugh Kenner, *Samuel Beckett*, pp. 167ff. But Professor Kenner overstates the argument that in this play for radio all living is an illusion, conjured up by voices and sound effects. In its conventions sound radio is no more 'illusionist' than the theatre.

in question the continued existence of a person (as in the Berkeley-derived ontological puzzle where what is unperceived may not exist, *esse est percipi*); the latter is a naturalistic device, the familiar mumbling of a tired old woman. Such is the range and assurance of this play.

One might wonder why Beckett attempted this kind of polyphonic dialogue only once. The answer must be that inner monologue – self talking to self or to a projected voice – has exerted the strongest pull in his art. *Krapp's Last Tape* compresses into one brief edited whole the painful incongruity between two broken monologues: the young voice with its finely cadenced record of 'quintessential' Proustian moments,[59] and the old voice, slangy and abrasive, at once mocking and lamenting the voice it has been listening to. The play must be seen or at least heard to bring out fully the dramatic irony of this juxtaposition. It should be heard as *solo dialogue* – the interlocking voices of two identities separated by thirty years – within the formal monodrama which is also the appropriate metaphor for the ultimate isolation of the speaker. Each of the two major interruptions of the young man's monologue by old Krapp – checking the dictionary for the word 'viduity' and recording his last tape – works as interaction between two voices and states of mind. As Krapp starts reading out the definition of 'viduity':

State – or condition – of being – or remaining – a widow or widower. (*Looks up. Puzzled.*) Being – or remaining?...(*Pause. He peers again at the dictionary.*) (p. 13)

The pause, the slow questioning repetition, is enough to give such emphasis to the words that we instantly see the connection: Krapp in his present state of 'remaining' is questioning (beyond the forgotten word) the attempt made, in that spoken diary, to express a state of 'being'. Thus, less than halfway through the short play, Beckett makes us aware of the essential dramatic link between the juxtaposed monologues; and we are made sensitive to the grotesque, sad power of Krapp's second interruption, which

59 See the excellent study '*Krapp's Last Tape* and the Proustian Vision', by Arthur K. Oberg, *Modern Drama* (Dec. 1966), pp. 333–8. I have briefly placed the play, in the context of withdrawal to minimal language, in '*Six Characters*: Pirandello's Last Tape', *Modern Drama* (May 1969), p. 4.

ends with mocking yet affirming echoes of the voice of mechanised memory: 'Be again' four times repeated, a life attempting to sum itself up:

Be again, be again. (*Pause.*) All that old misery. (*Pause.*) Once wasn't enough for you. (*Pause.*) Lie down across her. (p. 18)

Around this perfectly controlled inner structure, we respond – when the play is seen as a cycle – to the outer structure: a monologue heard backwards. At the beginning, the fragmented language of the present speaker (reading out his life as numbers on boxes); at the end, 'the strong, rather pompous' young voice with its cadences of attempted self-transcendence, its idle assertion of some peak achievement in his life and writing. The work is short enough for the opening and concluding monologue to interact with one another – to suggest a residual dialogue between two remote strata of self.

Happy Days is a near-monologue which draws into itself a dialogue that transforms the texture of the play. We become aware of three different dramatic devices, or three ways whereby Winnie's solo voice is energised by her meagre prospects of dialogue. First, there is the minimal and actual dialogue with Willie – six exchanges in all[60] – each mocking and yet affirming the possibility of question and answer, of speaking and being heard. Willie's monosyllabic 'It' (in answer to Winnie wondering whether hair goes with 'them' or 'it') his crude relish of 'formication', the pun on emmet's eggs, of the word 'sucked up', and of the self-involving definition of hog ('Castrated male swine...'), amount to a parody of dialogue. Yet these minimal encounters still work as dialogue, and, in performance, provoke the kind of laughter which usually greets a witty repartee. By contrast, the repetition of 'Fear no more' – in the 'audition' scene – has the resonances of a pathetically deflected colloquy in love; and this effect is paralleled by Winnie's final joy over the single syllable 'Win' which her decrepit partner just manages to utter, and by the failure of the couple to sing the *Merry Widow* duet together, though Willie hums it in Act I, and Winnie sings it at the end of the play.

60 Not counting Willie's reading out of newspaper adverts which are not directly answered by Winnie although they do start off a sequence of reminiscences in her monologue.

Secondly, and all-pervasively, we have what might be called Winnie's *as if* dialogue: the rich succession of addresses to a silent, and mostly invisible, Willie. The monologue is turned into a shadow-dialogue through the monologuist's simple need for an auditor:

So that I may say at all times, even when you do not answer and perhaps hear nothing, something of this is being heard, I am not merely talking to myself, that is in the wilderness, a thing I could never bear to do – for any length of time.[61]

This human need for an interlocutor who is barely present suffices to fill every page of the text[62] with an apostrophe of one kind or another; from the first hailing (Hoo-oo!) to the final, tender and anxious appeal ('What ails you Willie, I never saw such an expression...'). The transformation in the texture of the language cannot be overstressed for, in effect, Winnie's monologue, with all its inwardness, is turned outward, it turns on the person addressed and his being addressed releases most of the turns of phrasing. To illustrate the range briefly: we have such archaic mock-pathos as:

> Slip on your drawers, dear...before you get singed. (p. 14)
> Would I had let you sleep on; (p. 18)

repeated requests for confirmation, for shared knowledge:

> Is that not so, Willie, that even words fail at times? (p. 20)
> Was I lovable once, Willie? (*Pause.*) Was I ever lovable? (p. 25)

requests for requests:

> Bid me put this thing down, Willie, I would obey instantly... (p. 28)

instructions or spectatorial comments:

> Go back to your hole now, Willie, you've exposed yourself enough. (p. 20)
> Lift up your eyes to me, Willie, and tell me can you see me. (p. 23)
> Again, Willie, again! (*claps.*) Encore, Willie, please. (pp. 30–1)

[61] *Happy Days*, p. 18. Cf. also the quotation heading this section, p. 153 above.

[62] There is one exception: p. 33 of the English text does not have an address to Willie, for it is wholly given to the impersonation of Mr and Mrs Shower.

In such places the syntax itself has become fully dramatic, interpersonal. The immobilised woman's questions and imperatives as it were call out for dialogue (as if all speech called out for dialogue). Her static world is set in motion by this semblance of dialogue. All this goes with a constant modulation in tone, a musical pattern; it is the kind of 'scoring' that insists that the voice should be used as a subtle instrument.

Thirdly, there are Winnie's self-apostrophisings and impersonations which flow in and out of the quasi-dialogue just discussed. The plea for an encore, for example, is immediately followed by one of Winnie's characteristic self-addresses: 'How often I have said, in evil hours, Sing now, Winnie, sing your song...'; 'And something says, Stop talking now, Winnie, for a minute, don't squander all your words for the day...' This in turn modulates, after a silence, into the dramatic sketch of the cruel visitation from the Showers (or Cookers), with a vivid impersonation of their dialogue:[63] 'What's she doing? he says – What's the idea? he says – stuck up to her diddies in the bleeding ground – coarse fellow.' We have here what Eliot once hoped to find in drama: the vernacular as it might be conveyed by a Marie Lloyd in the role of a middle-aged woman going through the contents of her bag,[64] in a dramatic context as awesome as the *Prometheus Bound* of Aeschylus. And all the devices are given a natural human motivation: the solitary person's need to dramatise, to split into voices, to compel an otherwise inaccessible dialogue.

Beckett's transformations of the monologue in both *Krapp's Last Tape* and *Happy Days* offer the perfect fusion of a particular human predicament and a particular dramatic language. In this respect Beckett accomplishes something that neither Naturalist nor Expressionist dramatists have been able to accomplish before him. As Roy Walker says, *Krapp's Last Tape* 'solves the technical problem of the Expressionists who tried clumsily to cope with the consequences of depth psychology',[65] for example, in the afterthought soliloquies of O'Neill's *Strange Interlude*. One may add that naturalistically motivated monodramas are relatively

63 This technique is also used in *Embers*, but there the 'other voices' are spoken by others.

64 T. S. Eliot, 'Marie Lloyd', *Selected Essays*, p. 457.

65 *Op. cit.* n. 1, pp. 534–5.

slight works like Cocteau's *La voix humaine* (a woman's last telephone 'conversation' with the lover who does not answer) or O'Neill's *Hughie*, the instant confessional to the night porter. Beckett's soliloquies work both on the surface and in depth, have personal and universal resonances. They are unique in modern drama.

But taking his art to a further point of experiment, Beckett moved on to dramatise the solitary creative act itself. We have already discussed the depersonalised function of Words in the radio play *Words and Music*. All that needs to be added at this point is that *Cascando* presents, among other things, the sources of soliloquising, the tired creative effort to make a monologue dramatic, that is to say to split off the Voice – the voice that wells up in the mind – from the Opener, the creator of the voice. With elegant counterpoint the text insists that the Voice is distinct, its monologue both autonomous and in vocal competition with the Opener and with Music:

Opener: They said, it's his own, it's his voice, it's in his head.
(*Pause.*)

Voice: faster...out driving out...rearing...plunging nowhere... for the island...then no more...elsewhere...anywhere... heading anywhere...lights –
Silence.

Opener: No resemblance.
I answered, And that...

Music: (brief) –
Silence.

Opener: ...is that mine too?
But I don't answer any more.
And they don't say anything more.
They have quit.
Good.[66]

The reader or the listener – responding to the tonal invention – may accept the message: the Voice, longing for its own extinction, has its own dramatic function since it is *there*, since it has been called into being. Yet the distinction between 'Opener' and 'Voice' is microscopic; their affinity suggests a 'personless'

66 *'Play' etc.*, pp. 45–6.

soliloquy splitting up and then returning to soliloquy. The dramatic personae, with their compulsions, 'have quit'. There are only the rhythms of that panting Voice whose last words merge, appropriately enough, with the Opener and with Music: 'just a few more...don't let go...Woburn...he clings on... come on...come on – *Silence.*

It is as if Beckett had taken us behind the monologue itself, to the point where the weary latter-day genesis of words in the mind is perceived with such self-conscious clarity that, after such perception, even the monologue must cease – giving way to silence and the sound of breathing.[67]

[67] *Not I* (1973) is briefly discussed in my Conclusion, pp. 236–7.

4: Pinter

'I am pretty well obsessed with words when they get going', Pinter once said when an interviewer asked whether his creative imagination was not more visual than verbal. Pinter went on to stress the doubleness of drama: 'It is a matter of tying the words to the image of the character standing on the stage. The two things go very closely together.'[1] This dual stress is important, for Pinter has explored the whole scale of verbal–visual power in the different dramatic media: film scripts as well as plays for radio and television flank his major plays for the theatre. Yet one is entitled to single out that obsession with words. It is impossible to think of a Pinter play in terms of mime, for the groping attempt of two or more characters to mark out contested territory with indefinite words – as animals, we learn from Lorenz and Tinbergen, mark out territory with definite posture, movement, colour and sound – is central.[2] The new patterns of dialogue can be regarded as the principal interest in each play. All other interests – including structure and insight into character – are inseparable from the 'transactions' in the dialogue. Pinter has worked out his plays, and the plays work on us, through words.

On the level of artistic creation this means that Pinter has

1 'Harold Pinter Replies', *New Theatre Magazine* (Jan. 1961), p. 9.

2 A similar analogy is offered by Ronald Hayman in *Harold Pinter*, London, 1969, p. 91. (It occurred to me independently.)

a particularly acute sense of the 'blank page' as 'both an exciting and frightening thing. It's what you start from.'[3] The words on the page *are* the shaping medium of the play, occasionally showing a strain of inbreeding, words multiplying words in scenes that seem autonomous.[4] On the level of 'audience impact' the words compel patient listening, attention to *how* things are being said, sometimes against *what* is being said. For certain patterns in a Pinter play may gain an almost hypnotic hold on ear or mind, even though they do not inform, have no emotional charge, and offer only neutral clues to the speaker.

On the linguistic level proper Pinter's dialogue is precise enough to provide samples for a work on the Varieties of Contemporary English; and the conversational rhythms alone could be used to train 'aural perception' in foreign students of spoken English. (It would be a much less mechanical primer than the one that inspired Ionesco's *The Bald Primadonna*.[5]) The precision is matched by the social–cultural range of the dialogue across Pinter's entire work (only once, in *The Homecoming*, within the texture of *one* play): from the 'non-standard' and inarticulate

3 'Between the Lines', *The Sunday Times* (4 March 1962), p. 25, subsequently published in a revised form as 'Writing for the Theatre', *Evergreen Review* (Aug.–Sept. 1964), pp. 80–3. All further references will be to the second version.

4 Pinter himself says: 'Too many words irritate me sometimes, but I can't help them, they just seem to come out – out of the fellow's mouth. I don't really examine my words too much, but I am aware that quite often in what I write some fellow at some point says an awful lot.' Interview with Lawrence Bensky, *The Paris Review*, no. 39 (Fall 1966), p. 26. Cf. Shaw on letting 'the play write itself and shape itself', Ch. 1, p. 75. See also Richard Schechner's unqualified gloss on Pinter as the 'disinterested artist...He is meticulous in scenic structure and dialogue for their own sake.' 'Puzzling Pinter', *Tulane Drama Review* (Winter 1966), p. 184.

5 The contrast can be tested by setting the banal conversational opening of, say, *The Dumb Waiter* or *The Collection* against the opening scene of *La Cantatrice chauve*. Pinter's patterns, though 'empty', are at once casual-seeming and humanly authentic. Ionesco *starts* with the denatured logic of language, the talking machine. Cf. also 'La Tragédie du langage', *Notes et contre-notes*, Paris, 1962, pp. 155–60. The essay confirms Ionesco's primary interests: 'la démarche tout à fait cartésienne de l'auteur de mon manuel d'anglais' and 'les automatismes de langage', for example. By contrast Pinter *starts* with a seemingly 'raw' language, as if untouched by schooling. See also n. 12.

speech that keeps recurring in *The Room, The Dumb Waiter, The Birthday Party* and *The Caretaker*, to the euphemistic props of 'U-speech' in *A Slight Ache*, and to the sophisticated urban word-consciousness in plays like *The Collection, The Lover* and *Old Times*. Pinter has a facility for starting with a particular speech-style at a level of mimesis which Beckett found uncongenial and which Eliot could only achieve with strain. Yet a particular speech-style is not left 'to speak for itself', each is gradually made to exhibit its 'absurd' potentiality; the tramp's inarticulateness is intensified; the genteel phrases of Edward and Flora in *A Slight Ache* turn into a disturbed, mock-euphemistic litany by the end of the play; the mannered verbal games enacted by the married couple as adulterous lovers are underlined: 'To hear your command of contemporary phraseology, your delicate use of the very latest idiomatic expression, so subtly employed' (Richard in *The Lover*, p. 75). Not only is the dialogue 'idiomatic', it is saturated with idioms 'played' to show up their idiocy.[6] Similarly, jargon is used to draw attention to the misuse of language as a comic–aggressive smokescreen (Goldberg's cliché-patter, Mick's finance and interior-decorator terms; the academic jargon of Teddy, the cellarmanship of Duff).[7] The low slang in *The Homecoming* is arranged to sound as if the cloaca of language had been dredged to exhibit the 'underground' of ceremonious family talk. The words 'get going' with obsessive patterns.

One characteristic of Pinter's dramatic language has become

[6] Some examples: the idiom-catalogue of Edward on his wife in *A Slight Ache* (p. 24); Ben and Gus in sustained dispute over the phrase 'light the kettle' in *The Dumb Waiter* (pp. 47–8); Bill fencing with James over the extent to which he is a 'wow' at parties in *The Collection* (p. 22); or the variations rung on 'going the whole hog' in *The Homecoming* (p. 68) until Joey concludes that 'Now and again...you can be happy...without going any hog at all.' See also Martin Esslin's amusing account of 'Pinter Translated', *Encounter* (March 1968), and *Brief Chronicles*, pp. 190–5. The translators' howlers are all due to Pinter's dialogue being steeped in English idioms. Cf. Shaw on idiom and translatability, Ch. 1, n. 15.

[7] *The Birthday Party*, Act III (2nd ed.), pp. 77–8; and below: pp. 180–1; n. 42; p. 187; p. 189. *The Caretaker*, Act II, pp. 37–8; Act III, pp. 63–4, used again, with dramatic irony, p. 76; *The Homecoming*, Act II, pp. 51–2 and 61–2; *'Landscape' and 'Silence'*, pp. 25–7. (All page references to Methuen paperback edition.) See the main section in this chapter for further discussion of these points.

so familiar that terms like 'Pinterish' and 'Pinteresque' have come to denote – as Ronald Hayman reminds us – the irrationality of everyday conversation, its 'bad syntax, tautologies, pleonasms, repetitions, *non sequiturs* and self-contradictions'. Hayman goes so far as to claim that 'Pinter has capitalised in a way that no playwright had ever done before...on the fact that real-life conversations don't proceed smoothly and logically from point to point.'[8] Pinter certainly is an innovator, yet it needs to be stressed that what is original in his dialogue is the fusion of the minimal language in naturalism (Chekhov) and the aesthetic expressiveness found in implicit speech from the Symbolists to Beckett.[9]

Most important of all: we experience – and can only experience – the plays through listening to the way everyday language gets deflected by – and the way it alienates – the speakers from one another. In James Boulton's words:

> Evocative or disturbing speech, language which is an accurate reflection of colloquial English and yet reflects the mystery that Pinter sees as an inevitable feature of human relationships: this is a starting point for a consideration of his vision. It leads directly to what is perhaps the chief irony in his plays: the discrepancy between the implicit claim in any *patois* that it is the currency accepted and understood by all its users, and the dramatic fact that all such language in actual usage reveals not complete communication between man and man but their essential apartness.[10]

Pinter has, then, invented a drama of 'human relations at the level of language itself'. The phrase just quoted is taken from Jean Vannier's definition of what is really new in the theatre

8 *Harold Pinter*, London (2nd ed.), 1969, pp. 1–2 (a play-by-play discussion which *starts* with language). Attentive listening and systematic linguistic description both confirm that spoken English, at most levels of usage, is *inexplicit* – broken or jumbled-up syntax, word-searching, unrelated repetitions and overlaps are frequent. See David Crystal and Derek Davy, *Investigating English Style*, London, 1969, Part II, Ch. 4. The linguistic features are there, but not the dramatic shaping.

9 Cf. my Introduction, pp. 21ff in particular.

10 James T. Boulton, 'Harold Pinter: *The Caretaker* and Other Plays', *Modern Drama* (Sept. 1963), pp. 131–40. But Boulton does not develop this point on dialogue.

of Beckett and Ionesco: while the traditional theatre, says Vannier, presents 'psychological relationships which language only *translates*', in the new drama the characters' language is 'literally *exposed* upon the stage' so that there appears '*a theatre of language* where man's words are held up to us as a spectacle'.[11]

Yet Pinter stands in sharp contrast to Beckett and Ionesco.[12] Beckett – who seems to have been present at some latter-day Fall or Babel of literary language – has created his dialogue out of the stylised breakdown of hyper-literary styles.[13] Pinter, to develop the image, has taken the linguistic Babel for granted (perhaps too glibly at times) at the level of everyday exchanges, talk, chat, verbal games – with an ear for local usage, or rather abusage and verbiage. He seems to carry no literary 'burden of the past'. He has created his dialogue out of the failures of language that might occur *as* English is spoken, by frightened or evasive or sadistically playful characters. The words come much less from 'eavesdropping'[14] – that naive picture of the dramatist in the bus queue – than is sometimes supposed. The patterning in the dialogue frequently goes with violent or mannered distortion. Yet a Pinter character's speech can, eventually, be 'pinned down' to an identifiable person even when it is used to conceal identity. In sum, Pinter's dialogue tends to 'correspond' to what we hear outside the world of the play, even though it is made to 'cohere' with the overall rhythm of the play.

Consider a simple contrast, something like a paradigm. *The Caretaker* opens with a micro-naturalistically presented conversation between the host and the invited tramp (Aston and Davies) and

11 Jean Vannier, 'Theatre of Language', *Tulane Drama Review* (Spring 1963), p. 182. (Paraphrase with extracts.)

12 Pinter has explicitly stated: 'I'd never heard of Ionesco until after I'd written the first few plays.' *The Paris Review*, no. 39, p. 19. For this reason, and in keeping with the limits of this study, I shall not develop the brief contrast offered in n. 5. By contrast, the debt to Beckett is repeatedly acknowledged: in *The Paris Review* (p. 20); in 'Harold Pinter Replies' (*loc. cit.* p. 8); and in a cheerful private letter, in *Beckett at 60, A Festschrift*, London, 1967, p. 86.

13 Cf. Ch. 3, pp. 138–52.

14 Pinter on 'eavesdropping': 'I spend no time listening in that sense. Occasionally I hear something, as we all do, walking about. But the words come as I'm writing the characters, not before.' *The Paris Review*, no. 39, p. 26. That stress on *writing the characters* (here and elsewhere) accords with what we find in the dialogue.

after some Uuh-ing and Huh-ing the tramp bursts into this 'life-like' narrative: 'Ten minutes off for tea-break in the middle of the night in that place and I couldn't find a seat, not one. All them Greeks had it...' While *Waiting for Godot* begins with the stylised duologue of two literary tramps (or traditional clowns or questers) whose lines could be swapped around.[15] 'Nothing to be done' – Estragon's classical opening line – at once creates a 'gesture to the universe', with that literate non-personal passive voice. (No wonder that one down-to-earth producer insisted that the correct English must be 'Nothing doing'.[16]) Or take the exchange between Stella and James, the married couple in *The Collection* (1961), at one of the points where they are teasing out the verbal tangle created around Bill as a potential or hypothetical adulterous partner.

Stella: He dosn't matter.
James: What do you mean?
Stella: He's not important.
James: Do you mean anyone would have done? You meant it just happened to be him, but it might as well have been anyone?
Stella: No.
James: What then?
Stella: Of course it couldn't have been anyone. It was him. It was just...something...
James: That's what I mean. It was him. That's why I think he's worth having a look at. I want to see what he's like. It'll be instructive, educational.[17]

This sounds like a fusion of three areas of language: real-life conversation; conventional comedy of manners; and a certain elicitation technique (James's 'What do you mean?...Do you mean...You mean...That's what I mean'), suggesting a light parody of linguistic philosophers or 'linguisticians'. As conver-

15 As Gessner has done. See p. 156 and n. 52 above.

16 See Colin Duckworth (ed.), *En attendant Godot*, London, 1966, p. 91.

17 '*The Collection*' *and* '*The Lover*' (1963), London, 1966, pp. 29–30. Earlier, in the 'comedies of menace', 'what do you mean?' is always just that – comic evasion of threat. It is the question that greets a statement like 'tch, tch, tch, tch' (*The Birthday Party*, 2nd ed., p. 16; an imperative 'Pick it up' ('*The Room*' *and* '*The Dumb Waiter*', p. 45) and, most memorably, a question like 'Where were you born then?' (*The Caretaker*, p. 27).

sation between a couple probing into their marital insecurity – with a slight comedy of manner sharpening – it is nearer to early scenes in Eliot's *The Cocktail Party* than to anything in Beckett. (It is, however, less rhetorical than the 'angry scene' verbal duel between Edward and Lavinia which we contrasted with Beckett's adulterous triangle.[18]) At the same time, James' questions amount to a language game, or, more exactly, Pinter makes use of a layman's half-knowing, half-playful semantic test: can these evasive words (which seem to say nothing yet may imply too much: 'It was him...It was just...something ...') be pinned down, can they 'mean' an action? How different is Hamm's broken, still religious quest for meaning in *Endgame* – a question placed between Clov's report of a 'zero' sun and a surviving flea – 'We're not beginning to...to...mean something?' A speculative question derided by Clov: 'Mean something! You and I mean something?' For Beckett 'the meaning of meaning' is ontological, a leftover quest for essence; for Pinter it is linguistic, word-clues crossing word-clues.[19]

In the present context what matters is to see that the texture of Pinter's dramatic language is quite different from Beckett's. Yet clearly this is related to other important differences which can only be listed here. The structure of many Pinter plays – notably *The Caretaker* and *The Homecoming* – can be plotted as a half-submerged but otherwise forward-moving action (*implicit* exposition, denouement, and so on), while Beckett's plays turn in a static–perennial cycle. A Pinter character can nearly always be extrapolated (the dots can be connected to draw a familiar figure, as in the child's puzzle), and hours can be spent discussing quite traditional questions of motive and psychological interaction.

[18] Pp. 131–3 above.

[19] Walter Kerr sees Pinter as the only dramatist today who 'writes existentialist plays existentially'; Beckett builds his plays conceptually as a Platonist: *Harold Pinter*, New York, 1967, pp. 3–9. The affinity between Beckett and Pinter was, I think, overstated by Martin Esslin in 'Godot and his Children...' (*Experimental Theatre*, ed. W. Armstrong, London, 1963, pp. 128–46), though he did distinguish Beckett's 'highly stylised classical mode' from Pinter's 'tape-recording fidelity' which has 'opened up a new dimension of stage dialogue' (*op. cit.* p. 46). In a later article Esslin himself stresses the fusion of 'realism' and 'the absurd' in Pinter's work: 'Epic Theatre, the Absurd, and the Future', *Tulane Drama Review* (Summer 1964), p. 46, reprinted in *Brief Chronicles*, London, 1970, p. 231.

The time-scale for a Pinter play can be measured by the clock; there are no 'timeless moments', and no openings to time lost beyond redemption. Pinter's silences are perfectly timed to fit characterisation and to create a rhythm, but we do not feel – as we do in Beckett – that language is created out of a silence that is, in the end, all-consuming. (Though *Landscape* and even more *Silence* are Pinter's attempt at reaching this dimension.)

In sum, Pinter has little of Beckett's intense 'metaphysical' anguish; and, again, little of the sheer intensity of feeling – that to speak is to suffer and that all language is exhausted. But Pinter has learnt to exploit his own sense of language-nausea:

> Such a weight of words confronts us day in, day out, words spoken in contexts such as this, words written by me and by others, the bulk of it stale and dead terminology; ideas endlessly repeated and permutated, become platitudinous, trite, meaningless. Given this nausea, it's very easy to be overcome by it and step back into paralysis. I imagine most writers know something of this paralysis. But if it is possible to confront this nausea, to follow it to its hilt, then it is possible to say something has occurred, that something has been achieved.[20]

In his most authentic work Pinter succeeds in just that: in 'making something occur' out of the felt paralysis of words. He can re-create the rhythms of difficult or failing utterance with a detached, almost ego-empty method of writing, in a dialogue 'not subjected to false articulation'. This is a specialised, reduced version of one of the aims of classical naturalism:

> Given characters who possess a momentum of their own, my job is not to impose upon them, not to subject them to false articulation, by which I mean forcing a character to speak where he could not speak, of making him speak of what he could never speak.[21]

Paradoxically, the pursuit of this aim can also lead Pinter to indulgent pattern-making, and mannerism.[22] (I have refrained

[20] 'Writing for the Theatre', *loc. cit.* p. 81. [21] *Ibid.*

[22] See pp. 177–8; 181–2; 187 below. For an illuminating definition of Mannerism see *The Styles of European Art* (introduced by Herbert Read), London, 1965, pp. 248ff. For a critical attempt to relate the poetry of Donne to Mannerism in painting and music, see Daniel B. Rowland, *Mannerism – Style and Mood*, New Haven, 1964. Giorgio Melchiori finds a 'New Mannerism' in the early poetry of Eliot, and in the dramatic verse of Christopher Fry, but he sees

from using capital M, though in using this term here and elsewhere I do have in mind the style which has been so clearly identified in the realm of pre-Baroque architecture and painting, and applied in literature to the study of Metaphysical and Modernist poetry. The main point is that Mannerism is not just the sum total of 'mannerisms', but an inherent and consistent tendency to exploit 'conceits', linguistic complexity or modish *jeux d'esprit*, which a 'sophisticated' public can be expected to understand and enjoy. At the same time Mannerism is clearly parasitical on an earlier 'classical' art: it can develop 'line by line' or through richly ambiguous local scenes and texture only because the underlying structure is grasped with reference to an earlier form – in Pinter's case classical naturalism.)

In the early plays (as in *The Room*) it is the patterns of 'non-communication' that sometimes become decorative or facile. In the later plays, particularly in the 'sophisticated' television plays, the verbal games with their 'intriguing' sexual ambiguity are too dependent on the linguistic equivalent of 'suspense' – once the code is deciphered, we are left with a cliché.

Yet the progression of Pinter's work as a whole shows a determination to avoid cliché and self-repetition. Each of the four major stage plays has attempted to do something different – and the urge to innovate, to re-create the language in and for each new play is something Pinter shares with Eliot and Beckett. Pinter keeps renewing his dramatic form and language, at the cost of what looks like increasing critical self-consciousness. He himself has complained of the relative difficulty of writing *The Homecoming* and when that play was written he felt once more: 'I want to write a play, it buzzes all the time in me, and I can't put pen to paper.'[23] He connects this with the difficulty of

Eliot the dramatist as increasingly in search of 'Classical' form and language. See *The Tightrope Walkers*, London, 1956 (especially Introduction, pp. 133–49; and pp. 150–74). At the end of this work there is an interesting note on a passage from E. R. Curtius (*European Literature and the Latin Middle Ages*, London, 1953, p. 273) which suggests that Mannerism is a stylistic constant running through all periods of unbalance.

[23] *The Paris Review*, no. 39, pp. 35–6. Contrast Pinter on his early plays: 'It was a kind of no-holds barred feeling, like diving into a world of words.' 'In an Empty Bandstand', *The Listener* (6 Nov. 1969), p. 631.

avoiding 'the searchlights' in contrast with his direct concern with *writing* – 'completely unselfconsciously' – when he wrote his first three plays. We may assume that writing against 'the searchlights' means, among other things, the dramatist writing with intensified stylistic consciousness: aware of his own achieved work – and the public's attitude to it – as something inhibiting (the taboo on repetition colliding with the expectation of something 'Pinteresque'). But in the narrower sense of scrupulous attention to the words on the page Pinter has been a highly self-conscious writer from the outset. The price is recurrent mannerism. The achievement: the shaping of an essentially mimetic dialogue towards a new kind of expressiveness in a 'theatre of language'.

Pinter's 'double thing': shapes for listening

Ideas concerning his own dramatic language take up a good third of Pinter's tentative yet firmly thought-out article 'Writing for the Theatre'.[24] There are comments here on the ambiguity of dialogue, on the growth of language out of human indeterminacy, out of what is 'inexpressive, elusive, evasive, obstructive, unwilling' in the characters. This goes with a conscious exploration of a 'language where under what is said another thing is being said'. These points define genuine discoveries, and they remain essential keys to Pinter's dialogue. But so much has been heard of these ideas in our over-communicative time that they have become critical commonplaces (Pinter's 'failure of communication', 'subtext').[25] There is need for new questions, and a fresh inquiry, and it might as well start with a neglected point from Pinter's statement on playwriting:

24 *Evergreen Review*, no. 33 (cf. also n. 3 above).

25 The most sustained study on 'subtext' is John Russell Brown's 'Dialogue in Pinter and Others', *Critical Quarterly* (Autumn 1965), pp. 225–43, later used in the same author's *Theatre Language*, London, 1972, Ch. 1. See also Introduction, pp. 21–2. In 'Writing for the Theatre', Pinter himself has objected to the 'grimy, tired phrase, failure of communication' as applied to his work. Victor Amend points to the inherent dramatic limitations of 'demonstrating failure of communication through man's chief means of communication' in 'Harold Pinter – some Credits and Debits', *Modern Drama* (Sept. 1967), p. 173. In sum, the devices of non-communication tend to get obvious, contrived and self-exhausting.

> The function of selection and arrangement is mine. I do all the donkey-work, in fact, and I think I can say I pay meticulous attention to the shape of things, from the shape of a sentence to the overall structure of the play. This shaping, to put it mildly, is of the first importance. But I think a double thing happens. You arrange *and* you listen, following the clues you leave for yourself, through the characters.[26]

Just how does this 'double thing' happen – in particular dialogue sequences and across a whole play? How does Pinter solve the tension between 'spontaneity' and 'design' in language? In the context of this study this is to test, once more, a persistent tension in post-naturalist drama: between the diffuseness and fragmented banality of most 'conversation', and the need for dialogue to concentrate and express, to quicken the beat in the action – so that in under two hours a pattern of experience may be felt upon our pulses. There is here an affinity between Pinter's 'double thing' and Eliot's early hope for 'a new form...out of colloquial speech' (first attempted in *Sweeney Agonistes*). But Pinter has no interest in formal 'verse drama', and he seems to be free from the pains of Eliot's linguistic dualism: that partial taboo on 'the language of the tribe', the hollowness of words against the Word.[27]

We may first define the two poles of Pinter's dramatic language: moving from the seeming record of eavesdropping towards rhythmic abstraction. One can point to two distinct, as it were nuclear, styles, to be seen at their simplest in Pinter's revue sketches (each sketch being homogeneous enough to make us perceive the 'shape' of the dialogue instantly). Contrast, for example, the rambling, inane, yet humanly authentic conversation of two old women in an all-night café:

Second: Yes, there's not too much noise.
First: There's always a bit of noise.
Second: Yes, there's always a bit of life.

[26] 'Writing for the Theatre', *loc. cit.* p. 82.

[27] See Ch. 2, pp. 108ff. Raymond Williams draws an evolutionary line from Eliot's early comic-strip characters, and the first scene of *The Cocktail Party*, to *The Birthday Party* – Pinter taking further the stylisation of 'the dead phrases, the gaps of an accepted articulacy', etc., in the context of ordinary English speech. *Drama from Ibsen to Brecht*, London, 1968, p. 325.

(where the pattern is woven 'along with' and 'from within' the conversation) with the comic-parodic build-up of the cross-examination of the Applicant by a secretary, equipped with nerve-testing electrodes and earphones:

After a day's work do you ever feel tired? Edgy? Fretty? Irritable? At a loose end? Morose? Frustrated? Morbid? Unable to concentrate? Unable to sleep? Unable to eat? Unable to remain seated? Unable to remain upright? Lustful? Indolent? On heat? Randy? Full of desire? Full of energy? Full of dread? Drained? of energy, of dread? of desire?[28]

The applicant is caught up in a crescendo of bewilderment, he 'can't get a word in edgeways', and finally collapses – after trying to cover up his earphones – to the sound of drum-beat, cymbal, trombone and a piercing buzz. Such a simple situational convention (aptly called, in relation to Pinter's early plays, 'comedy of menace') is enough to enable Pinter to exploit the energies of rhythmic formalisation, in this instance a question-catalogue.

In *The Dumb Waiter* (a one-act play, much more complex than any revue sketch, but more immediately 'transparent' than any of the major plays) the guided inconsequentiality of the dialogue between Ben and Gus is transformed into a sharper pattern when – following the comic food orders received through the dumb waiter – the speaking tube is introduced. That ill-functioning instrument of communication 'dictates' a parodic ritual, with its own rhythm of pauses, as Ben listens, holds the tube to his ear and to his mouth, alternately:

Ben: The Eccles cake was stale.
The chocolate was melted.
The milk was sour.

Gus: What about the crisps?

Ben: The biscuits were mouldy.
Well, we're very sorry about that.
What? What? Yes. Yes. Yes certainly. Certainly. Right away.[29]

28 Quoted, respectively, from *The Black and White* and *The Applicant*, in *'A Slight Ache' and Other Plays* (1961), London, 1966, pp. 126 and 135. Among the other revue sketches *Request Stop* and *Last to Go* resemble the first, *Trouble in the Works* the second pattern.

29 *'The Room' and 'The Dumb Waiter'* (1960), London, 1966, p. 62.

Such 'shapes for listening' are several removes from casual conversation, from some putative 'tape-recording ear'. (One could make a rough analogy: Pinter's speaking tube is nearer to Eliot's telephone in *Sweeney Agonistes*[30] in its function than to the concealed tape-recorder of the descriptive linguist.) And it can hardly be an accident that it is immediately after the little food-litany induced by the unseen and unheard presence in the speaking tube that the play reaches a rhythmic crescendo: the ritualistic reiteration of orders:

> Shut the door behind him.
> Shut the door behind him.
> Without divulging your presence.
> Without divulging my presence (. . .)

and the anguished litany of the victim's unanswered questions (ending with 'What's he playing these games for?').[31]

Through his entire work Pinter has been working out different kinds of dialogue 'shaping'. In the early plays, particularly in *The Birthday Party*, *The Dumb Waiter* and *A Slight Ache*, quasi-ritualistic patterns are used repeatedly to give a rhythmic intensity to climactic scenes. Yet the rhythms of ritual – responses, catechismic cross-examination, litanies – are used parodistically or playfully to dehumanise speech. (One is reminded of what Huizinga said about the *formal* similarity of 'ritual' and 'play': 'Formally speaking there is no distinction between marking out space for a sacred purpose and marking it out for sheer play.'[32]) Then, in *The Caretaker* – as I shall try to show – a language of lived encounter is created out of the fragmented speech of two inarticulate persons: Aston and Davies set against the sadistically elaborate jargon-speeches of Mick. To that extent *The Caretaker* is Pinter's most valuable achievement in unified 'listening' and 'shaping', in fusing the human and abstract attributes of dramatic language.

'Design' is more palpably or ingeniously imposed in all the later plays, in which we may distinguish three dominant interests, pressing to shape the dialogue. There is the ritualised interplay between decorum and scatological violence in *The Homecoming*

[30] Cf. Ch. 2, pp. 110–11, Dusty's telephone conversation.
[31] *Loc. cit.* pp. 64–5.
[32] Johan Huizinga, *Homo Ludens*, London, 1949, pp. 19–20.

(the language of the tribe in para-animal display within one family). Then there are the highly patterned, though colloquially based, verbal games people play,[33] taken from and presented to a psycho-sexually 'sophisticated', knowing society: in *The Collection* and *The Lover* (1961, 1963), later in *The Tea Party* and *The Basement* (1965, 1967), all originally written for television, and so exploiting visual clues (devices of close-up, mixing, fading and quick scene-shift) to intensify the omission of verbal clues. In all these plays the conventional comedy of manners is 're-packaged' as a modish language of hints and guesses, nourished by the energies of imagined or potential adultery. Such patterns of verbal fantasy and near-farcical titillation make up much of the texture of *Old Times* (1971), where the mannerist dialogue – the many-coloured bubbles of talk from three corners of the triangle – is shaped to re-enact a still unpurged trauma, with gathering intensity. The third way of shaping dialogue can be seen in the 'word-painting' and 'sound-painting' patterns of *Landscape* and *Silence* (1968, 1969): a semi-abstract scoring of speech fragments in a small-scale 'musical' design, as precise as Webern or Boulez.

I propose to discuss the essential features in this spectrum of styles by concentrating on three full-length plays – *The Birthday Party*, *The Caretaker* and *The Homecoming* – and then looking at the 'new direction' in *Landscape* and *Silence*.

When *The Birthday Party* was first performed,[34] critical response included the feeling that there was a violent yet imperfectly controlled style-switch in the play. This seemed to amount to an abrupt change from microscopic naturalism (typified by the opening exchanges of Meg and Pete on cornflakes and 'nice bits' from the newspaper), to highly stylised 'absurdist' patterns

33 I am alluding to Eric Berne's book *Games People Play* (1964), London, 1966, because these plays by Pinter seem to be working exactly on that level of serio-sophistication. Also, Pinter's 'games' can be seen – as in Berne's work – as open-ended forms of ritual. If ritual provides fixed rhythmic patterns, 'games' are a source of half-ritualised ambiguity – in situation and language. I think that *Old Times* (1971) – first performed after the completion of this chapter – is comparable in approach and method, in a sustained and complex way.

34 Arts Theatre, Cambridge, April 1958. The response here recorded is based on a note I wrote after the first performance.

reaching a climax in the Goldberg–MacCann brainwashing patter of Act II, and the final incantation with its orchestrated clichés in Act III. The two styles then actually seemed to work negatively against one another, instead of creating a theatrical counterpoint: for Stanley's situation as a persecuted and guilty figure was never worked out on the human level 'promised' by the seeming naturalism, while the Goldberg–MacCann variations stood out too blatantly as an already familiar theatre style. Now, with repeated hearing and reading, one can see that Pinter does in fact control his 'two styles' with skill, but the controls are precariously dependent on performers (and auditors) having learned the 'codes' of early Pinter. And, in later plays, Pinter developed a subtler and more unified 'shaping' for the dialogue.

One way in which Pinter controls the two styles can only be appreciated when seeing the play whole – in practice, seeing it twice or reading it backwards. One then sees, with sudden clarity, that the 'ordinary' conversational opening and ending are a frame for, a connivance at, the 'extraordinary' events in the house. The empty, natural-seeming but denatured talk – which goes with stupor, with Meg's sentimental naiveté and Pete's good-natured impotence – makes the atrocious inquisition possible.

Another kind of control turns on emphasis. Take, for example, the phrase 'This house is on the list', repeated like a *leitmotif* four times, in increasingly alarming contexts, and amounting to gradual intensification. First we have the casual-seeming exchange between Meg and Pete:

Meg: This house is on the list.
Pete: It is.
Meg: I know it is.

The pattern is next used in a teasing exchange between Meg and Stanley, when the latter is trying to cast doubt on Meg's talk of 'visitors':

Stanley: (...) I'm your visitor.
Meg: You're a liar. The house is on the list.
Stanley: I bet it is.
Meg: I know it is.

And it re-emerges in Stanley's first anxious questioning about the visitors ('Why?' 'This house is on the list.' 'But who are they?')

and in his panicky questions after the arrival of Goldberg and MacCann:

Stanley: (*turning*) But why here? Why not somewhere else?
Meg: This house is on the list.
Stanley: (*coming down*) What are they called? What are their names?[35]

On the simplest level these are just signals (don't miss 'the list' – it is sinister like a 'black list'.) But something else is also happening: the gradual stylisation – in the last two examples an insistent, 'catechismic' questioning – prepare the way for the fully stylised ritual inquisition later in the play.

Then there is the rather simple yet often effective heightening: the chain of idiomatic – and idiosyncratic – phrases, where the 'chain' amounts to a stylised verbal smokescreen, what Pinter himself calls that other silence, a 'torrent of language'.[36] Here is Goldberg, on arrival in the house:

(*sitting at table*) The secret is breathing. Take my tip. It's a well known fact. Breathe in, breathe out, take a chance, let yourself go, what can you lose? Look at me. When I was an apprentice yet, MacCann, every second Friday of the month my Uncle Barney used to take me to the seaside, regular as clockwork, Brighton, Canvey Island, Rottingdean – Uncle Barney wasn't particular. After lunch on Shabbus we'd go and sit in a couple of deck chairs – you know the ones with canopies – we'd have a little paddle, we'd catch the tide coming in, going out, the sun coming down – golden days, believe me MacCann...(Act I, p. 27).

We recognise here, on the naturalistic level, the complacent clichés and rhythms of a semi-educated Jewish dealer with a flair for 'flannelling'. ('What can you lose?', and the raconteur's use of *would*: 'on Shabbus we'd go...') Yet it is highly patterned, and the cumulative effect of Goldberg's speeches (and they tend

35 *The Birthday Party*, 2nd revised ed., London, 1965, pp. 12, 17, 20 and 34 respectively. (I note that the build-up of the 'catechism' is slightly more marked in the first edition – 'I mean, why...?' following 'But who are they?' in the third 'list' exchange. (Cf. 1963, p. 21 and 1965, p. 20.) More significantly: the third exchange is followed (in both editions) by Stanley's onslaught of Where/What/What/Who/Who questions over his tea. The whole sequence is rhythmically heightened and in effect establishes Stanley himself as the first inquisitor.

36 'Writing for the Theatre', *loc. cit.* p. 82.

to dominate the play) is to parody a type of culture-patter: the sinister complacencies of the successful Head of Family and Business. So a highly individual language is used to expose the way elements in our language compel conformity. In Act II the function of Goldberg's speeches is quite clear: the farcical paean about the joys of boyhood ('I'd tip my hat to the toddlers...') and the fit man's cheerful waking to sunshine ('all the little birds, the smell of grass, church bells, tomato juice...') amount to a verbal limbering up for the verbal torture of Stanley; and the birthday celebration speeches, after the inquisition inflicted on the victim, are experienced as a black ritual.[37] But by Act III Goldberg's patterned loquacity becomes more arbitrary. In particular, Goldberg's speeches when left alone with MacCann seem to have little function apart from 'creating a scene' and reinforcing the cultural bankruptcy of Goldberg through making him mouth a medley of slogans – Judaic, British and miscellaneous culture-props – with the dramatic breakdown over 'Because I believe': logorrhoea into vacancy. There is a strong local interest here but the connection with the context of the whole play is tenuous. It is, more than anything else, a verbal and rhythmic bravura act.[38]

In the cross-examination of Stanley, and, even more clearly, in the Goldberg–MacCann incantation in the penultimate scene of the play, we see the extent of Pinter's attraction to the patterns and rhythms of ritual – apparently without wishing to evoke (as Eliot wished to do)[39] a primitive or sacred rhythm of sacrifice. Nor do these scenes have the human pressure – the political–religious terror – which we find in such a work as *Darkness at Noon*, and in authentic documents of persecution. The pressure is induced through rhythmic intensification, through the paralysing spell of a disconnected language, for example the jump from random cliché-questions to random fantasy-questions ('What about the Albigensenist heresy?/Who watered the wicket at Melbourne?'). But the cross-examination scene at least externalises

[37] *The Birthday Party*, pp. 43, 44–5, 56.

[38] *Ibid.* pp. 77–8. As far as I am aware no published criticism has seen this dialogue-sequence in context. A critic friend, Christopher Gillie, has suggested to me one possible function of this scene: Goldberg and MacCann are demoralised in and by the absence of Stanley, the victim they need.

[39] See Ch. 2, pp. 97 ff.

that sense of 'meaningless proceedings' which Kafka's K.[40] – never interrogated – so resents. The final incantation is, however, more gratuitous:

Goldberg: We'll watch over you.
MacCann: Advise you.
Goldberg: Give you proper care and treatment.
MacCann: Let you use the club bar.
Goldberg: Keep a table reserved.
MacCann: Help you acknowledge the fast days.
Goldberg: Bake you cakes.

followed by those spell-unbinding parodic responses: 'We'll provide the skipping rope./The vest and pants./The ointment./The hot poultice./The fingerstall./The abdomen belt./The ear plugs./The baby powder...'

We do respond here to the violent parody of institutionalised caring. But the detail of the mumbo-jumbo is so far-fetched (or farcical) that is is only in performance – through the image of the helpless victim and his reduction to gurgling speechlessness – that we connect this ritual with any pattern of felt persecution. The 'shaping' is preponderant, the texture of the language mannerist.

The only difference between *The Birthday Party* and *The Caretaker*, Pinter has pertly suggested, is that in the latter he has cut out the dashes and used dots instead. Neither dash nor dot can be heard in performance, yet the critics can 'tell a dot from a dash a mile off'.[41] One may not always be sure about those dots, but one can see a difference: in *The Caretaker* Pinter moves much nearer to dialogue 'in character'. The shaping is now all in the gradual intensification of the given – ultra-naturalistic – language; it is inseparable from the structure of the play. Moreover, such patterning is used for quite traditional aims: to express a character's life on the stage through speech – speech that is the signature of a mind, unmistakable, unique, even if it takes some time to decipher. So even the dots (those graphic–psychological–musical signs) are used and developed in the two patterns of hesitancy which meet, interact, and part company in the

[40] *The Trial*, Ch. II (especially pp. 54–5, Penguin ed.).
[41] 'Writing for the Theatre', *loc. cit.* p. 80.

verbal encounter of Davies and Aston. For most of Act I these two characters are interlocked in a groping conversational exploration of one another, which reaches its first intensity when Aston offers the tramp a bed to sleep in:

Davies: How long for?
Aston: Till you...get yourself fixed up.
Davies: (*sitting*) Ay well, that...
Aston: Get yourself sorted out...
Davies: Oh, I'll be fixed up...pretty soon now...

This between two pauses; and the whole sequence takes up about a quarter of an hour of slow playing time. (Pp. 16–21. The effect of tempo is an essential factor in the rhythmic structure.) The pattern is further intensified – the groping reaches its own regressive climax – in Act II, when Davies is offered the job of caretaker:

Aston: Well, there's things like the stairs...and the...the bells...
Davies: But it'd be a matter...wouldn't it...it'd be a matter of a broom...isn't it?
Aston: You could have a duster...
Davies: Oh, I know I could have that...but I couldn't manage without a...without a broom...could I?
Aston: You'd have to have a broom...
Davies: That's it...that's just what I was thinking...
Aston: I'd be able to pick one up for you, without much trouble... and of course, you'd...you'd need a few brushes.
Davies: You'd need implements...you see...you'd need a good few implements...
Aston: I could teach you how to use the electrolux, if you...wanted to learn...
Davies: Ah, that'd be... (p. 45)

Out of context, this looks like the simple stylisation of comedy – underscoring the fumbling style of two 'hesitators'. But in the movement of the whole play this is taken further, to reveal – through that groping for clues, through the linguistic pattern – the hidden psychological pattern: Aston's pathological slowness after electric current treatment; Davies' paranoid suspiciousness. But the essential point is this: we continue to experience – to 'work out' – all this through the language; we listen to the words *as* symptoms, the diagnosis or aetiology is contributed by us. There is a double movement. Aston, in his ill-timed confession about mental illness, re-creates the feel of breakdown (as if speaking out of his illness and not after it). The pattern of hesitancy is at the same time movingly transformed at the end of Act II:

They used to come round with these...I don't know what they were ...they looked like big pincers, with wires on, the wires were attached to a little machine. It was electric. They used to hold a man down, and this chief...the chief doctor, used to fit them on either side of the man's skull. There was a man holding the machine, you see, and he'd ...he'd do something...I can't remember now whether he pressed a switch or turned something, just a matter of switching the current ...I suppose it was...(p. 59).

Against this, there is the transformation in Davies: the manic fluency of his 'pecking' speeches (when he thinks he can exploit the sickness of Aston, his benefactor) culminating in the rhythms of violent rejection, in the long outburst that ends with 'I never been inside a nuthouse!' Then, with the punitive intervention of Mick[42] and the expulsion of Davies, his wave of fluency breaks again, and the play ends – in a complete fusion of the psychic and rhythmic pattern – with the tramp's broken words.

In *The Homecoming*, the next major play, there is a shift away from the human–artistic balance of *The Caretaker* – to greater ingenuity in the 'shaping', with a language at once more violent and more mannered. A black family ritual – the initiation of the new mother–whore, with all due ambivalence – provides the climax for the meeting between hosts and homecomers; and the action – more indirect, more fragmented, and more dependent on gradual clue-assemblage than the earlier plays – is almost entirely verbal.

42 The economy of Mick's jargon speeches needs to be stressed. It is doubly effective: as a voice, a 'torrent of language' counterpointing the speech of both Davies and Aston, and in the way Mick's interior-decorator patter is used again in a comic but sadistic climax (cf. n. 6). Contrast the speech-torrents of Goldberg (p. 180 above) and of Lenny (p. 187 below).

On the affinity of these monologues with the monologues of Dan Leno and other music hall artists, see Peter Davison, 'Contemporary Drama and Popular Dramatic Forms', in *Aspects of Drama and the Theatre*, Sydney University Press, 1965, pp. 160ff.

True, one character, Ruth, warns her stage audience that her lips move and 'Perhaps the fact that they move is more significant ...than the words which come through them' (pp. 52–3). But words are used to underscore those lips, and for the rest, every character is a speech-maker. Pinter himself has implied that there is less 'writing' (in the sense of wordy or gratuitous writing) in this play than in *The Birthday Party* or *The Caretaker*, saying that it is the only play that comes 'near to a structural entity which satisfies me'.[43] But we may add that this 'structural entity' goes with a highly elaborate texture woven out of the dehumanising abuses of speech.

The ritualised language of the family lies at the centre of the play, and it is arranged in broadly juxtaposed patterns of ceremony and its violation.[44] It can best be seen in Max's schizoid-seeming shifts from the language of celebration to verbal defecation (and the other way round). There is something like a key-change at the end of Act I when Max suddenly switches from the abuse of Ruth as a whore ('We've had a smelly scrubber in my house all night. We've had a stinking pox-ridden slut in my house all night.') to the mother-ceremony ('You a mother?...How many you got?') and then to the father-ceremony: 'You want to kiss your old father? Want a cuddle with your old father?...You still love your old Dad, eh?...He still loves his father!' The repetition, the rhythmic intensity – as much as the change from bawdy to baby-talk – alerts us. By the opening of Act II the contraries become quite clear. Max's long, decorative speech (that rare thing, a subtle, comic pastiche) intensifies the ceremony: 'Well, it's a long time since the whole family was together, eh? If only your mother was alive...'

The speech (too long to quote in full) draws on a whole thesaurus of sentimental clichés in its evocation of 'fine grown-up lads', 'a lovely daughter-in-law', grandchildren who – if only they were present and Jessie, the first mother-figure, were alive – would be 'petted', cooed over', 'fussed over', 'tickled'. The mother-figure herself taught the 'boys' 'every single bit of the moral code they live by', she was 'the backbone of this family...

43 *The Paris Review*, no. 39, p. 26.

44 See also Kelly Morris: 'Within the format of excessive decorum, the idiom is aggression.' '*The Homecoming*', *Tulane Drama Review* (Winter 1966), p. 186.

with a will of iron, a heart of gold and a mind', to be attended in her lifetime with tribal ceremonies:

she put her feet up on the pouffe and I said to her, Jessie, I think our ship is going to come home, I'm going to treat you to a couple of items, I'm going to buy you a dress in corded blue silk, heavily encrusted in pearls, and for casual wear, a pair of pantaloons in lilac flowered taffeta. Then I gave her a drop of cherry brandy. I remember the boys came down, in their pyjamas, all their hair shining, their faces pink, it was before they knelt down at our feet, Jessie's and mine. I tell you, it was like Christmas.

The counter-images follow at once, in the just as elaborately patterned, and comically violent, speech abusing his brother Sam and the whole 'crippled family, three bastard sons, a slut-bitch of a wife', with retroactive curses (pp. 44–51). There follows an immediate switch-back to the celebration of the homecoming pair – as if they were newly wed and in need of paternal blessing – in an almost orientally ornate tone (beginning 'But you're my own flesh and blood...'). Such sudden switches not only make up a whole scene but clarify the 'shaping' in the play; and they foreshadow Max's final great contraries, the wish to expel and then incorporate the new mother–whore:[45]

A.: Where's the whore? Still in bed? She'll make us all animals.
B.: But you...Ruth...you're not only lovely and beautiful, but you're kin. You're kith. You belong here.

The point to stress here is that these rites of transformation are enacted entirely through *naming*, through a switch in the evocative range, as if using language magically. This resembles the way Othello transforms Desdemona's room into a brothel by going through the 'appropriate' gestures and naming (*Othello*, IV, ii, 24–96). But in *The Homecoming* the to-and-fro shifts of language cumulatively create a playful mood, a series of *as if* situations or simulated transformations, including the central transformation of the home into a family brothel. The effect is that of 'op art': rapidly flickering style signals which yield this

[45] The ensuing quotes: pp. 68 and 75 respectively. For a full discussion of the theme of Ruth as queen-bee, mother and whore, see Hugh Nelson, '*The Homecoming*: Kith and Kin' in *Modern British Dramatists* (ed. John Russell Brown), Englewood Cliffs, N.J., 1968, pp. 145–63.

or that pattern, depending on the angle of vision. It is only in retrospect that the spectator or reader can see that each of those shifts in language has been as precisely coded as traffic signals – green into red and so on – and it is only then that the 'shaping', and with it the meaning of the play, is seen.

This account underlines the virtuosity – and the mannerism, once more – in the structure and texture of the dialogue. And there are other aspects of the dialogue that support this reading. First, the excessive use of pastiche not so much in Max's speeches just discussed, as in Lenny's. There are too many of these, and it is only late in the play that we are able to make the connection between the pimp and the style-monger. Then we see the point of these appropriately centreless pastiches: the facility in assuming any tone, in using words seductively, as in the three 'stories' of his initial encounter with Ruth in Act I (pp. 28–33), or in the manner of a glossy ad, as in the taunting of Ted in Act II (p. 64). Secondly, conventional comedy-of-manner lines seem to be over-distributed. Max's manic slips of the tongue ('I gave birth to three grown men.' – p. 40) and comic antithesis ('I've never had a whore under this roof before. Ever since your mother died.' – p. 42) match his ornate ceremony speeches; and Lenny's elaborate inquiry into the facts of his conception (p. 36), may be justified as father-baiting; but even a deliberately low-toned and barely articulate character like Joey becomes a goonish phrase-maker on sexual intercourse, ringing speculative changes on 'going the whole hog' (rising to 'Now and again...you can be happy...without going any hog at all').

Cumulatively, such effects tilt the play too far towards parody and away from empathy or the shock of recognition. There is a 'too-muchness' on the surface. This may be the price of an over-conscious ingenuity in the post-naturalist idiom of the play, where the links between the overall shape and the detail of the dialogue are deliberately teasing and tenuous.

The compensating achievement of the play is the subtly worked out counterpoint which brings different kinds of dehumanised speech into collusion. The grossly perverted vernacular of Max and Lenny is balanced by the homogenised academic jargon of Teddy, which goes with an attitude ('It's a question of how far you can operate on things'), and provides a stylistic clue (the only one we get) to his at once clinically detached and voyeurish connivance at his wife's imagined prostitution. Between these two patterns hovers Ruth, whose gradual transformation is shown through the transformation in her language: from the slow, desultory marital conversation of her arrival, to the seductive innuendos and the fragmented story of her modelling in the two key encounters with Lenny, and then, at the end of the play, switching to the farcically clear-cut mercenary jargon of her professional terms, a mark of triumphant self-assertion. In the final effect, the play language of a comedy of manners is weighted by the cumulative imagery of flesh: Max's butcher-talk, Lenny's pimp-talk. Their scatological invective saturates the play with an almost Jacobean exposure to corruption of the body, and its vocal organ – the tongue.[46] And after such exposure Pinter is flexible enough to end the play with what comes over as an authentic human voice: 'I'm not an old man. Do you hear? Kiss me.' moans Max, crawling on the floor as his verbal fantasies collapse.

After *The Homecoming* Pinter turned from such large-scale and complex shaping to scene-plays with minute inner 'shaping' in the dialogue of *Landscape* and *Silence* (and the bagatelle *Night*). It seems clear that the miniature scale – probably influenced by Beckett's late plays for radio[47] – has been deliberately chosen so that the musical and rhythmic pattern – the sound of words

46 Hugh Nelson draws a parallel between *The Homecoming* and *Troilus and Cressida* (*loc. cit.* pp. 157–60); and Ronald Hayman says about the play: 'In mood, it's rather like a *Troilus and Cressida* taken over entirely by Thersites and Pandarus.' (*Op. cit.* p. 67.) Perhaps the language of the play, 'coming from below', releases one of Wilson Knight's 'Dionysian' powers: 'some dialect that has not been attenuated by modern sophistication' – though the sophistication is there in the shaping. (See Wilson Knight, 'The Kitchen Sink', *Encounter* (Dec. 1963), pp. 48ff., written before *The Homecoming* appeared.) One can understand why Pinter objects to 'this scheme afoot on the part of many "liberal-minded" persons to open up obscene language to general commerce. It should be the dark secret language of the underworld.' (*The Paris Review*, no. 39, p. 34.) Pinter's attitude to 'the dark secret language' is thus the opposite of what D. H. Lawrence wanted.

47 Cf. Ch. 3, pp. 152 and 163–4. *Landscape* and *Silence* were given a distinguished stage performance by the Royal Shakespeare Company (July 1969) which has, however, only confirmed that the dialogue is for the ear.

emerging out of timed pauses and silences – may be played out, may become the play.

Despite the general move towards a 'musicalising' of language *Landscape* still has a clear, *dramatic* counterpoint: the interweaving of the two contrasted voices of Beth and Duff.[48] The classic female/male 'Yin and Yang' opposites provide the overall design; and it is worked out on every level – structure, image and rhythm.

Beth's interior monologue – almost psychotically withdrawn and regressive – reconstructs the fragmented memory of gentle love-making in the sand; Duff – addressing Beth and unsuccessfully attempting to engage her in colloquy (p. 21) – moves from two aggressively recounted episodes (a walk with the dog, an argument in the pub) to the fantasy of violently possessing Beth in the hall, against the banging of a gong. They are antithetical in every utterance: she is all inwardness, he a verbal Tarquin.

Their opposed 'stories' and psychic patterns are communicated through indirect 'word-painting', or through one of the basic principles of drawing invoked by Beth: 'as objects intercepting the light cast shadows' (pp. 27–8). Beth's words are taken from a 'landscape' of lyrical images: sea, sand, unremembered faces, light touch of arm and neck or withdrawal from touch, standing in the mist, in the sun; while Duff talks of walking through the 'racket' made by the birds, on paths covered 'with all kinds of shit' before he gets to boasting of his cellarmanship, of forcing Beth after violent complaining and swearing. In places the rhythmic pattern clearly supports this divergent 'duet'. For example:

Beth: Still misty, but thinner, thinning.
Duff: The bung is on the vertical, in the bunghole. Spile the bung. Hammer the spile through the centre of the bung. That lets the air through the bung, down the bunghole, lets the beer breathe.
Beth: Wetness all over the air. Sunny. Trees like feathers. (p. 25)

where Duff's aggressive jargon, with its emphatic stress on action words and on 'bung' (the repetition, the plosives, the back

[48] What follows is a reassessment of what I wrote about the first radio performance of *Landscape* for *Modern Drama* vol. 11, no. 4 (Feb. 1969), pp. 445–6. I now think that I then overstated Pinter's move to abstraction.

vowels, the suggestion of dung and bang, the slang sense, all working together) is intercepted by Beth's low-toned and broken phrases, with their sibilants and front vowels. The two patterns culminate in the poetic inversions and vocatives given to Beth at the end of the play, while the rhythmic crescendo of Duff's verbal attack can only be shouted or barked. The nine silences – one of them marked *long* silence – insulate the speakers from one another, and create an inner space in the 'soundscape' – time for the inwardness of Beth's words to work on the listener.[49]

Silence lacks this contrapuntal strength. The dream-like 'stream of consciousness' that is only one part in the opposed voices of *Landscape* is now extended to two speakers – to Rumsey, the older man, and Ellen – and the more violent slangy language of Bates tends to get submerged in the dominant minor mode. ('I walk in my mind. But can't get out.' – p. 39). The shaping of the whole playlet is intricate. There are three fragmented sequences, each giving the 'tone' of a mind; three episodes are enacted in minimal dialogue; and in the final section the memory-fragments are further fragmented and re-played until the three tones are gradually diminished and engulfed by silence. It makes good listening; and it does suggest the gradual fade-out of memory or the conversion of 'events' into barely traceable verbal smudges in the mind. Yet, it lacks the subjective power – the sense of suffered action – which gives even Beckett's most abstract pieces (from *Play* to *Cascando*) an emotional immediacy. So, even though Pinter retains his mastery of concrete words – the mental landscapes, for example, can be visualised, the residual dialogue might be 'overheard' – it is as if the play had been written for the sake of the rhythmic pattern.

Landscape and *Silence* can be seen as a concentration – or distillation – of Pinter's concern for 'shaping', both as overall design and as insistent patterns of sound and rhythm. At the same time these plays point, once more, to one of the polar extremes of modern drama: the 'infolding' of language, at once reduced and musicalised, within a miniature play. The urge against

49 Martin Esslin states: 'When Pinter asks for a *pause*...he indicates that intense thought processes are continuing, that unspoken tensions are mounting, whereas *silences* are notations for the end of a movement, the beginning of another, as between the movements of a symphony.' *The Peopled Wound*, London, 1970, p. 220.

explicit or rhetorical language which was first expressed by the Symbolist poets ('De la musique avant toute chose')[50] and by certain modern novelists ('I begin to long for some little language ...broken words, inarticulate words...' says a character in *The Waves*)[51] has finally found expression in a carefully limited dramatic language.

[50] Verlaine's *Art Poétique* opens with these words. The affinity between *Landscape* and *Silence* and certain pieces of modern music would have occurred to many people. Pinter himself says: 'I feel a sense of music continually in writing, which is a different matter from having been influenced by it. Boulez and Webern are now composers I listen to a great deal.' *The Paris Review*, no. 39, p. 20.

[51] Virginia Woolf, *The Waves* (1931), London, 1955, p. 169: preceded by 'How tired I am of stories, how tired I am of phrases that come down with all their feet on the ground!' For further discussion, see Introduction, pp. 22ff.

5: Osborne

There is critical insight in one of Osborne's rare judgements on his own work: 'Although *Look Back in Anger* was a formal, rather old-fashioned play, I think it broke out by its use of language – Harold Pinter does that now.'[1] This brief and seemingly casual self-criticism links up with two key points in this study: the revitalisation of drama through language, and the growing self-consciousness, precisely about language, of even such an intuitive dramatist as Osborne. For Osborne's point of departure was intuitive: filling the old naturalistic form with the new wine of a highly theatrical and ego-charged rhetoric (a linguistic variant of 'pouring new ideas into old forms', the formula that was found inadequate by Strindberg nearly seventy years before *Look Back in Anger*).[2] And if the first play 'broke out by its use of language' – creating the appearance of newness in 1956 – language has remained an interesting element in Osborne's plays, even in plays that are flawed in structure or erratic in their flow of imaginative life.[3]

1 'That Awful Museum', *Twentieth Century*, CLXIX (Feb. 1961). See also *John Osborne: 'Look Back in Anger', a Casebook*, London, 1968, p. 66.

2 '[In other countries] men have tried to create a new drama by pouring new ideas into old forms. But this has failed...' Strindberg, *Miss Julie* (translated by Michael Meyer), London, 1967, p. 19. The point is also discussed by Raymond Williams in *Drama from Ibsen to Brecht*, London, 1968, pp. 77–8, 320, 338 (4).

3 The linguistic breakthrough has been claimed as a break with the whole literary drama – including Shaw and Eliot (see John Kershaw,

In that critically self-conscious comparison with Pinter's language Osborne implicitly accepts that there is some intrinsic value in 'making it new' through language. We may link this with his eclecticism and restless search for a style.[4] Among the published plays[5] only *Look Back in Anger* and *Epitaph for George Dillon* (1958, but written earlier, in collaboration with Anthony Creighton) exhibit the relatively simple formula: histrionic rhetoric thrust into conventional naturalism. (It was a style that so to speak chose itself, partly as a relatively direct vehicle for self-expression, partly because 'it was there' at the time as a dominant mode for a writer who, at one and the same time, admired the energies of neurosis in the plays of Tennessee Williams,[6] and seemed to accept that there was some affinity between naturalism and social concern.) Then came a series of experiments: the 'folk art' of the music hall, intended to 'cut across the restrictions of the so-called naturalistic stage'[7] in *The Entertainer*; the infusion of Luther's own prose into the dialogue, along with the epic/chronicle material, in *Luther*; the subtly textured monologue which absorbs all dialogue in *Inadmissible Evidence*; the attempt at 'Chekhovian' scoring for the cross-talk of a group in *The Hotel in Amsterdam* – to focus on the more interesting stages. (Osborne's attempts to move into other styles – the 'costume language' of a period, declining Austria–Hungary, in *A Patriot for Me*, and the attempt to intensify the voice of

The Present Stage, London, 1966, pp. 34–5). Yet Osborne's anti-literariness is itself literary; at any rate, it often parodies the literary and is, to that extent, stylistically self-conscious. For example, Jimmy Porter, when limbering up for his most violent tirades, speaks of his skit ('a poem') which is 'soaked in the theology of Dante, with a good slosh of Eliot as well'; and the opening round in the onslaught on Helena is 'Pass Lady Bracknell the cucumber sandwiches, will you?' (*Look Back in Anger*, II, i, pp. 51–2).

4 See also Gabriel Gersh, 'The Theater of John Osborne', *Modern Drama* (Sept. 1967), pp. 137ff.

5 In a suppressed early play, *The Devil Inside Him*, the central character, Huw, the would-be poet, speaks in singsong cadences which set him apart from others. Gersh, p. 139.

6 See Osborne's review of Tennessee Williams, 'Sex and Failure', in *The Observer* (20 Jan. 1957), p. 11. (There Osborne attacks the 'adjustment school' who smooth out the facts of human failure; and the 'emotion snobs who believe that protest is vulgar and to be articulate is to be sorry for oneself'.)

7 See Osborne's prefatory note to *The Entertainer*.

vituperation, through Lope de Vega's violent world, in *A Bond Honoured* – are also relevant, though these near-failures will not be discussed here.)

All these are attempts at innovation in one sense: Osborne has tried not to repeat himself, among other things not to repeat his initial naturalism-and-rhetoric formula. Cumulatively, we recognise in the succession of plays idiosyncratically domesticated models from an 'imaginary museum'. At the same time Osborne's will to extend his resources of form and language has created a tension – comparable to what we found in Shaw[8] – between the 'naive' dramatist and the conscious explorer of styles: the scope of modern drama tugging against Osborne's personal limitations.

There appears to be something improvised, even haphazard, in the way Osborne moves from one play-style to another. There are no long-deliberated changes from one mode of language to another (as in Eliot), nor does there seem to be a compelling inner movement (as in the gradual compression of language in Beckett and Pinter). Yet one can see in Osborne's zig-zagging line of development[9] two main play-forms – the room-based and the open-stage play – and two distinct stage languages – histrionic self-expression and the dialogue of characters intended to be socially, or historically, representative. The tension between these two modes of language keeps recurring in both types of play. Sometimes Osborne attempts to create an interplay between the two modes of language within a double or shifting structure: in *The Entertainer* through connecting Archie Rice's domestic talk with his music hall 'turns', in *Luther* through the shift from the private interior of Act I to the 'epic' propensities of the other two acts. The histrionic monologuist keeps re-entering the large-scale 'open' plays; and the dialogue of more or less monologue-

[8] Cf. Ch. 1, p. 00. While Shaw kept going back to past styles 'atavistically', Osborne does show awareness of contemporary dramatic languages. There is – one may add – nothing in the entire critical writing of Shaw to compare with Osborne's brief remark on Pinter – on the language of a contemporary. (Cf. also Ch. 1, n. 90.)

[9] A glance at the chronology of the plays reinforces one's perception of the 'zig-zags'. For example: *Inadmissible Evidence* (1965), the most consistently mono-centric play, was written between two clusters of large-scale and outward-pointing plays; the second cluster (*A Patriot for Me* and *A Bond Honoured*) is followed by a return to 'private interiors'.

centred plays keeps expanding (or thinning out) to catch, in almost gratuitous sketch-like scenes, the *language*, the up-to-date idiom, of this or that *contemporary*[10] cartoon type (from the smoothly religious admirer of Billy Graham: 'I simply ask myself whether their [people's] lights are shining?' to the Castro-loving hippie actress: 'So we dropped in at Wig Creations for the moustache, then got a taxi to Carnaby Street.')[11] In all this we find versatile inventiveness at the cost of imperfect artistic control. And we recognise Osborne's at once generous and anxious urge to embody *both* the inner and the outer world; to express troubled psychic states and to represent all kinds of 'interest' – voices, social movements, scenes. In brief, the urge towards wholeness.

Yet it is precisely in his language that Osborne has been least able to develop, to match his ideal conception of a drama that is at once personal and social or communal. There is a recurrent loss of 'felt life' in his dialogue of relationship, group, and large-scale public events, both in the contemporary and the historical or quasi-historical plays. (In the latter Osborne has found it particularly difficult to give life to 'the potentially fascinating dialectic'[12] between an ideology or an institution and the principal character – the potential Brechtian direction.) By contrast, he has given a new voice to the isolated or wounded character, the play seen through a temperament,[13] the line from Strindberg.

10 From the language of the 'posh' Sunday papers in *Look Back in Anger* to the hippie jargon in *Time Present* Osborne obsessively parodies this or that *contemporary* lingo. I think it could be shown that there is a linguistically conservative impulse behind Osborne's way with 'new words' – instant absorption and rejection. The impulse seems to be epitomised in Bill Rice's backward-looking remark: 'We all had our own style, our own songs, and we were all English. What's more, we spoke English.' (*The Entertainer*, p. 81.)

11 *Epitaph for George Dillon*, Act II (the scene with Geoffrey Colwyn-Stuart, pp. 42–9), and *Time Present*, Act II (Abigail's appearance, pp. 74–8 – to be compared with Pamela's portrait of the actress, pp. 37–9).

12 The quoted phrase is from the Author's Note to *A Bond Honoured* – and could also be applied to *Luther* and *A Patriot for Me*.

13 I am using Toby Cole's gloss on Strindberg's definition of the 'great naturalism', *Playwrights on Playwriting*, London, 1960, Introduction, p. xvii; cf. Strindberg's 'On Modern Drama and Modern Theatre' (1889), *ibid.* p. 17.

There is something like critical consensus on the existence of that 'voice',[14] though its quality remains to be examined. A more general question may be asked here. In a witty simplification, Mary McCarthy wrote that Osborne 'like a coloratura or counter-tenor, finds that he is limited to parts of experience, as it were, already written for his voice's strange timbre'.[15] In other words, Osborne cannot extend the range of his dramatic language – though he keeps straining to do so – through a personal creative limitation. Yet, is it not possible that such a limitation is intensified by the difficulty, in our time, of creating a language that has dramatic life *both* on the personal and on the communal plane?

In attempting to answer this question, we may briefly consider two of Osborne's statements on drama, spanning a decade of creative life. At one point in his confident manifesto-like contribution to *Declaration* (1957) Osborne asks a series of questions – characteristically offered as the dramatist's approach to socialism: questions, experiment, not dogma.

> What is their relationship with one another, and with their children, with their neighbours and people across the street, or on the floor above? What are the things that are important to them, that make them care, give them hope and anxiety? *What kind of language do they use to one another?* What is the meaning of the work they do? Where does the pain lie? What are their expectations? What moves them, brings them together, makes them speak out?...[16]

Here the question of language is just one question, seemingly unproblematic, and interlinked, as in classical naturalism, with the dramatist's questions about the meaning of individual lives. In practice, such an almost Chekhovian ideal of embodying lived meaning in 'the kind of language they use to one another' keeps

[14] Raymond Williams, *op. cit.* p. 319; Gersh in the article cited; Alan Carter in *John Osborne*, Edinburgh and London, 1969. (He oddly calls it the 'public voice' in the chapter under that heading.)

[15] *The Observer* (4 July 1965). Later Osborne himself called his speeches 'arias' in Interview (Part I), *The Observer* (30 June 1968), p. 21.

[16] 'They Call it Cricket', in *Declaration* (ed. Tom Maschler), London, 1957, p. 84, reprinted in *Playwrights on Playwriting*, p. 144 (my italics). Cf. also: 'a writer's job today...is to try and get over to as many people as possible'. 'The Writer in his Age', *The London Magazine*, IV (May 1957). This quote is from *Casebook*, p. 61.

eluding Osborne. In the plays there was 'a problem of language' from the start. On the one hand, much of the dialogue of relationship turned out to be perfunctory or inert 'satellite' dialogue around the central rhetorician (who as it were incorporated in his own speech-flow answers to questions like 'What is *their* relationship?'). On the other hand, the intensified language of the central characters, from Jimmy Porter on, was histrionic and ambivalent enough to justify Osborne's self-defence – earlier in the same article – against the 'shallow heads with their savage thirst for trimmed-off explanations' who took dramatic statements (like 'There aren't any good brave causes left') at their face value, 'incapable of recognising the texture of ordinary despair, the way it expresses itself in rhetoric and gestures that may perhaps look shabby, but are seldom simple'. And that rhetoric – exploiting the energy of self-dissociation from communal life – asserted itself *against* 'the kind of language *they* use'.[17]

In various statements made some ten years later Osborne spoke of the fragmentation of society, of the anti-verbal theatre and the 'verbal breakdown' as increasingly threatening to the dramatist who wants to *write* for the theatre. Seemingly in the context of defending experiment in drama (against that old-bogey form, the well-made play) Osborne writes:

> Landseer, o.k.: si. But Bacon si, Picasso si also. We live in a society of such lurching flexibility that it is no longer possible to construct a dramatic method based on a shared social and ethical system. The inexorable process of fragmentation is inimical to all public assumptions or indeed ultimately to anything shared at all. A theatre audience is no longer linked by anything but the climate of dissociation in which it tries to live its baffled lives. A dramatist can no longer expect to draw many common references, be they social, sexual or emotional. He can't generalize in the old way. He must be specific to himself and his own particular, concrete experience.[18]

As a diagnosis this must be familiar; but it is Osborne who is making it, dedicated to some form of participatory drama, yet

[17] Osborne's central characters are meant to move on a higher plane of awareness *and* expressiveness – sometimes recalling Eliot's method of 'two planes' as defined at the end of *The Use of Poetry and the Use of Criticism* (cf. Ch. 2, n. 19). But see also pp. 208ff. below on four Osborne characters and their ambivalent self-awareness.

[18] 'On the Thesis Business...', *The Times* (14 Oct. 1967).

pointing to his own difficulty in creating a drama of shared values with a language of common reference. Elsewhere he names the discouragement that made him abandon a projected play (*Coriolanus*, set in an African republic, Brecht territory presumably involving experience mediated by newspapers): 'I didn't know whether I wanted to write a play about public feeling when all my instincts were focussing down on interior things and people's inner self.'[19] At the same time he deplores the new non-verbal experiments – happenings and mixed media – which are supplanting and corrupting verbal drama, his art.[20] And he affirms his own 'allegiance to words' in an age when 'the verbal breakdown is getting to the point where it's dangerous and nonsensical'.[21]

These statements indicate the way in which Osborne's personal limitations are crossed by 'the frightening limitations of a one-sided existence' – in Hebbel's phrase, which Lukács uses to sum up the condition of the modern *theatre of environment*. In that theatre, dialogue is split off from environment; the dialogue is less and less able to express the being and destiny of characters, while the social and historical world appears merely as an increasingly hostile environment.[22] Osborne's drama, which keeps striving towards some balance of the personal and social in the dialogue itself, repeatedly makes one conscious of an acute imbalance. Frequently, the imbalance is exactly what is being dramatised. In the early and contemporary plays the hyper-articulate character (George Dillon, Jimmy Porter) defines himself by rejecting, with ribald contempt, the language as much as the values of a group (the clichés of the Elliot family, the genteelisms of Alison and her sort). In a later play like *Inadmissible Evidence* Osborne goes much further – towards a curiously externalised form of solipsism: the self-alienated monologue of Bill Maitland absorbs solid clusters of vocabulary from the social world – technology, legal jargon and so on – only to spit them out again as alien stuff. Then we have this for example:

19 Interview (Part I), *The Observer* (30 June 1968).

20 *Ibid.* 'We have managed to revive traditional theatre for a while, and now it is a corrupt art.'

21 Interview (Part II), *The Observer* (7 July 1968), quoted more fully on p. 204 below.

22 Georg Lukács, 'Theatre and Environment', *The Times Literary Supplement* (23 April 1964).

I hereby swear and affirm. Affirm. On my... Honour?
By my belief. My belief in... in... the
technological revolution, the pressing, growing,
pressing, urgent need for more and more
scientists, and more scientists, for more and
more schools and universities and universities and
schools, the theme
of change, realistic decisions based on a highly
developed and professional study of society by
people who really know their subject...
(*flails, the Judge looks at him reassuringly and
he picks up again.*) In the ninety seven per cent
ninety seven, of all the scientists who have ever
lived in the history of the world since the days
of Euclid, Pythagoras and Archimedes. Who,
who are alive and at work today, today, now,
at this time, in the inevitability of automation
and the ever increasing need, need, oh, need
for, the stable ties of modern family life,
rethinking, reliving, making way for the motor
car, forty million by nineteen...[23]

This speech – a parodic oath or creed in Maitland's self-indictment – has a 'texture of despair' which can be placed between late Shaw and Beckett. In Shaw, we may recall,[24] even the disillusioned rhetoric in the late plays had a cadenced syntax that in itself tended to reassure or anaesthetise. Osborne gives Maitland, the isolated speaker or 'disengaged man'[25] a broken syntax whose jerky rhythms create, in this opening scene of the play, at least the feeling of some yet un-diagnosed malaise. More precisely, Maitland's speech can be placed between Shaw's automata in *Back to Methuselah* v (with their monstrous reflex-language used, by the still confident parodist, to 'debunk' mechanistic thought), and Lucky's speech in *Waiting for Godot* (where the fragmented syntax is only one element in a subtly

23 *Inadmissible Evidence*, pp. 10–11. A good brief example of the parody of contemporary clichés: 'The practical dangers of pre-marital in the commanding heights of the declining objects' (cf. also n. 10).

24 Cf. Ch. 1, pp. 75–84, particularly the speeches of The Elder and Aubrey in *Too True to be Good* (1931).

25 The phrase used by Robert W. Corrigan, who sees *Inadmissible Evidence* as one example of 'The Drama of the Disengaged Man' in his anthology *The New Theatre of Europe 3*, New York, 1968. (Introduction, pp. 20ff.)

self-exhausting language that reduces all thought to a broken machine).[26] In all three speeches the mechanism of language itself is used to parody some meaninglessly 'mechanical' process. The texture of Maitland's speech seems coarse-grained when set beside Lucky's speech; Osborne is using the broken syntax, with its repetitions and word-piles, superficially. At the same time Osborne has cut himself loose from the clearly and ideologically targeted Shavian parody. The emphasis shifts from the 'target' (trivial-sounding rejection of modern science) to the *personal* voice of a mediocre but intensely despairing man 'caught up in the mechanics of a half-understood jargon'.[27]

In her comparative study of Shaw and Osborne, Katharine J. Worth – who puts the stress firmly on the resemblances between the two dramatists without focussing on the language – remarks that in his more pessimistic sensibility 'Osborne seems to begin at about the point reached by Shaw during the First World War'.[28] One can go further than that, and say that the difference in sensibility corresponds to a shift in style: in Osborne's plays even the rhetoric of verbal theatricality gets gradually introverted; it loses both the reassuring syntax of witty discourse (the 'euphemistic grace' of the old rhetoric[29]) and the operatic propensities of 'verbal music'. Osborne shifts rhetoric away from abstraction, dips it into that idiomatic, half-slangy uninhibited 'vernacular' which at times becomes Wilson Knight's 'Dionysian' speech from below,[30] an urban lumpen-proletarian dialect, non-literary but aware of the literary, and drawing on the imagery, often hyperbole,[31] of emotional disturbance. In this

26 Cf. Ch. 1, pp. 77–8; and Ch. 3, pp. 140ff.

27 Quoted from Simon Trussler, *The Plays of John Osborne*, London, 1969, p. 123. Mr Trussler rightly says that this Lucky-like speech is *less* typical of Bill's 'abrupt, egocentric, strongly associative idiom' than a later speech in the same scene. I chose the speech in this place to make several points clear with economy; for the more typical idiom see pp. 208–9 below.

28 *The Shavian* (Oct. 1964), pp. 29–35 (quote from pp. 29–30).

29 Roland Barthes links 'euphemistic grace' with an unproblematic classical language. *Writing Degree Zero* (1953), London, 1967, p. 68, etc.

30 Cf. Wilson Knight, 'The Kitchen Sink', *Encounter* (Dec. 1963), p. 48. (Cf. Ch. 4, n. 46.)

31 Alan Carter, *John Osborne*, pp. 153–60, offers an over-mechanical classification of Osborne's imagery (which I cannot use).

sense it is Osborne who has acted out a recognition of one of Shaw's characters: 'Since the war the lower centres have become vocal' (cf. Ch. I, n. 91).

This point can be briefly clarified by looking at Osborne's dramatic language in precisely those plays that have been considered most 'Shavian'.[32] For example, there is at least an initial similarity between the rhetoric of odium turned on multiple targets by John Tanner in *Man and Superman* and by Jimmy Porter in *Look Back in Anger*. But Tanner's tirade on the upper-class daughter and her mother – which parodies itself, both by being mounted on an ironical platform, and by exhibiting what I called the 'comic pathology of verbal excess[33] – even the balanced syntax carrying the string of negative but generic epithets has a euphemistic undertow:

> A horrible procession of wretched girls, each in the claws of a cynical, cunning, avaricious, disillusioned, ignorantly experienced foul-minded old woman whom she calls mother, and whose duty is to corrupt her mind to the highest bidder. (*Man and Superman*, Act II)

While Jimmy Porter's pointedly domestic tirade on the middle-class daughter (his wife) reaches a climax in the quick beat of colloquial picture-language:

> Did you ever see some dirty old Arab, sticking his fingers into some mess of lamb fat and gristle? Well, she's just like that. Thank God they don't have many women surgeons! Those primitive hands would have your guts out in no time. Flip! Out it comes, like the powder out of its box. Flop! Back it goes, like the powder puff on the table... She'd drop your guts like hair clips and fluff all over the floor.
>
> (*Look Back in Anger*, Act I, p. 24)

and the tirade against the mother – who is cast, as in Shaw, in the role of the unscrupulously class-conscious protectress – throws up a crescendo of ribald, person-directed similes ('she'd bellow like a rhinoceros in labour'...'She's as rough as a night in a Bombay brothel'), and culminates in a manic hyperbole as Jimmy elaborates his image of worms feasting on the mother.[34] It is not simply that Osborne's language is more violent, image-borne

32 By Katharine Worth, article cited (n. 28).

33 Cf. Ch. I, p. 66.

34 *Look Back in Anger*, Act II, pp. 51–3.

and vernacular than anything in Shaw; the over-charged invective is closing in on the personal conflict, drawing attention away from the supposed social target to the speaker's condition: *his* misogyny, *his* need to use words as instruments of torture. At the same time, the ironic platform is being undercut.[35] The pathological element in the comic verbal excess is being intensified.

In *Luther* Osborne clearly wanted to move towards epic drama.[36] There are signs that he wanted the distancing (or 'alienation') this form requires, with the dialectic of a theological/cultural revolution drawn into the open structure and the outward-reaching dialogue of the play. The style-shift becomes theatrically palpable with the change from the 'private interior of Act One, with its outer darkness and rich personal objects', to the second and third acts, 'sweeping, concerned with men in time rather than particular man in the unconscious; caricature not portraiture', as Osborne tells us in a Decor Note.[37] Yet it is the language coming from the 'private interior' that has most life, in performance as much as in reading; and the open scenes, partly through Osborne's relative failure to capture the language of ideas, seem frequently hollow. Even the sustained discussion scene between Luther and Cajetan on the fear of an intellectually torn world (Act II, Scene iv) lacks the dialectical *and* verbal force of Shaw's debates on heresy in the tent and trial scenes of *Saint Joan*. Yet Osborne intuitively reaches the language of inner conflict which Shaw hardly attempted; it is enough to recall that Joan in her first moment of isolation is given a long speech

35 The acting tone and the context of these tirades is as important as the texture. Osborne's Shavian-sounding stage direction calls for the climax of the 'worms' speech to be spoken 'In what he intends to be a comic declamatory voice'. But the intention is being outstripped by the manic intensity. Further, Tanner's tirade establishes an ironic complicity between Anne and Tanner ('You talk so well.' /'Talk! Talk!') and leads to the comic denouement of the shared motor cruise; Jimmy's tirade is primarily fuelled by his sense of isolation from his stage audience – an isolation which (taken with the two subsequent tirades) the language itself intensifies.

36 *Luther* is not 'epic theatre' in the Brechtian sense. This is convincingly argued by Simon Trussler (*op. cit.* pp. 95–100) and by Martin Esslin in 'Brecht and the English Theatre', *Tulane Drama Review* (Winter 1966), p. 69 (also in *Brief Chronicles*, London, 1970, pp. 93–4).

37 *Luther*, p. 46.

on the triumph of being alone ('I am alone. France is alone. God is alone.') in the hammered rhetoric of affirmation.[38]

By contrast, in Martin's broken confession – interwoven with the communal confession of trivia by other monks (Act I, Scene i) – Osborne succeeds in re-transmuting thought into dream, into the concrete imagery of the tormented body–mind – flesh, bone, bowels. The debt to Luther's own language and to psycho-analytic studies of the 'excremental vision' is of secondary importance;[39] what matters is that the language, stylised yet natural in the context, re-creates the experience of isolation and spiritual despair. The bare statement 'I am alone. I am alone, and against myself' is 'embodied' in Martin's telling of the nightmare about the crushing pile of people, in speech rhythms that communicate anxiety, and in a fragmented lament:

My bones fail. My bones fail, my bones are shattered and fall away, my bones fail and all that's left of me is a scraped marrow and a dying jelly.

where the imagery recalls Psalm 22,[40] and where the rhythms of auto-hypnotic repetition express a personal trauma, controlled and counterpointed by the confessional ritual.

As one of the recurrent motifs in Luther's inner conflict, Osborne dramatises, with empathy, the young monk's obsessive wrestle with words; his constant fear of the wrong word, equated with sin – 'It's the single word that troubles me'; the alternate shock and release when he can speak the words of a text as it were for the first time; the persistence of doubt: 'Father, I'm never sure of the words till I hear them out loud.'[41] Thus in

[38] *Saint Joan*, end of Scene V.

[39] Osborne used Erik H. Erikson, *Young Man Luther*, New York, 1958, as source-book. The phrase 'excremental vision' is the title of the chapter in Norman O. Brown, *Life Against Death*, London, 1959, which precedes a study of Luther's famous *Turmerlebnis* (Ch. XIII and XIV).

[40] Psalm 22.14: 'I am poured out like water, and all my bones are out of joint; my heart is like wax; and it is melted in the midst of my bowels.' The physical imagery is at once personal and universal; so is the dramatic gesture of self-rejection. Cf. Martin's 'If my flesh would leak and dissolve...' (the fragment preceding the one quoted) with 'O that this too too sullied flesh would melt', *Hamlet* I, ii, 129ff.

[41] The word-motif recurs in the following places in *Luther*: I, ii, pp. 26–9 (from where the first quote is taken); I, iii, pp. 38–40; II, i, p. 60 (second quote).

Luther's language Osborne re-creates something of the questing scripture-based Protestant (paralleled only by the text-conscious Talmudist or the Mandarin) making the inward understanding of the words an essential issue.

There is much in Osborne's dramatic language that seems to connect with the desire to 'hear the words out loud', in order to reach some certainty (if only the reassurance of 'I talk, therefore I am' – as Mary McCarthy suggests).[42] Histrionic rhetoric in particular is inseparable from the *feeling* that words are self-authenticating. Further, Osborne is essentially a verbal dramatist:

> words are important. They may be dispensed with, but it seems they're our last link with God. When millions of people seem unable to communicate with one another, it's vitally important that words are made to work. It may be old-fashioned, but they're the only things we have left...[43]

Perhaps it is no accident that the term 'old-fashioned' – also used by Osborne about the form of his first play – is now applied to his 'allegiance to words', in a context that makes it clear that Osborne is aware of the shrinking area of meaning through words. The power of language is asserted against its felt decline. The texture of Osborne's rhetoric itself embodies this tension – the attempt to gain new theatrical vitality for what is, after all, an 'old-fashioned' language.

The rhetoric of self-dramatisation

> Gifted people are always dramatising themselves. It provides its own experience, I suppose. *Epitaph for George Dillon*, Act II

It will be helpful to recall Eliot's early essay '"Rhetoric" and Poetic Drama' (1919) for a number of reasons. First, the essay contains the clearest short definition of one kind of rhetoric: 'where a character in the play *sees himself* in a dramatic light'.

42 Cf. n. 15 above.

43 Cf. n. 21 – A creed reminiscent of Shaw on the theatre as a temple: 'Think of the theatre...as one of the few acts of communion left to us. Imagine that this may be the last time the Host is raised before your eyes.' 'On Critics and Criticism', *The Sunday Telegraph* (28 Aug. 1966), reprinted in *Casebook*, pp. 69–71.

(Othello's 'And say, besides, – that in Aleppo once...' is the first of several examples.) Through such a speech we gain 'a new clue to the character, in noting the angle from which he views himself'; quite a different thing from the 'vicious rhetoric' we get 'when a character *in* a play makes a direct appeal to us'. Further, Eliot makes a significant connection between the first kind of rhetoric and people's awareness of themselves – in actual life – as actors; and he rightly defends the half-humorous tirades in Rostand's *Cyrano* as successfully exploiting this self-conscious dramatic rhetoric. Finally, Eliot in effect offers us some criteria for judging the quality of rhetoric. We can ask whether, in a particular dramatist's work, the rhetoric shows something of the variety, the growth that Eliot found in Elizabethan rhetoric: 'partly an improvement in language and...partly progressive variation in feeling.'[44]

In Osborne's revival of the tirade, the rhetoric of self-dramatisation *plays* the most vital part. At certain emotional climaxes, the central character is made to verbalise his feelings; that is, he will dramatise, but not rationalise, his self-awareness (usually an ambivalent awareness of being both 'exceptional' and exceptionally inadequate). He is, to change Eliot's definition, looking for a clue to his character, noting the angle from which he *speaks*. It is an essentially histrionic self-projection, nourishing various kinds of verbal theatricality.

At its most direct, Osborne (himself an actor) resorts to the actor-character: George Dillon, Archie Rice, Pamela. It is a simple device, for it offers a naturalistic pretext for both the verbal excess and the self-conscious address (the way a character times a speech and watches its effect on his audience); and, at the same time, it offers the quickest way for a transfusion of theatrical clichés into the dialogue. In this way George Dillon, the failed actor, not only sees and mocks himself theatrically (and doubly so) as actor *agonistes*:

I know I've got to fight every one of those people in the auditorium. Right from the stalls to the gallery, to the Vestal Virgins in the boxes! My God, it's a gladiatorial combat. Me against them! Me and mighty them!

44 *Selected Essays*, pp. 37–42. The brief quotations in this paragraph are, respectively, from p. 39; p. 40; p. 39. (See also Ch. 2, n. 2.)

but he is also 'permitted' to denounce the family that has offered him hospitality in terms of a cheap play-analogy ('like living in one of those really bad suitable-for-all-the-family comedies they do all the year round in weekly rep. in Wigan'). In the end he can only express himself through histrionic rhetoric, and he turns the personal duologue with Ruth – a potentially 'real' relatedness – into verbal posturing.[45]

Archie Rice imports the clichés, the tone, the rhythms of his jejune music hall 'turns' into his domestic talk. For example, the refrain of his song in Number Five – 'Thank God I'm normal' – reappears in the drunken but authentic piece of self-exposure at the climax of Act II, and starts off a new refrain in the same style:

> Say, aren't you glad you're normal? I've always been a seven day a week man myself, haven't I Phoebe? A seven day a week man...I'm a seven day a week man myself, twice a day.[46]

(As if apologising for his now habitual manner of speaking, Archie is earlier made to say: 'If you can dodge all the clichés dropping like bats from the ceiling, you might pick up something from me.'[47]) The cumulative effect is that we begin to see Archie's relationship with his family as an 'extension of that with his audience, treating them to a string of unfunny and inconsequential remarks, talking all the time to avoid the pain of silence.'[48] In sum, his talk is an extended revue sketch, underscoring the 'low theatricality' of his private world.

Pamela, the actress-heroine of *Time Present*, projects herself in terms of two opposed theatrical styles: the twittering world of 'Show-business', which now embraces 'everybody',[49] and the moribund theatre and life-style of her dying father. What verbal vitality there is in this ill-organised play comes from the way Pamela sees the world as a stage and dramatises her negatives:

45 *Epitaph for George Dillon*, Act II, pp. 49–65 – quotation from pp. 56–7.

46 *The Entertainer*, end of Act II (p. 73). Cf. also the refrain of Archie's song 'Number one's the only one for me!' and 'You'd better start thinking about number one, Jeannie' (pp. 32–3 and 68).

47 *Ibid.* p. 62.

48 Martin Banham, *Osborne*, Edinburgh and London, 1969, p. 32.

49 *Time Present*, p. 48: 'You're all of you in Show Business now. Everybody...' Cf. Osborne himself: 'We're all in show-biz now. It isn't a closed metaphor any more.' First *Observer* interview (30 June 1968).

as she parodies the vocabulary and gestures of a 'mean time'. Even a casually picked-up political slogan, the title of a pamphlet, is introverted with a comic–dramatic negative: 'Striding into the Seventies. I haven't got used to hobbling about in the Sixties yet.'[50] The posture is perhaps epitomised in: 'No, I'm not [Abigail]. But if I were, I'd be what I'm not – a whopping, enduring, ironclad, guaranteed star!'[51] – the dramatic syntax of dissociation, in this instance from the 'spurious gestures', the fashionable style of Abigail, a rival actress (in classical comedy this would be the central posture). Against the 'mean' contemporary scene, Pamela sets the old style, like a mundane version of Beckett's Winnie, clinging to fragments from the past. The verbal legacy of this style turns out to be: a collection of stale captions, with bits of cliché-dialogue from hack plays (which Pamela reads aloud from her father's cuttings-book, as an elegy for her father and the age of elegance he is supposed to represent).[52] The character placed at the centre seems only able to express herself by echoing either one or the other style – the megalopolitan lingo of 'the scene', or the old theatricality.

We may now go on to more extended, and less directly histrionic, examples of the rhetoric of self-dramatisation. A character creates for himself a theatrical platform, even if he is not formally – only instinctively – an actor (Jimmy Porter, Bill Maitland) and even if his rhetoric is not placed in a formal theatrical framework with explicit play-metaphors in its texture (*Inadmissible Evidence*). A dramatic view of the self – a broadly

[50] *Ibid.* p. 33, followed by a fuller self-dramatising speech: 'But what about the mean-time? We've got to get through that, haven't we? I don't know about striding off anywhere. I seem to be stuck here for the moment...'

[51] *Ibid.* pp. 38–9.

[52] *Ibid.* end of Act I, pp. 52–3. The argument is rewritten from my article 'Old and New in London Now', *Modern Drama*, vol. 11, no. 4 (Feb. 1969), pp. 442–3. There I also argue that Pamela's histrionic language tends to disperse the current of feeling, so that the more personal, broken dialogue, pointing to lack of love or meaning – which Osborne is almost certainly trying to write – cannot surface. I further connect Pamela's tendency to make a collage of contemporary voices with the art of *bricolage* (cf. also Introduction, n. 84). I have since noticed that Osborne himself claims to admire collage art, at least in Picasso: who can *play* with 'bits of newspapers and bottles' ('That Awful Museum', *Casebook*, p. 65).

externalised inner conflict – remains a constant element. The following passages, set side by side, seem to insist on asking whether we do not find in the texture of the rhetoric a progressive *variation* in language and feeling. Does the theatrical posture permit nuances of self-expression?

(A)
No, wait. Shall I recite my epitaph to you? Yes, do recite my epitaph to me. 'Here lies the body of George Dillon, aged thirty-four – or thereabouts – who thought, who hoped, he was that mysterious, ridiculous being called an artist. He never allowed himself one day of peace...He made no one happy, no one look up with excitement when he entered the room. He was always troubled with wind round his heart, but he loved no one successfully. He was a bit of a bore, and, frankly, rather useless. But the germs loved him. – Even his sentimental epitaph is probably a pastiche of someone or other, but he doesn't quite know who. And, in the end, it doesn't really matter.

Epitaph for George Dillon, Act III, p. 87

(B)
I rage, and shout my head off, and everyone thinks 'poor chap!' or 'what an objectionable young man!' But that girl there can twist your arm off with her silence...One of us is crazy. One of us is mean and stupid and crazy. Which is it? Is it me? Is it me, standing here like an hysterical girl, hardly able to get my words out? Or is it her?... I want to stand up in your tears, and splash about in them, and sing. I want to be there when you grovel. I want to be there, I want to watch it, I want the front seat. *Look Back in Anger*, Act II, Scene i, p. 59

(C)
I never even liked that kind of music, but to see that old black whore singing her heart out to the whole world, you knew somehow in your heart that it didn't matter how much you kick people, the real people, how much you despise them, if they can stand up and make a pure, just natural noise like that, there's nothing wrong with them, only with everybody else. I've never heard anything like that since. I've never heard it here. Oh, I've heard whispers of it on a Saturday night somewhere...But you won't hear it anywhere now. I don't suppose we'll ever hear it again. There's nobody who can feel like that. I wish to God I could, I wish to God I could feel like that old black bitch with her fat cheeks, and sing... *The Entertainer*, Act II, p. 71

(D)
But, and this is the but, I still don't think what you're doing will ever, even, even, even approach the fibbing, mumping, pinched little worm

of energy eating away in this me, of mine, I mean. That is: which is that of being slowly munched and then diminished altogether. That worm, thank heaven, is not in your cherry rose. You are unselfconscious, which I am not. You are without guilt, which I am not. Quite rightly...[53]

Inadmissible Evidence, Act II, pp. 105–6

In the first passage the device of the third-person[54] 'epitaph' provides an instant platform for self-dramatisation. It is to justify – in naturalistic terms – a virtual soliloquy, lifting the speaker's voice above the banalities of the surrounding dialogue. At the same time the epitaph offers partial self-parody: the self-mocking posture goes with a particular self-conscious judgement on his style: 'sentimental...probably a pastiche of someone or other'. (One may contrast this with Dubedat's dying creed – where Shaw gives unselfconscious pastiche to another artist-figure.[55]) So there is here a certain emotional complexity: the character despairing of his own pose. Yet the texture of the speech remains relatively mechanical and 'prosy'; there is little inner variation to generate the feeling advertised.

By contrast, the manic intensity of Jimmy Porter's speech is communicated as much through the rhythm as through the emotional hyperboles. The histrionic posture is embodied in the whole movement of the speech: its rapid changes in pace, from declamatory self-reportage to the reiterated questions – with their nervous, percussive beat – to that crescendo of self-excitation in the closing harangue. (The movement recalls Hamlet's ranting 'Hecuba' speech – there too there is accelerating declamation,

[53] In discussing these passages I have taken into account both the context and the length. Excessive length will be indicated. Briefly, the immediate context is as follows: in (A) George Dillon is addressing Ruth who leaves before the end of the speech: so a quasi-soliloquy turns into formal soliloquy; in (B) Jimmy Porter is addressing Alison and Cliff, and 'provokes' silence from both; Archie Rice in (C) and Bill Maitland in (D) is addressing his daughter – but while (C) is placed in a vestigial duologue, (D) is formally a monologue. Thus each 'tirade' deflects, or displaces, a central relationship in the play concerned.

[54] Sudden shifts from 'I' to 'he' also occur in Jimmy Porter's speeches – for example Jimmy talking of himself as a 'bewildered little boy', *Look Back in Anger*, p. 58. It is the counterpart of talking about a person present (Alison) in the third person to the stage audience (Cliff).

[55] Cf. Ch. 1, pp. 69 (3) ff.

a roulade of questions, a self-induced verbal hysteria judged by the speaker: 'I...like a whore unpack my heart with words.' *Hamlet*, II, ii, 578–99.) Jimmy is conscious of his own theatricality ('standing here like an hysterical girl, hardly able to get my words out') and makes us in turn conscious that his rhetoric calls out for an imaginary audience over the heads of the characters addressed. From one point of view, Jimmy's histrionic rhetoric compensates for his impotence in speaking the words that might reach another person. It is a verbal 'displacement activity' – the furibund rhetoric 'displaces' the original function, the attempt at personal communication.

Archie Rice's long drunken speech gains its effects through a run-down 'ramble', and not, like the other passages, through the energies of the run-on tirade. One might say it is hardly 'rhetoric'. But the ramble is controlled and theatrically self-expressive: the professional story-teller keeps pointing back to himself, clarifying his own feeling through the blur of his incoherent thinking, and carefully 'timing' his effects through the seeming diffuseness.[56] (We have seen earlier how the tone and the rhythms of Archie's stage style account for his domestic talk – here the attention-seeking repetitions.) Something is trying to break through from the obvious 'maudlin sentimentality' – an attempt to recover a lost meaning; the song he talks about seems to be pitted against his own feeble songs and habitual patter. The situation resembles the conclusion of Sartre's *La Nausée*,[57] where Roquentin pits the song of the Negress against a lifetime drained of meaning, and his sickness of language. And it further recalls the speech Christopher Fry once singled out to illustrate what verse can do in the theatre: the speech in *The Dark is Light Enough* where the Countess evokes the memory of her father dancing to a gipsy band, until he reaches 'a comprehension as wordless as the music'.[58] The point of the comparison

56 Osborne's stage direction says: 'Archie is drunk and he sings and orchestrates his speech as only a drunken man can, like a conductor controlling his own sound.' *The Entertainer*, p. 70.

57 Jean-Paul Sartre, *La Nausée* – conclusion. The Negress sings 'Some of these days', and Roquentin reflects on the song as a possible way out: 'La Négresse chante. Alors on peut justifier son existence?'

58 'Why Verse?', *Vogue* (March 1955), pp. 136–7, reprinted in *Playwrights on Playwriting*, pp. 125–30, quoting *The Dark is Light Enough*, Act II, Oxford, 1954 (1971 paperback ed. pp. 131–2).

is that in Archie's speech there is nothing of Sartre's explicit conceptual clarity, nor of Fry's stylised pointing. The speech has to work through the speaker's poverty of understanding and language – using chiefly his histrionic control over a tone of voice – to make a moment of experience dramatically significant.

In the brief extract from Bill Maitland's marathon soliloquy (it is that, though his daughter is mutely present) we see again[59] the way rhetoric 'turns in on itself', as the syntax and punctuation are distorted for emphasis. The resulting rhythm distinguishes this passage from the other examples of rhetoric. Here normally colourless functional words (but–but; still–will; the 'even' cluster, the odd pronoun paradigms; 'that is: which is that'; 'this me, of mine') are as much carriers of intense self-dramatisation as the highly coloured content-words. It is the rhythm of a disordered but still effect-conscious (effect-seeking) voice, alternately halting and exploding. The usual predominance of 'I' statements is here pointedly, even crudely, underlined by the way statements about 'you' are placed in antithesis with the speaking 'I', in wearily assertive clauses. All these linguistic effects fit in with the context, the flow of emotion in the whole speech. We are listening to a man who is in the process of converting his potential love for his daughter into an aggression which is self-destructive. Such a psychic conversion seems to be fuelled or catalysed by the language. So that we are constantly attending to dramatic *symptoms* – in this case something very much like auto-suggestion – as we listen to the modulations of this rhetoric.

In sum, there is considerable stylistic variation[60] in feeling in Osborne's rhetoric of self-dramatisation, both in particular speeches and from one play to another. It may not be what Eliot called 'an improvement in language', but it does amount to a revitalisation of rhetoric.

The limitations of Osborne's rhetoric seem to be these: it is an over-externalised rhetoric, which cannot accommodate 'thinking aloud' or genuine inwardness: it has 'no time for' pauses and silences, reflection and implicit self-seeing. (Contrast the Elizabethan soliloquy: 'the expression of an individual who, thinking

59 Cf. pp. 198–9 above.

60 This has been ignored even by eulogistically pro-Osborne critics (e.g. Carter, *John Osborne*, p. 150).

aloud, renders account of his most intimate feelings and thoughts'.[61]) It is a rhetoric which amplifies a mediocre speaker, or intensifies a naturalistically based idiom; it does not create a new dramatic language capable of expressing unexpected states of mind and experience – though that might be too much to expect. At the same time the energies of this rhetoric seem to be too much at the mercy of moments of empathy releasing the right kind of verbal paroxysm – with the risk of sheer exhaustion. By now Osborne himself seems to have got tired of rhetoric. *Inadmissible Evidence* was the last play where rhetoric was consistently expressive; the later plays either avoid, or (as in *Time Present*) look back on that style fitfully.

It is probable that Osborne would be more at home in a theatre which still had a central rhetorical convention – somewhere between Elizabethan drama and Victorian melodrama. As it is, his persistent naturalism has tended to inhibit; and his 'restless search for a style' has only rarely – in *The Entertainer* and in *Inadmissible Evidence* – led to a roughly satisfying fusion between the structure of the play and texture of the dialogue – releasing and controlling a 'full-blooded' theatrical language.

61 Schücking's definition, quoted in Thomas Van Laan, *The Idiom of Drama*, Ithaca, N.Y., 1970, p. 31.

6: Arden

We are here with a word. That's all. That's particular. Let the word dance...

(*Serjeant Musgrave's Dance*, I, iii)

Arden's work can be seen as a critically conscious attempt at revitalising drama, partly through the primitive sources of the language: releasing the energies of the ballad, of rough verse and song, set in and against a highly coloured prose dialogue which is itself frequently drawn from the rich speech patterns of an archaic or exotic dialect. It is a literary attempt to create a language that has seemingly pre-literary qualities – 'primary colours', a tough lyricism, a popular poetry-in-the-theatre.

The aim itself is not new. It springs from the hope that 'the popular dramatic tradition'[1] can bring about a revival of the drama. Yeats – at a time when he still hoped for a popular theatre – saw the connection between a living 'theatre of speech' and the need for a renewal of drama as an art form by reaching back towards 'a time when it was nearer to human life and instinct, before it had gathered about it so many mechanical specialisations and traditions'.[2] Just as poetry may be made new by going back to an earlier, less literary language (and Yeats specifically recalls the use Wordsworth and Coleridge made of

[1] I am appropriating Bethell's well-known title. Arden would certainly share the view that 'it is to the despised popular theatre that we must look for a revival of the drama...'. S. L. Bethell, *Shakespeare and the Popular Dramatic Tradition*, London 1944, p. 29. For a general definition see also my Introduction, p. 30 with n. 73 referring to renewal through 're-barbarization'.

[2] *Explorations*, London, 1962, pp. 210ff. (*Samhain*: 1906.)

the old ballad-writers), so drama may gain new life through capturing speech that still has the feel of a pre-literary language. 'Before men read...they loved language, and all literature was then, whether in the mouth of minstrels, players or singers, but the perfection of an art that everybody practised, a flower out of the stem of life. And language continually renewed itself in that perfection, returning to daily life...'[3] Though Arden might not go all the way with that dream of a traditional and communal dramatic language, he does aim, quite centrally, at a theatre that can draw on a language that is rooted in the past (like the ballad), and on the kindred language of 'primitive' speakers (like the 'anachronistic' vagrants of *Live Like Pigs* whose talk is as 'rich-and-strange' as that of Synge's peasants).[4]

What is new in Arden is the attempt to regain touch with an all but lost pre-industrial language in and for our own pan-industrial society, with all its urban complexities of speech. On the one hand, this involves a conscious unearthing of a half-buried, no longer truly popular, poetic tradition (with the risk of archaism), and a deliberate going outside 'standard' English and even the more central forms of non-standard English (with the risk of exoticism). On the other hand, Arden is a critically conscious post-Brechtian dramatist, a student of drama who has rediscovered for himself an 'imaginary museum' of popular drama stretching from Aristophanes through the Mummers' plays, the medieval Moralities, and Elizabethan/Jacobean drama, to the 'Victorian penny-gaff melodrama'.[5] Brecht himself was not so much a direct influence as a mediator, making it easier for Arden to go back to sources he was naturally drawn to: not

3 *Ibid.* p. 212.

4 The comparison with Synge was also made by Katharine J. Worth, in 'Avant Garde at the Royal Court Theatre', *Experimental Drama* (ed. W. A. Armstrong), London, 1963, pp. 206–7. See also below: p. 227. When Arden was asked to name the dramatists who had an impact on him, he listed, among others, 'Lorca, Synge, O'Casey, Yeats to an extent'. Interview with Walter Wager, *Tulane Drama Review* (Winter 1966), p. 46.

5 See Arden's long letter to *Encore* (May–June 1959), pp. 42–3. My selection from Arden's much fuller account of the 'popular tradition'. I shall not include in this discussion Arden's own use of 'penny-gaff melodrama' – *The Workhouse Donkey* (1963) and *The Hero Rises Up* (1968) – partly because it is not essential to the argument, partly because I think they offer only vitality.

just the epic and the popular theatre in general, but – particularly relevant in the present context – to the English ballad, folk or folksy song, irregular verse juxtaposed with prose dialogue, and period language for parables set in the past.[6] And if Arden was originally drawn mainly by the backward-looking lyrical expressiveness of the ballad – his first and still unpublished radio play *The Life of Man* (1956)[7] sounds like an extension into full ballad-play of the dramatic resources of *The Ancient Mariner* – he has tried to develop a multiple-style dramatic language for plays that speak to a modern audience.

Such an approach to drama and language sets Arden consciously apart from his contemporaries. 'Telling a True Tale' – his manifesto-like defence of the ballad as the 'bedrock of English poetry', and as a (poetic) tradition that can still be a source for the language of drama – opens with the words:

> To use the material of the contemporary world and present it on the public stage is the commonly accepted purpose of playwrights, and there are several ways in which this can be done. Autobiography treated in the documentary style (Wesker). Individual strains and collisions seen from a strongly personal standpoint and inflamed like a savage boil (Osborne). The slantindicular observation of unconsidered speech and casual action used to illuminate loneliness and lack of communication (Pinter). Tough analysis of a social disease (Ibsen/Arthur Miller). And

6 For Arden on Brecht see Interview with W. Wager (n. 4); *Plays and Players* (Aug. 1963); 'Brecht and the Brass Trade', *The Guardian* (29 July 1965). Martin Esslin considers Arden 'The truest follower of Brecht', in 'Brecht and the English Theatre', *Tulane Drama Review* (Winter 1966). A detailed and generous study on the influence of Brecht (which I read only after completing this chapter) can be found in Margrit Hahnloser-Ingold, *Das englische Theater und B. Brecht*, Bern, 1970 (Ch. 6 on Arden). I could only do justice to the differences in the *dramatic language* of Brecht and Arden in a further study; briefly, I still consider that Arden is more bound by the traditional ballad and by outlandish dialect than Brecht was.

7 This radio play creates a rich 'sound tapestry' out of verse, song, and 'poetic prose', the latter including the religious rhetoric of the Ahab-like Captain of the doomed ship (Captain Anthract) and the riddle-like images of a 'shining dead man' – a Welsh seaman killed through the captain's agency. Arden gives *coherence* to this play by firmly anchoring the language in the ballad world, in folk-lore and myth (stretching back to Homer's *Hymn to Dionysus* and Ovid's *Metamorphoses*). It is the kind of coherence that he fails to achieve in many of the published plays.

so on. What I am deeply concerned with is the problem of *translating the concrete life of today into terms of poetry that shall at the one time both illustrate that life and set it within the historical and legendary tradition of our culture*. I am writing in English (British English) and primarily for an English (British English) audience.[8]

The point of immediate interest is that central concern with something more precarious than Arden seems to realise: 'translating the concrete life of today into terms of poetry...', showing the modern world '*within* the historical and legendary tradition'. How does Arden's art of 'translation' work? – this seems to be the corresponding critical question.

The theatrically explicit juxtaposition of sharply distinct modes of language – verse and prose, heightened and naturalistic, traditional and contemporary elements – is one way in which Arden attempts this art of 'translation'. It follows that Arden's greatest artistic problem is to achieve a poetic or rhythmic unity – usually within a loose structure – to hold otherwise discordant modes of language in meaningful relation within each play. Ideally, Arden would aim at the kind of free-flowing unity which can be found in the rich texture of Shakespeare's histories (his own example is *Henry V*) where verse and prose, ceremonious and low speech, are set in counterpoint; but he accepts that prose must now be the dominant element.[9] Arden wishes to make a sharp distinction between the functions of verse and prose: verse uses 'the associations of words and images as strengthened by our metre and rhyme to remind us of an almost unlimited range of associations over and beyond their surface significance; in prose, however, each word simply means what it says and nothing else.'[10]

Thus Arden is opposed both to Eliot's late verse pattern 'based on the Noel Coward conversation line' and to Pinter's complex 'vernacular dialogue' where 'prose is beginning to work out of prose into poetry', with a 'desire to use straightforward

8 'Telling a True Tale', *Encore* (May–June 1960), pp. 22ff., reprinted in *The Encore Reader*, London, pp. 125ff. (my italics).

9 'Verse in the Theatre', *New Theatre Magazine* (April 1961), pp. 12ff. – one of Arden's key critical writings to be read against his similar observations on language in 'Building a Play', an interview, *Encore* (July–Aug. 1961), pp. 28–30.

10 *Ibid.* p. 12 (Arden's opening definition).

prose to say things that prose does not normally say'.[11] Or, to use two shorthand terms: a 'univocal' language, with subtle variations of intensity, and an 'infolding' language, with inner complexities and resonances, are emphatically excluded from Arden's idea of dramatic language. By contrast, Arden admires *Murder in the Cathedral* for its multiple prose and verse styles; but, in practice, Arden is aiming at a much more rough-and-ready juxtaposition of styles, with seemingly improvised transitions within a casual-seeming overall design. He wants to achieve a kind of folk art, akin to 'the Celtic tradition of epic writing, in which the bard would tell the story in improvised prose, with, interspersed in the story, certain passages of emotional tension which are composed in verse and which were verbatim and invariable'[12] – that is, fixed by tradition.

This interesting approach to the language of drama may be tested in a number of ways. We may begin by looking at a particular pattern in Arden's loosely textured tapestry of styles. How appropriate is Arden's use of traditional ballad-like verse (often sung to traditional tunes) in the most relevant plays? How does it function: how does it express heightened 'emotional tension', and how well does it 'translate'?

It seems clearly more difficult to achieve appropriateness, and the other values that make up felt coherence, in the roughly contemporary than in the 'period' plays. To appreciate the difficulty I will take first what seems to be an example of incongruity: Krank's sung verse on the Nazi death camps in the opening scene of *The Waters of Babylon* (1957, Arden's first published play). Krank has just been presented – through his opening prose speeches – as a crooked-sounding, picturesque stage-foreigner, and after the song the scene immediately races on, through a farcical exchange with a stage-Irishman, to the complex intrigue of a picaresque melodrama, in the course of which Krank turns out to be pimp, brothel-keeper and ex-guard from Buchenwald, and keeps changing his speech-style (in different kinds of prose and verse). But early on, at the point indicated, in response to a request made by a beautiful West Indian whore, Krank sings:[13]

[11] *Ibid.* pp. 13–14.

[12] *Ibid.* p. 13. See also 'Telling a True Tale' (*loc. cit.* p. 127).

[13] *The Waters of Babylon*, Act I, in *Three Plays*, Penguin ed. pp. 21–2.

As I went down by Belsen town
I saw my mother there
She said, go by, go by my son, go by,
But leave with me here
Your lovely yellow hair.

As I went down by Auschwitz town
My brother looked out of the wall
He said, go by, go by my brother, go by,
But leave with me here
The lovely strong tooth from your skull.

As I went down by Buchenwald town
And there for my sweetheart I sought
But she whispered, go by, Oh my darling go by,
You leave with me here
The lovely red blood of your heart.

Now the inappropriateness here is not only a matter of context, important though that is, since the verse is both 'out of character' and makes only one forced connection with the fact, revealed later, that Krank was a guard at Buchenwald. One asks: is anything gained locally from setting the images of mass murder in our time – hair, teeth, blood – in the frame of those traditional images, rhythms and burdens: 'Lovely yellow hair'...'Lovely red blood of your heart'? Does the discord illuminate or 'translate' anything at all? It seems that Arden's willed conjunction of the contemporary and the traditional here points to certain ultimate limits of language: there are experiences and events that are too complex or far-reaching to fit into the old language, the more-or-less inherited framework of ballad imagery and rhythm. It is the kind of mistranslation that ends by traducing both the modern use and the traditional language.[14]

Even in *Live Like Pigs* (1958), the contemporary play that is most successful in shaping into a rhythmic unity the heterogeneous elements in the language, the balladry is to some extent forced upon the play: the songs that open each scene form an easily detachable folk-art frame. (Arden himself is aware of this when

14 Contrast: Peter Weiss, *The Investigation*, briefly discussed in the concluding section of my introduction. I am aware that in this instance my personal value-judgement is inseparable from the stylistic judgement.

he asks the producer to integrate or else cut out these songs.[15]) Yet some of these ballads have a simple strength of their own, for example the opening:

> O England was a free country
> So free beyond a doubt
> That if you had no food to eat
> You were free to go without.

which, taken with the succeeding verses, attempts to draw a parallel between the condition of 'the sturdy beggars of the sixteenth century' and the Welfare State misfits of the play (whose exotic prose dialogue is in tune with the language of the ballad-world). Within such a frame, Arden shifts the emotional *and* the linguistic centre of the play away from the 'contemporary' to the 'anachronistic',[16] in part, one supposes, for the sake of an old-world expressiveness. We enter a world – the world of the Sawneys and their still nomadic Gipsy guests – where everybody sings a traditional song. The songs have several functions. Some, like Sailor Sawney's song on mermaids (end of Scene i) and Rosie's lullaby (end of Scene xvi), are chiefly decorative – rounding off their respective scenes like a musical coda. The songs *within* the scenes create a rhythmic excitement, or rather a series of climaxes throughout the play: song links up with song in a Dionysiac rhythm (whose ultimate climax is the scene where screaming women want to tear Col to pieces – Scene xvi).

The attempt is made to 'prove upon our pulses' the otherwise uncertain continued existence of a world where a young man displays his sexual vitality through a soldier's song, 'Tow-ri-ah-di the doodle-ay' (Blackmouth, Scene v); where a girl answers an objectionable neighbour's frightened question with a riddle-like taunt-song (Daffodil, Scene xiv); and a forty-year-old woman, half asleep in bed, ends her soliloquising, on an old lover, by singing some verses from a game (Rachel, Scene xii). One of the characters, Old Croaker – whose very name suggests a voice –

[15] Introductory note to *Live Like Pigs*, *Three Plays*, Penguin ed. p. 102.

[16] I find myself in agreement with Richard Gilman: 'the cards may be stacked against the Sawneys socially but dramatically they have all the aces'. See the whole argument (disagreeing with John Russell Taylor), 'Arden's Unsteady Ground', *Tulane Drama Review* (Winter 1966), reprinted in *Modern British Dramatists* (ed. J. R. Brown), pp. 104ff. (quoted from p. 112).

sings 'Tom Tom the piper's son' the moment she arrives on the stage (Scene iv), and singing and chanting her way through the play, contributes to the final rhythmic climax of action by reciting 'words' she calls 'rhyming' (a spell to protect the house from the fury of neighbours):

> Window close and window true
> In and out and who comes through?
> Mary and Jesus and the Twelve Tall Riders
> Nobody else nobody else nick nack noo! (Scene xvi)

Perhaps there is an element of spell-binding in Arden's primitivism. We do not find here an ironic or critical (Brechtian) use of ballad opera, we find, rather, the passionate invocation of a word-dance. The spell may work, but when it fades one is left with the awkward, partly extra-literary question: is this not a 'hot-house' language, which we experience like a festival of folklore in the suburb?

Arden may have realised that there was something forced or inappropriate about the balladry in *Live Like Pigs*; at all events he never again used the ballad either as a framework or as a method of intensified expression within a play that has an approximate contemporary setting. Instead, he turned to periods and situations that had in them the makings of a ballad play. In *Serjeant Musgrave's Dance* (1959) the time and the place – and with it the language – are sufficiently distanced to create, in the reader or audience, a feeling of apparent timelessness (despite the approximate late-nineteenth-century mining town setting).[17] *Armstrong's Last Goodnight* (1964) – which grew directly out of the ballad[18] and where much of the language is precisely located in the sixteenth-century Border Country – the sense of a 'period language' is so strong that it risks being taken as pastiche, a text from the museum of language.

17 The play's subtitle is *An Un-Historical Parable*; and Arden stresses the deliberate approximateness of the period in his Introduction (second paragraph) and in the information given to G. W. Brandt; see 'Realism and Parables: from Brecht to Arden', *Contemporary Theatre* (ed. J. R. Brown and B. Harris), London, 1962, p. 53.

18 See Arden on the origins of the play in his interview with Simon Trussler – the second interview in *Tulane Drama Review* (Winter 1966), p. 50. The play began with a reading of the ballad, which Arden subsequently connected with Conor Cruise O'Brien's book about Katanga.

There is, then, a coherence of vision and language in these two plays. Each of them is conceived as a whole in terms of 'primary colours': the setting and the costumes (black-and-white coal town with the red uniforms; the medieval stage emblems of castle, palace and forest) match the leading characters who seem to spring straight from the ballad world and who can speak the language of pre-rational artifice 'naturally'. The transitions from prose dialogue to verse or song seem unforced and well-integrated in their dramatic context. We may take as an example Annie's verse on war and soldiering:

Annie: I'll tell you for what a soldier's good:

To march behind his roaring drum,
Shout to us all: 'Here I come
I've killed as many as I could –
I'm stamping into your fat town
From the war and to the war
And every girl can be my whore
Just watch me lay them squealing down!
And that's what he does and so do we.
Because we know he'll soon be dead...

What good's a bloody soldier 'cept to be dropped into a slit in the ground like a letter in a box. How many did you bring with you – is it four?

Bargee: Aye. Four.
Annie: That's four beds in the house?

. . . .

Annie (*in a sudden outburst*): Then you'd do well to see they stay four nights because I'll not go with more nor one in one night, no, not for you nor for all of Egypt!

(*Serjeant Musgrave's Dance*, Act I, Scene ii)[19]

Here the verse can be felt to erupt with a distinct pictorial and rhythmic force; it is quick-moving, yet individual lines can stand out with a memorable explicitness and connect with the key ideas of the play ('I've killed as many as I could'). In the transition to prose dialogue the image-pattern of the verse seems to be carried over, though the rhythm is changed ('dropped into

[19] Methuen ed. pp. 17–18. Arden seems justified in saying that when Annie speaks in verse she is making an 'oracular pronouncement': turning her own experience into a generalised comment on soldiers. 'Verse in the Theatre' (*loc. cit.*), pp. 13–14.

a slit in the ground like a letter in a box'). And then the heightened prose modulates into the girl's ordinary speech, direct and simple, but sufficient to convey her obsession or derangement. At the same time, the physical images of killing and stamping and whoring soldiers 'point a moral' without any need for didactic pointing: they add up to a short local parable on war. The incident itself adds up to a scene-within-the-scene which, in context, stands out like a ballad from the surrounding public house speech-making (for example, the Mayor's consciously cynical set speeches with the worn clichés on soldiering: 'there's loyal hearts and true here, and we're every man-jack of us keen to see our best lads flock to the colours' – p. 23).

Musgrave's climactic scene is similarly integrated in the design of the whole play. The song itself has a primitive stamping rhythm (as Musgrave stamps around the dead soldier's swinging skeleton) and evokes the 'shudder' of the gallows as in a popular woodcut or, again, in a ballad:

> Up he goes and no one knows
> How to bring him downwards
> Dead man's feet
> Over the street
> Riding the roofs
> And crying down your chimneys...
>
> (Act III, Scene i, pp. 84–5)

But even though this does evoke the remote-yet-familiar ballad world, it is felt as something 'new'. We have not heard just this rhythm, just these images before, and yet we hear echoes as in certain art versions of a folksong. In other words, it is the kind of 'imitation' that is re-creation and not 'pastiche'. Further, as in the Annie scene, the verse has affinities with the prose language: it arises in a natural-seeming transition from Musgrave's preceding speech:

Musgrave (*at the top of his passion*): D'ye hear me, d'ye hear me, d'ye hear me – I'm the Queen of England's man, and I'm wearing her coat and I know her Book backwards. I'm Black Jack Musgrave, me, the hardest serjeant of the line – I work my life to bugle and drum, for eighteen years I fought for one flag only, salute it in the morning, can you haul it down at dark? The Last Post of a living life? Look – I'll show it to

> you all. And I'll *dance* for you beneath it – hoist up the flag, boy, – up, up, *up!*

The emphatic energy of this prose speech – its rhythm of repetition, its 'I'-centred exclamations and rhetorical questions, its fusion of military and religious emblems – is something we recognise as the 'Musgrave music' (we have heard it before, especially in the two soliloquies: his solitary prayer at the end of Act I, and the sleep-talking scene in Act II, Scene iii). So the language of the verse that follows is 'in character', yet it undergoes a change of key and moves 'beyond character'. Further, it provokes a double awareness: an immediate, physical or 'naive' revulsion, and a distanced and complex need to reflect on Musgrave's paradoxically violent brand of pacifism (made clear in the context). At that point the 'primitive' language becomes a language of parable to be *re-translated* – by the 'sophisticated' reader/spectator – into some contemporary parallel, making a connection, for example, with a certain type of propaganda speech that declares war on war. In other words, the tradition-based language is, here, successfully dramatising universal issues.[20]

Serjeant Musgrave's Dance succeeds in creating a tradition-based language in a way that is not obtrusively 'regional' or 'exotic' or 'antiquarian'. By contrast, *Armstrong's Last Goodnight* constantly risks being bracketed in some such way. The play is Arden's most ambitious dramatisation of the traditional ballad world on an epic scale; it has grown out of the ballad of *Johnie Armstrong*, verses from which are effectively used at the end of Act II and in the scene, near the end of the play, where Armstrong,[21] trapped by the King's treachery, is hanged, slowly singing as if it were a lament for himself and his anarchic and archaic world:

> To seek het water beneath cauld ice
> Surely it is ane great follie
> I hae socht grace at a graceless face
> And there is nane for my men and me.[22]

[20] See also C. W. Brandt, *loc. cit.* n. 17. But Brandt illustrates the function of the ballad language through the song of a minor character, Attercliffe.

[21] I shall continue to refer to Gilnockie as Armstrong for the sake of clarity.

[22] *Armstrong's Last Goodnight* (1965), Act III, Scene xiv, Methuen ed. pp. 119ff. Cf. the ballad *Johnie Armstrang*, no. 106 in *The Oxford Book*

until the words are broken up in the struggle with his executioners. After further verses from the ballad and his last words (in prose), the noose tightens around Armstrong's throat. This scene has great power, and makes effective use of the language of the ballad in its traditional context. But it does not point beyond itself – does not ask to be 're-translated' in the way Musgrave's song does.

The various types of period and regional language – which make up much of the texture of the dialogue – are outlandish and decorative in the most obvious sense. But Arden uses dialect and 'idiolect' with emblematic sharpness and a clear dramatic function – especially in the conflict between the courtly Lindsay and the barbaric Armstrong, amounting to a collision of two verbal worlds.

When the two protagonists are confronted with one another, the distance that separates their mental and social worlds is brought out by a sharp contrast between their diction and their voices: Lindsay's precise, finely cadenced poet–diplomat's language (that comes 'trippingly off his tongue') confronts the singing and the wild staccato of Armstrong's ejaculations, the strangeness of his dialect intensified by a stammer and a barely human roaring.[23] No wonder that Armstrong needs an interpreter; and at certain points the dialogue hinges on internal translation. When Armstrong, made docile by Lindsay's smooth talk, utters these words of reconciliation: 'Your wame, I heard it nicker' it is not only Lindsay but many members of an English audience

of Ballads (ed. James Kinsley), 1969, second quatrain of stanza 10. The lines used by Arden at the end of Act II are based on the opening and concluding quatrains of the original ballad. There are many ballad-like verses scattered through the play; the National Theatre production opened with the horns and hunting verses of Act I, Scene iii, thus appropriately suggesting a ballad-world framework for the whole play.

23 *Ibid.* Act I, Scene vii, to be contrasted with Act III, Scene xii (marking Lindsay's transformation). Arden pushes Armstrong towards the inarticulate through this double effect: dialect and speech impediment. Cf. *Live Like Pigs* where the noises made by several characters are woven into the tapestry of speech and sound: Rachel makes animal noises; Col is 'much given to uncouth noises to supplement his speech'; Blackmouth howls like a dog (Scene x); The Old Croaker not only croaks but cackles. Intense speech in Arden sometimes recalls the origins of human speech in animal noises and ululation.

that benefit from the interpreter's gloss in a somewhat less outlandish dialect: 'The Laird wad speir, Sir David, whether or no ye've eaten the day.'[24] By contrast, at one of the climaxes of the play – when Armstrong is deceived by the king's 'fraternal' letter, delivered by Lindsay – Armstrong's own delighted translation of the unexpected and alien-sounding word 'fraternal' as 'That means he calls me his brither' clinches the point of his fall[25] through his vanity and misplaced trust.

Lindsay's spare morality-type verse – with its clear-cut pastiche of the language of the historical Lyndsay's *Thrie Estaits* (1540) – is skilfully woven into the texture of the play, at once contrasting with and complementing other 'period' styles. There is an emblematic – or heraldic – clarity about this verse too. For example, in the lines that convey to the audience Lindsay's inner transformation – from an easy-going and hedonistic courtier into a ruthless royal politician – the moral point is made in terms of 'primary colours':

> A like coat had on the Greekish Emperour
> When he rase up his brand like a butcher's cleaver:
> There was the knot and he did cut it.
> Ane deed of gravity. Wha daur dispute it?[26]

This picture language goes with a visual 'demonstration' (the audience sees the royal herald's tabard), and the cliché-metaphor of 'cutting the Gordian knot' serves as a form of 'action poetry': when the verses end, Lindsay proceeds to destroy Armstrong – by guile, in prose. Further, the 'emperor' image exactly echoes one of the heraldic images ('He is ane Emperour complete', III, i, p. 94) applied to Armstrong by the Lady who earlier says to him: 'You are indeed heraldic, Sir' (II, ix, p. 78). It is as if Lindsay, in becoming decisive enough to outwit Armstrong, had acquired his opponent's emblems and attributes. The traditional

24 *Ibid.* p. 51. Non-linguists would not quite understand the interpreter either (e.g. speir = ask).

25 *Ibid.* pp. 112–13. Other internal language jokes are: Armstrong making fun of Gaelic (e.g. I, vii, p. 43) and the English Commissioners and Clerk – in the opening scenes – flat and formal to the point of parody.

26 *Ibid.* Act III, Scene ii, p. 112. Contrast Lindsay's opening verse speech, as he takes off his herald's coat (Act I, Scene ii, pp. 26–7).

language portrays this transformation with combined moral and pictorial directness.

Yet from the point of view of Arden's concern with 'translating' (and Arden came to write this play because he perceived a parallel between the ballad world of Johny Armstrong and Tshombe's Katanga) the language of the play seems to make few felt connections between traditional and contemporary modes of consciousness. The traditional language is not 'made new' from within; but neither does the play offer an effective counter-language (apart from the local contrasts mentioned in note 25) to the extended use of the ballad and the varieties of sixteenth-century Scots dialogue. There is an inner balance of styles, but no counter-balance: there is, so to speak, no extra-territorial or ironic play-language 'to shock the audience out of their complacency', like the device of the Knights' platform speeches in *Murder in the Cathedral*, or the historicising voices in *Saint Joan* and in Brecht's *Galileo*.[27] (There is nothing even to correspond to the gay juxtaposition of the biblical, folk and *modern* idiom in Arden's nativity play, *The Business of Good Government*: where we have, for example, Joseph singing the carol about himself; the angel changing from his Biblical role to consciously quoting from the Bible, and assuming the role of prompter to the Magi and palace official to Herod (with corresponding changes in idiom); while Herod himself is made to switch from a colloquy with the Angel to the political rhetoric that initiates the massacre of the innocents. And such style-shifts are held within the opening and closing carols, in the 'naive art' frame of a medieval shepherd's play.[28])

Through his refusal to 'historicise' in *Armstrong's Last Goodnight*, Arden tends to seal off his predominantly archaic–exotic dialect

27 The statement concerning *Murder in the Cathedral* is Eliot's. (Cf. 'Poetry and Drama', *Selected Prose*, p. 78.) Shaw, Eliot and Brecht have all chosen themes from history that are central in our culture, myth-like in combining the 'known' with an invitation to re-making. Arden's choice of border-line history underlies the burden his language has to carry.

28 John Arden and Margaretta D'Arcy, *The Business of Good Government, A Christmas Play*, London, 1963. Examples, respectively: Joseph, pp. 29–30; Angel, p. 31, in contrast with the various roles and languages assumed: pp. 45–53; Herod, pp. 49–50. (Cf. the earlier switch into political rhetoric: p. 18.)

as, in effect, a period reconstruction. It is no doubt for this reason that the language of the play has been called pastiche, and even compared to Van Meegeren's fake art.[29]

This links up with a more general limitation in Arden's use of exotic language in drama. In his approach to prose dialogue Arden certainly intends to achieve that combination of vernacular vigour and flexibility which he admired in Goethe's *Götz*: a play 'that varied [the vernacular prose] from the stately conversation of princes and emperors to the slang of soldiers and the regional dialect of peasants, and that included in its scope not only battles, chivalry and romantic love, but also . . . wide-ranging historical questions'.[30]

In practice, few would question that Arden has a marked predilection for 'the regional dialect of peasants', and that his own creative energy is released – is joyously employed – in re-creating patterns of speech that are either backward-looking or cut off, through some social accident, from the pressures of contemporary consciousness felt, by now, in most types of every-day English (and not merely in 'metropolitan' or 'educated' speech). And this marked creative bias – seen at its clearest in *Live Like Pigs*[31] but a main current in Arden's drama – represents a form of nostalgia for heightened or poetic prose, for speech 'fully flavoured as a nut or apple'.[32]

Technically, such exotic prose works through local heightening to achieve a local intensity in imagery and rhythm.[33] It yields

[29] See, respectively, John Russell Taylor, *Anger and After* (revised ed.), London, 1969, p. 102, and Frederick Lumley, *New Trends in 20th Century Drama*, London, 1967, p. 266.

[30] Introduction to *Ironhand*, 1965, p. 5. The language of Arden's adaptation is vigorous, but it has, I think, an excess of expository or 'chronicle' dialogue, which is *not* in Goethe, nor is the ballad-like final lament of Metzler (III, vi), nor the gipsy spells (III, viii). As this is characteristic of Arden's dialogue one is tempted to think that Arden – like Götz at his trial speaking of the court proceedings – desires to 'write it *all* down, boy; we'll make it into a ballad and we'll sing it in the streets'. (II, xv, p. 113) – the ballad is to counteract the word-excess in the 'proceedings'.

[31] E.g. Rosie talking to Rachel about Sailor, *Live Like Pigs*, Scene ii (Penguin ed. pp. 111–12).

[32] From Synge's Preface to *The Playboy of the Western World* (cf. n. 4 above).

[33] See also Bamber Gascoigne on heightened prose (he too draws a line from Synge to Arden), *Twentieth Century Drama*, London, 1962,

less interest in terms of interaction between characters, in the movement of dialogue from speech to speech. And it lacks the inner complexity, the nervous concentration or evasiveness, the ambiguity and stylistic many-sidedness, which does stamp much modern speech; features that have been exploited in some of the most interesting dialogue techniques of our time. In this respect Arden is – as he himself has implied[34] – at the opposite pole from Pinter. We may value his achievement – the vigour and occasional beauty of his language – and still remain aware of a limitation. In so far as such things can be summarised, Arden's 'tradition', by leaning too much on archaic or regional languages, risks insulating itself. With all its liveliness, it is a language not 'open' to the way language is being lived and re-made under the pressure of new modes of thought and being. From this point of view Arden's dramatic language seems highly specialised.

Yet the potential direction of Arden – and his actual achievement in *Serjeant Musgrave's Dance* and in the best scenes of *Armstrong's Last Goodnight* – is an interplay of languages: the opposite of a 'specialised' language. In attempting to revitalise a 'popular dramatic tradition' Arden may be said to be aiming at reaching his audience on several levels, through a 'principle of multi-consciousness' (to use Bethell's term[35]). In such a drama both traditional and modern, popular and literary, robust and lyrical, modes of expression would interact. The language of a play would have 'straight lines, as it were, in contrast to curved': it would be communal and yet speak to the audience with one man's voice.[36]

Behind that aim we sense the Shakespearean ideal – and Arden has on occasions invoked Shakespeare as an influence or a term of reference in his own critical statements. Yet the Shakespearean ideal introduces a set of critical values that would be damaging

pp. 68–70. It is also interesting to recall Ronald Peacock pointing to the way Synge's drama was limited by his lack of contemporary consciousness and his use of 'extremely local' speech. *The Poet in the Theatre*, London, 1961, pp. 115–16.

34 In 'Telling a True Tale' and 'Verse in the Theatre'. See pp. 216–217 above.

35 *Op. cit.* p. 29, and pp. 50–2 on 'duality of time' in *Henry IV*.

36 John Arden, 'Poetry and Theatre', *The Times Literary Supplement* (6 Aug. 1964).

and out of scale in judging Arden – or, indeed, any dramatist of our time. It is sounder to think of Shakespeare as having left us an image of wholeness, where the sensuous and the intellectual, the inward and the public are equally at home. That wholeness can serve as a measure – as it did for Francis Fergusson – which points to the 'partial perspectives of the modern theater',[37] in language as in so much else. In the very process of evaluating the limited languages of modern drama we come to accept – along with the limitations and the 'crisis' – the value of each dramatic language in its own terms; and end by affirming the value of each dramatist's search for authentic expression. Wholeness, in the Shakespearean sense, is an unattainable ideal, which, as Eliot said in a comparable context, 'provides an incentive towards further experiment and exploration, beyond any goal which there is a prospect of attaining'.[38]

37 *The Idea of a Theater* (1949), Part II.
38 'Poetry and Drama' (Conclusion), *Selected Prose*, p. 85.

Conclusion

'Any general statement', said Pound in *ABC of Reading*, 'is like a cheque drawn on a bank. Its value depends on what is there to meet it.' With this warning in mind, what I want to do in this final chapter is to re-think some of the general questions raised in the detailed argument of the foregoing chapters: not a recapitulation but a continuing inquiry. The appearance of new work by both dramatists and critics in the interval between writing the main chapters and this Conclusion has given a new perspective to this inquiry.

The value of the words in drama – to begin by drawing a big cheque – seems to be vindicated. Language survives as an essential element in drama under various, often extreme, pressures: from outside, the pull of non-verbal or anti-verbal theatre, the unscripted 'happening', the physical or 'concrete language' (of Artaud and his successors) freed from writing, speech and dialogue; from within, the critique of language, the intensification of doubts about words as a living and workable medium. In the broadest sense, one concludes that language renews itself each time a dramatist succeeds in bringing the 'talking animal' to life in the demanding context of the play. Action and the act of speaking – men speaking to men, or one man speaking to himself, or to God – are contrapuntal. As Kenneth Burke asserts, in a different context:

Once you have a word-using animal, you can properly look for the linguistic motive as a possible motivation in all its behaviour, even in such *actions* as could be accounted for without this motive in the corresponding motions of a non-linguistic species.[1]

If we accept that all action connects with verbal action at a certain level, drama and language are interdependent, and the connection is indestructible.

In what sense, then, can we speak of a 'crisis of language' in drama? (The phrase itself is for shorthand, and should be avoided in glib company.) First, the various versions of a linguistic 'fall' – the experience of a new Babel in our time – seem to have had value more as myths *for* verbal creativity than as generally valid statements about language or literature. It is a particular writer in a precise situation who experiences language as 'exhausted' (Eliot) or 'abstracted to death' (Beckett) or as a cause of nausea and paralysis (Pinter). The experience is authentic and disturbing; it is transformed when it is allowed to enter and shape the act of writing, the texture of dialogue. Then the crisis becomes a condition of creativity. On the human and creative level, the dramatist, like other writers, may also find himself in the plight of the artist in Henry James' *The Middle Years*: 'It wasn't true, what he had for renunciation's sake to believe, that all the combinations were exhausted. They weren't by any means – they were infinite: the exhaustion was in the miserable artist.' On the level of dramatic theory, what is interesting is, precisely, how the miserable artist produces new 'combinations' – new play-modes and play-languages – partly out of and against the seeming exhaustion of 'all the combinations'. And on the stylistic level, what is interesting is what kind of new 'combination' comes out of the supposedly depleted pool of language.

A new dramatic language so to speak leans against both an

[1] Kenneth Burke, *Language and Symbolic Action*, Berkeley, 1966, pp. 456ff. The extremist, Artaud-type attack on language in drama is probably dying out. In recent writing see: (i) Herbert Marcuse's defence of aesthetic form – supported by texts from Brecht and Beckett – in 'Art and Revolution', *Partisan Review* (Spring 1972), and (ii) John Lahr's defence of the American avant-garde theatre as a place where our language is renewed; dialogue in Pinter, Beckett, and Humpty-Dumpty's language game are singled out for praise. *Plays and Players* (Dec. 1972), p. xvi; *Acting out America, Essays on Modern Theatre*, Harmondsworth, 1972, pp. 22–3 and 170.

'old style' and the 'common language'. Even at an extreme point – Lucky's pathological speech, with its deviant syntax and diction – dramatic language connects with all language (the 'public' language we have, at various levels, learned and shared, from babble to rhetoric, from symbolist poem to advertisement). In short, the study of dramatic language confirms – what Wittgenstein and Roman Jakobson, among others, have affirmed – that there is no such thing as a 'private' language. Even the solipsist monologue springs from and returns to the 'language of the tribe' in the verbal action of drama.

It may be considered that drama performs, among other participatory functions, verbal mediation of a special kind. The relative stability of the 'common' language enters into and sets in relief the elements of distortion (or deviation) in the play-language: the boldly non-grammatical patterning, the over-elaborate or else minimal speech, and all that is deliberately mannered or 'unspeakable' in utterance. In return, drama has been and is being enriched by the stylistic marks of language-consciousness: the texture of dialogue *can* now be complex, multi-layered and ambiguous or polysemic without the risk (faced earlier by the non- or anti-naturalistic dramatist) that the play will end up with a merely esoteric and, in consequence, *un*-dramatic language.

The choice of styles – the imaginary museum – seems to have become a permanent condition of creativity in our culture, in drama as well as in poetry and the novel. And it now seems less necessary to dwell on the attendant fear of 'burdens': the burden of too many past styles, the burden of innovation, the burden of having to invent a new language, as it were, for each new play. There are several reasons for seeing, here too, a tamed or domesticated crisis, something like a 'period of consolidation'.[2] At one level, this links up with the earlier point that the 'exhaustion' of a style or language is either a myth or an over-simplified doctrine. It is much sounder to begin with Northrop Frye's dictum: 'the resources of verbal expression are limited... by the equivalents of rhythm and key, though that does not

[2] Bamber Gascoigne states: 'The theatre today is in a period of consolidation', and then specifically excludes subject matter and *dialogue* from this generalisation. *World Theatre*, London, 1968, p. 263.

mean, any more than in music, that its resources are artistically exhaustible'.[3] In short, it is necessary to be aware, *simultaneously*, of both the resources and the limits that govern any successful 'combination', in the present context – any new play-language.

When the resources as well as the limits are understood, the expanding 'choice of styles' does offer 'great potential artistic freedom'[4] to the dramatist both *within* a particular work, and *across* his works. We have, at different points, seen the interest of plays like *Sweeney Agonistes* and *Waiting for Godot* partly as a fusion or cross-fertilisation of 'popular' and 'poetic' modes of language (the former making use of the music hall and the minstrel show, the latter of the circus clown and the *commedia dell'arte*). If anything, the resourcefulness of this kind of combination needs further emphasis; it has been underscored by certain recent plays. Pinter's *Old Times* (1971) is a particularly clear example, with its interweaving of snatches from old hit songs (*Lovely to Look At*, *The Way You Look Tonight*, etc.) and the knowingly mannered dialogue with its collection of period clichés 'shaped' towards a final intensity. What we have called an 'infolding' language and the language of 'theatrical collage' are here effectively fused.

The dramatist's freedom to change his form and language from play to play (the Picasso-like shift across the spectrum of styles) remains precarious. We recall certain costs: Shaw's eclecticism was inseparable from inadequately controlled style-shifts within hybrid forms; Eliot's search for the right dramatic language was over-strained ('the intolerable wrestle with words') and led, in the final comedies, to a diminished naturalism in verse; Osborne's restless shifts of style seem at times merely improvised. By contrast, the carefully limited yet systematic inner development of a language in Beckett's drama seems to be

3 Northrop Frye, *Anatomy of Criticism* (1957), New York, 1965, p. 133. We may find further confirmation of the way past theatrical genres (which include modes of language) become creative resources, in what has been seen as 'one of the salient characteristics of the newer British drama...revivification of forms of the past, reclaiming for serious attention techniques and genres which have fallen into disuse' (e.g. farce and melodrama). John Russell Taylor, *The Second Wave, British Drama for the Seventies*, London, 1971, p. 155.

4 Cf. Introduction, p. 2, where this phrase is qualified by the burden of language-consciousness.

free from misjudged choices, at the cost of a diminished 'external world'. But, whatever the balance of gain and loss, in the post-Beckett drama an increasing pluralism of styles is likely to prevail. This can be seen in the work of a number of contemporary English dramatists (not discussed in this study): Peter Nichols, David Storey and Edward Bond, among others. Bond, for example, has moved from the ultra-naturalistic dialogue of *Saved* (1966) to the stylised form and many-layered language of *Narrow Road to the Deep North* (1968) and *Lear* (1972), respectively using the Noh-play (as Yeats and Brecht did before Bond), and *King Lear* as imaginative points of departure. Bond's *Lear* also confirms what the 'imaginary museum' *can* do for the dramatist: it can release a creativity that interacts with the parent-play, and exploits both oblique affinities and correspondences.[5] And, as Eliot had hoped, the inhibiting imitation of Shakespearean tragedy in blank verse (the choice of so many nineteenth-century poets) has been replaced by a more open interaction between the old and the new in the play's vision, structure and language.

The fusion and flexibility of dramatic languages just stressed does not exclude the continued life of certain specialised or divergent modes of play-language. Rumours concerning the death of 'naturalism' have been – to adapt Mark Twain's remark concerning his own death – exaggerated. The autopsy itself sounds clear (for example: 'English realistic drama is characterised by halting prose and fumbling dialogue'[6]) but the patient refuses to accept it in this simple form. We need to distinguish at least two kinds of survival for naturalistically based dramatic dialogue. There is the relatively simple mirroring – or parody – of 'the way we speak now', as in the later plays of Osborne. This kind of dialogue does have a certain vitality; but its interest seems local or superficial partly because it is inadequately shaped or embodied in the structure of the whole play. (The local interest,

5 The 'licence' to give a character a simple metaphoric speech (e.g. Lear's 'There is a wall everywhere', III, 2) may be more effective than the attempt to expand imaginatively lines found in Shakespeare (e.g. 'Then let me anatomise Regan', *King Lear*, III, vi, 77 – turned into a short scene in *Lear* II, 6). See Edward Bond, *Lear*, London, 1972, p. 80 and pp. 58–9 respectively.

6 Robert Brustein, 'The Limits of English Realism', *The Observer* (11 Feb. 1973).

incidentally, sometimes goes with a specific language-consciousness, as in the concluding scene of *West of Suez* (1971) where Osborne offers us in Jed's violent, pseudo-revolutionary jargon, a simplified type of anti-language: a character verbally defecates on the dying English language, for 'words, yes I mean words, even what I'm saying to you now, is going to be the first to go'.[7])

The other offshoot of naturalism is a distillation, or a simplification, of the dialogue of minimal speech – the line from Chekhov to Pinter. To place it in this way is not to underestimate its value when we meet it in a play like David Storey's *Home* (1970), where the reduced dialogue, 'the meticulous notation of everyday speech'[8] with its evasions, uncertain clues, hints and guesses, cuts into an aspect of the human condition in a new and still moving way. The genteel and self-screening generalities in the speech of the male inmates, Harry and Jack, cumulatively reach an intensity (they mirror what E. M. Forster, in *Howards End*, called 'panic and emptiness'); and when the fading, euphemistic speech of the two old gentlemen is crossed by the rawly inquisitorial Cockney speech of the two women, the underlying pressures are gradually made clear.[9] It may be said, over-simply: here is a new play made out of an old dramatic language. More precisely, we get a modification – some conventions of verbal mimesis are re-shaped *for* one play, a unique play – and, surely, we cannot mean *that* by an exhausted language. We should say, rather, that wherever we find fragments of the 'living language' shaped and embodied with artistic coherence in a play, we also find a living mode of dramatic language.

Certain characteristics of an 'infolding' language – implicitness, playfulness, the comic–pathetic struggle for words – have been absorbed by several modes of dramatic language (including the

7 John Osborne, *West of Suez*, London, 1971, pp. 82–4. See also Ch. 5, nn. 10 and 23.

8 John Russell Taylor's phrase, in *The Second Wave*, p. 144.

9 David Storey, *Home* (1970), Harmondsworth, 1972, pp. 44–5, 62 or 71, for example. The general argument cannot be taken further here, but one could liken the cumulative power of 'shaping' on 'minimal speech' to Marlow's account of Kurtz's words: 'They were common everyday words... But what of that? They had behind them, to my mind, the terrific suggestiveness of words heard in dreams...' Joseph Conrad, *Heart of Darkness* (1902), Ch. III, London, 1967, p. 144.

kind of naturalism just discussed). And there now exists a wide audience that accepts – or even expects – a dramatic language that 'plays' with itself, cannot be 'fixed' in one setting, cannot be simply paraphrased or 'verified' on one level only. Some 'principle of uncertainty' may be an essential element in what makes a particular speech or dialogue dramatic. In this way the contemporary equivalents of the Jacobean feeling for words, for complex verbal patterns – in short, for a 'poetic' complexity in language – have been brought into play again. This can be said, even if we remain aware of the risks: mannerism, banality, the clichés of 'non-communication', the involutions of a language-mirroring language.

Beckett's short play *Not I* (1973) seems to offer an implicit epilogue to the 'drama of speech' both in vision and in language. And it demonstrates, once more, the dramatic values of the solipsistic monologue and of stylistic compression.

The Mouth had been 'practically speechless' all her days; yet suddenly, and incomprehensibly to the consciousness behind those lips:

> Words were coming...imagine!...words were coming...a voice she did not recognise...at first...so long since it sounded...then finally had to admit...could be none other...than her own...certain vowel sounds...she had never heard...elsewhere...[10]

There follows an incessant stream of words – still fragmented and barely comprehended – and in old age (approaching seventy) the speaker seems to be on the threshold of some precarious verbal epiphany. The Mouth is 'straining to hear...the odd word' (like 'God is love') amid uncertain yet unmistakable signs ('the buzzing'; 'the dull roar in the skull'; 'the sudden flash'). It is as if, against all the odds, there was 'something she had to tell...could that be it?...something that would tell...how it was...how she...what?...had been?'. And this sudden urge to speak does not seem to be cancelled out by the contrary fragments that assert, through that Mouth: 'nothing she could tell...'.

This parable of language is only one pattern in the closely woven texture of the play. The stylistic features in that texture

10 Samuel Beckett, *Not I*, London, 1973, p. 10. All further quotations are from this text, primarily from pp. 13–14.

seem to recombine features we recognise from earlier works of Beckett: the broken yet urgent rhythms, words-to-breathing; the spare diction with a flicker of lyrical phrases ('and a ray of light came and went...such as the moon might cast...drifting ...in and out of cloud'); the elegant clichés of the 'old style' ('should she feel so inclined'; 'lest it elude her'; 'tender mercies'; 'new every morning'); the *leitmotifs*, the carefully placed repetitions to establish inner connections in the rapid movement (as in *Lessness*, but, as befits a play, in a more natural, less rigorously schematised way), and, in total effect, an elliptical coherence, a constant suggestion of the unspoken, the 'unspeakable' arc of utterance.

The still-increasing flexibility of modes of language in drama – the wider spectrum, the inner complexity – calls for a correspondingly flexible or pluralistic body of criticism. We need, and to some extent already have, a criticism that can adjust its 'speculative instruments', change its focus and even its critical language to do justice to this or that play-language. We need, further, what we still do not have: more *correlation* between different approaches, criteria and methods relevant to the study of dramatic language. I should like now to discuss, briefly, some of the problems and aims of such correlation in the still relatively underdeveloped criticism of dramatic language.[11]

The first sustained criticism of language in modern drama, Raymond Williams' *Drama from Ibsen to Eliot* (1952), appeared before the polar opposites of Brecht and Beckett had given us a new spectrum, before 'the expansion of dramatic action and

[11] A recent critical anthology, *20th Century Literary Criticism* (ed. David Lodge), London, 1972, includes much less on drama than on any other 'literary form of topic'. Further, some of the most far-reaching studies of drama – e.g. Francis Fergusson's neo-Aristotelian, action-centred *The Idea of a Theater* (1949) – barely attempt to discuss dramatic language. Out of nearly a hundred critical works I have read on drama in recent years, only a dozen or so had anything to say on dramatic language. By coincidence, three major studies appeared after the completion of my work (all late in 1972): John Russell Brown's *Theatre Language*, Ruby Cohn's *Dialogue in American Drama*, and, reaching me the day I concluded this Conclusion, Pierre Larthomas' *Le Langage dramatique*. It is exhilarating to discover simultaneous work in three countries, but their approaches are, necessarily, un-correlated, and only the third book deals with critical method. (See Bibliography I.)

speech to a more vital and extended human range'.[12] This gave the book a distorted perspective, which Raymond Williams has, in valuable revisions and additions, attempted to correct (no longer seeing verse drama as 'the main revolt against naturalism', among other things). Yet, in all the mutations of his criticism Williams seems not to have taken any further the critical method of the original book, where most relevant to the study of dramatic language: 'a working experiment in the application of practical criticism methods to modern dramatic literature'.[13] (If anything, his later preoccupation with the 'structure of feeling' and the social context of drama goes with reduced attention to language as an element in drama.)

Williams' application of *practical criticism* to modern drama was innovatory and often powerful. Yet it also showed up some of the limitations of practical criticism when dealing with dialogue in large-scale and complex works. One limitation is the presence of too much 'rhetoric' and too little 'stylistics' in that criticism. (At one point, in the chapter on Shaw, there is a jump from *Candida* (1894) to *Back to Methuselah* (1921), which ignores all the intervening plays – the crucial parable-comedies – and leads on to an extended judgement on Shaw's immature sense of life and art. And though this value-judgement on Shaw's sensibility is supported by quotation from the dialogue, the texture of the dialogue is left unexamined. (There is, admittedly, a linguistic joke linking Shaw's He- and She-Ancients with goats by way of the pronoun prefix.) There would be no point in recalling, at this stage, such a limitation – with a local and 'loaded' example – if it did not illustrate a risk that persists: the risk of a divorce between 'moral' and 'stylistic' criteria in the precarious marriage we call practical criticism. In Williams, the primary pull tends to be 'moral'; but that does not mean that giving in to the contrary pull (if it is to end up with patient donkeywork on Shaw's pronoun prefixes alone) would solve the critical difficulty.

The marriage of large concern and precise method in the study of dramatic language remains precarious. Indeed, taking a general

12 Quoted from the revised edition, Harmondsworth, 1964, p. 303. This edition (with its new Conclusion), *Drama from Ibsen to Brecht* (1968), and other works are included in my reference to revisions and additions.

13 *Ibid*. p. 14.

view, increasingly specialised methods of description bring the risk of a final divorce from interpretation and evaluation. In the criticism of drama it is sometimes difficult even to find room for adequate quotation and analysis of speech and dialogue within larger and value-bearing contexts. It is difficult to devise critical optics which can keep a sharp enough focus on the *contexts* of the dialogue while its *texture* is being examined under a magnifying glass. The one-dimensional page of small-scale criticism must simulate the other dimensions in the 'theatre of the mind': the whole action must be felt in the interaction of pauses or the effect of dots and dashes in the dialogue...[14]

What advance there has been in the study of dramatic language, in the twenty years since Raymond Williams' book appeared, has been more a matter of learning from the new dramatists than a crystallisation of new critical approaches and methods. Perhaps this is as it should be: the critical language as it were mirrors the new dramatic language. And the right kind of response may carry with it an extension or refinement of method. It is possible to approximate such conditions, and still live in a world where criteria and methods remain unrelated, keep springing up in fertile multiplicity. Perhaps that too is a sign of health (we may even congratulate ourselves on now having a museum of criticism to correspond with the *musée imaginaire*). Yet, I think, the effort towards synthesis, a more commonly shared notation in the criticism of dramatic language, will have to be made.

The attempt to 'stiffen' practical criticism with linguistically informed analysis of style seems one promising direction. But what methods are relevant? The conceptual difficulties of bringing together linguistic and literary criticism have become part of a central debate,[15] and need not be rehearsed here. But it seems to me clear just why linguistic critics have, so far, made such

14 For studies of the effect of pauses and punctuation in dialogue, see, respectively, Martin Esslin, *The Peopled Wound, The Plays of Harold Pinter*, London, 1970, pp. 220ff., and J. D. Dawick, '"Punctuation" and Patterning in *The Homecoming*', *Modern Drama* (May 1971).

15 See, for example, the exchange between Roger Fowler and F. W. Bateson in *Essays in Criticism*, XVII (July 1967) and XVIII (April 1968), reprinted in Roger Fowler, *The Languages of Literature*, London, 1971, pp. 43–79. The term verbal analysis is one used by Mr Fowler.

George Steiner's 'Linguistics and Poetics' in *Extraterritorial*, London, 1972, pp. 126–54, offers an imaginative discussion.

a slight contribution to the study of dramatic language, and why, in revenge (as the French say), the critics of drama have not made more use of precise *verbal analysis*. It is not simply that the latter tends to be too microscopic to be used extensively, or too little concerned with aesthetic and human values to be used exclusively. The subtle context of dramatic speech itself eludes those who only record 'linguistic features'. One may quote one typical programme, which would seem to turn its back on dramatic speech altogether:

> a particular message is used in two different situations. A beggar wanting something to eat and a child who wants to postpone going to bed at night both say 'I'm hungry'. Is the difference in situation sufficient to establish a difference of style? We think not. The style of a message will be described in terms of the relations of the linguistic features to one another, not in terms of the relations of linguistic features to non-linguistic features, so that questions of truth, intention, etc., will fall in a different area of literary analysis. Just as a particular message has a variety of performances, so on the other hand it has a variety of *interpretations*. Both seem to lie beyond stylistics in this admittedly limited conception of what constitutes style.[16]

But the phrase 'I'm hungry' – if we do not consider who says it, how it is said, to whom (if not in soliloquy), with what effect on the listener in the moment and in the total sequence of responses – is not dramatic language at all. For instance, when we hear or read Lear's words:

> I will have such revenges on you both,
> That all the world shall – I will do such things, –
> What they are, yet I know not; but they shall be
> The terrors of the earth (*King Lear* II, iv)

how much does a notation of linguistic features contribute to our understanding? We note, quickly, the 'ungrammatical' syntax of the second line, standing in contrast with – underscored by – Lear's otherwise still grammatical speech (his repeated use of will/shall, for example). Does this help? A little. It reinforces our understanding of the immediate context: Lear approaches

16 Sol Saporta, 'The Application of Linguistics to the Study of Poetic Language', in *Style and Language* (ed. Thomas E. Seboek), Cambridge, Mass., 1960, pp. 88–9.

his first breaking point, the daughters make no reply, and his threat is not acted on (is never acted on in the full context). Thus syntax and rhythm, situation and the speaker's dramatic posture, all interact in the rhetoric and pathos of Lear's unfulfillable threat to the universe. But, clearly, this still needs to be connected with all the large contexts – actional and symbolic – including the whole gamut of Lear's threats against the daughters/the universe, the interplay of microcosm/macrocosm in those threats, and so on.

One concludes, once more, that verbal analysis can make a contribution, but only a limited one – chiefly in testing and reinforcing through exact notation – to the study of dramatic language. The real task is to make the linguistic account 'tally' with all the other accounts: to show the interplay of structures within our text. My own account of Lucky's aphasiac speech in several contexts – the rundown of language and the efficacy of pathological speech, in the play, in Beckett's whole work, in our whole culture – was, it now seems, an attempt at such 'tallying'. Perhaps this was an unwitting exercise in 'structuralist' criticism. But it was only later that I came to see, in the teeth of sceptical reading, that *structuralism* – identifying all the 'structures' or 'codes' in the text, like peeling off the layers of an onion – may be offering some of the integrating methods that we need. (It is probably a historical accident – the close connection with the *nouveau roman* – that structuralism has contributed very little to the study of drama so far.[17]) There are at least three aspects of structuralism that seem relevant to the study of dramatic language. First, it promises a method for studying the hidden mimetic powers of words by showing the way the two 'axes' of language – syntactic or combining, and associative or selective powers – interact.[18] At the very least, critical accounts of dramatic speech must attend to the energies

17 But see Stephen Booth, 'On the Value of *Hamlet*', in *Reinterpretations of Elizabethan Drama* (ed. Norman Rabkin), New York and London, 1969.

18 My definition is deliberately simplified for the present purpose. A brief and valuable critical discussion of *selection/combination* – linking I. A. Richards' *The Philosophy of Rhetoric* (1936) and Roman Jakobson's 'Two Aspects of Language'... (1956) – can be found in W. K. Wimsatt, 'Battering the Object: The Ontological Approach', in *Contemporary Criticism* (ed. Malcolm Bradbury and David Palmer), London, 1970, pp. 76ff.

of syntax, and not merely to 'diction' or 'imagery'. Secondly, it promises a method for seeing the old text woven into the new text – the quotations, the layered writing – as though it were a palimpsest (an aspect of language we studied in Beckett, and discussed in connection with parody, pastiche, and theatrical collage). Thirdly, on the level of aesthetic theory, it promises to help us out of the long hangover of thinking dualistically, in terms of representation/expression. The invitation to concentrate on the multiple layers of a text is at least congenial to those who attempt to think through a spectrum of styles, beyond certain historical polarities (naturalism/symbolism for example).

There is another aspect of dramatic language that needs to be studied: the interaction between 'everyday' and 'literary', the spoken and the written language. The whole question of 'shaping' in dialogue is involved here: how do fragments of utterance fit into a dramatist's grammar? Roland Barthes remarked, at a recent symposium on literary style: 'the opposition of speech and writing has never been completely clarified'.[19] He sees the opposition inherent in both philosophy (different ontologies of speech and writing) and in linguistics (it has a lot to say about sentences, but little about 'subsentence' language). Whoever comes to study dramatic language will meet this 'opposition' everywhere: from the opening lines of *Hamlet* to the broken speech-flow of the Mouth in Beckett's *Not I*.

We need, further, a more precise notation for 'language as gesture' (to use R. P. Blackmur's phrase). We know that dramatic dialogue works through various implicit codes that signal this or that gesture, changing tone, tempo, all the qualities of enactment; and there exist some good studies of gesture and movement, for example by J. L. Styan and John Russell Brown.[20] There may be further promise in studying the complete triad of the 'speech-act': the words uttered, the frame of utterance (asking, asserting, promising, and so on), and the effect of the utterance on the hearer in the play. (Richard Ohmann's application of a model

19 Roland Barthes, 'Style and its Image', in *Literary Style, A Symposium* (ed. Seymour Chatman), London and New York, 1971 (quoted from p. 7).

20 J. L. Styan, *The Elements of Drama* (1960), Cambridge, 1967, Ch. 2. John Russell Brown, *Theatre Language*, London, 1972, Ch. 2 (drawing on Rudolf Laban's exercises for actors, in relation to Pinter).

taken from linguistic philosophy – in particular Austin's illocutionary action, which corresponds to what I call the 'frame' of utterance – is exactly what one means by promise; yet, so far, it has done nothing that cannot be as well, or better, done by approaches less ambitious in terminology.[21])

The attempt to correlate the study of dramatic language will, then, need to remain open to approaches from several disciplines. It should be envisaged as a work of gradual clarification through constant critical dialogue. The growing currency of the word 'dialogue', in its extended sense of attempting communication, reaching out towards consensus, fits in with the desired openness. Anyone studying the verbal dialogue of drama knows that a larger and continuous dialogue – between the 'work' and the 'audience' – surrounds it. Criticism, in turn, enters and may become part of that other, continuous dialogue. 'The semantic or linguistic nature of literature', argues Malcolm Bradbury,[22] 'its character as discourse, can still be emphasised, but its structure and form can be taken as aspects of the communal or social structure of language as a species of ordering and perceiving.' We must study not only the internal energies of dramatic language, but also its relation to *all* language, whose fitness (including fitness in art) is one of the shared concerns of our larger dialogue.

In the Ardens' morality play *The Island of the Mighty*[23] there is an ironic scene (Part II, Scene 2) in which Arthur discovers, from a wordless grin and a look of outrage, that two blindfolded English prisoners understand his dying tongue. Like Arthur's empire, the verbal arts are in decline – Merlin is corrupt, another Chief Poet is ungrammatical, all the chief poets are old, their 'Bones and brains complain'. But Arthur derives some comfort from the signs of verbal understanding witnessed: 'It is possible our civilisation does not lapse into complete savagery quite as rapidly as I feared.'

21 Richard Ohmann, 'Speech, Action and Style', in *Literary Style*, pp. 241–54, especially concluding section. (Ohmann is to develop this approach in a forthcoming book, *Philosophy and Rhetoric*.)

22 Introduction to *Contemporary Criticism*, p. 32. (My context.)

23 John Arden with Margaretta D'Arcy, *The Island of the Mighty, A Play on a Traditional British Theme in Three Parts* (text first published in *Plays and Players*, Feb. 1973 – main quotation from p. xviii).

Bibliography

I. DRAMA AND DRAMATIC THEORY

Abel, Lionel, *Metatheatre*, Hill and Wang, New York, 1963.
Archer, William, *The Old Drama and the New*, Heinemann, London, 1923.
Aristotle, *Poetics* (see Butcher).
Armstrong, William A. (ed.), *Experimental Drama*, Bell, London, 1963.
Artaud, Antonin, *Le Théâtre et son double* (1938), Gallimard (Idées), Paris, 1964.
Bentley, Eric, *The Playwright as Thinker* (1946), Meridian Books, New York, 1955.
The Life of the Drama, Methuen, London, 1965.
(ed.), *The Theory of the Modern Stage*, Penguin Books, 1968.
Bethell, S. L., *Shakespeare and the Popular Dramatic Tradition*, King and Staples, London, 1944.
Block, Haskell M., *Mallarmé and the Symbolist Drama*, Wayne State University Press, Detroit, 1963.
Bradbrook, M. C., *English Dramatic Form*, Chatto and Windus, London, 1968.
Brecht, Bertolt, *Brecht on Theatre*, Methuen, London, 1964.
Kleines Organon für das Theater (1948), Suhrkamp, Berlin, 1953 (cf. also Ronald Gray).
The Messingkauf Dialogues (transl. John Willett), Methuen, London, 1965.
Brook, Peter, *The Empty Space*, MacGibbon and Kee, London, 1968.
Brown, John Russell (ed.), *Modern British Dramatists* ('Twentieth Century Views'), Prentice Hall, Englewood Cliffs, New Jersey, 1968.
Theatre Language – a Study of Arden, Osborne, Pinter and Wesker, Allen Lane, The Penguin Press, London, 1972.
Brustein, Robert, *The Theater of Revolt*, Little, Brown, Boston, 1964.
Butcher, S. H., *Aristotle's Theory of Poetry and Fine Art* (1895), Macmillan, London, 1907.

Calderwood, James L., and Toliver, H. E. (ed.), *Perspectives on Drama*, Oxford University Press, New York, 1968.
Clark, Barrett H., *European Theories of the Drama*, Appleton, New York, 1929.
Cohn, Ruby, *Dialogue in American Drama*, Indiana University Press, Bloomington, 1971.
Cole, Toby (ed.), *Playwrights on Playwriting*, MacGibbon and Kee, London, 1960.
Cornford, F. M., *The Origin of Attic Comedy*, Arnold, London, 1914.
Craig, Gordon, *On the Art of the Theatre*, Heinemann, London, 1911.
Dawson, S. W., *Drama and the Dramatic*, Methuen, London, 1970.
Donoghue, Denis, *The Third Voice: Modern British and American Verse Drama*, Princeton University Press, 1959.
Edel, Leon, *Henry James: Les années dramatiques*, Jouve, Paris, 1931.
Introduction to *The Complete Plays of Henry James*, Rupert Hart-Davis, London, 1949.
Introduction to Henry James: *Guy Domville*, Rupert Hart-Davis, London, 1960.
Ellis-Fermor, Una, *The Frontiers of Drama* (1945), Methuen, London, 1964.
Else, G. F., *The Origin and Early Form of Greek Tragedy*, Harvard University Press, 1965
Esslin, Martin, *The Theatre of the Absurd* (revised and enlarged ed.), Penguin Books, 1968.
Fergusson, Francis, *The Idea of a Theater* (1949), Doubleday, New York, 1953.
Gascoigne, Bamber, *Twentieth Century Drama*, Hutchinson, London, 1962.
Gaskell, Ronald, *Drama and Reality*, Routledge and Kegan Paul, London, 1971.
Gassner, John, *Directions in Modern Theater and Drama*, Holt, Rinehart and Winston, New York, 1965 (expanded ed. of *Form and Idea in the Modern Theater*, 1956).
Gray, Ronald, *Brecht* ('Writers and Critics'), Oliver and Boyd, Edinburgh and London, 1961.
Hahnloser-Ingold, Margrit, *Das englische Theater und Bertold Brecht*, Francke, Bern, 1970.
Hoy, Cyrus, *The Hyacinth Room*, Chatto and Windus, London, 1964.
Ionesco, Eugène, *Notes et contre-notes*, Gallimard, Paris, 1962.
Kershaw, John, *The Present Stage*, Fontana, London, 1966.
Kesting, Marianne, *Bertolt Brecht: Dargestellt in Selbstzeugnissen und Bild-dokumenten*, Rowohlt, Hamburg, 1959.
Kitchin, Laurence, *Drama in the Sixties*, Faber, London, 1966.
Mid-Century Theatre, Faber, London, 1960.
Kitto, H. D. F., *Greek Tragedy, a Literary Study* (1939), Methuen, London, 1961.
Kott, Jan, *Shakespeare our Contemporary*, Methuen, London, 1965.
Krutch, Joseph Wood, *'Modernism' in Modern Drama* (1953), Cornell University Press, 1966.
Langer, Suzanne K., *Feeling and Form* (Ch. 17), Routledge and Kegan Paul, London, 1959.

Lessing, Gotthold E., *Hamburg Dramaturgy* (transl. H. Zimmern), Dover Publications, New York, 1962.
Lumley, Frederick, *New Trends in 20th Century Drama: A Survey since Ibsen and Shaw* (3rd revised ed.), Barrie and Jenkins, London, 1972.
McCarthy, Mary, *Sights and Spectacles 1937–1958*, Heinemann, London, 1959.
Magarshack, David, *Chekhov the Dramatist*, Hill and Wang, New York, 1960.
Marowitz, Charles, Milne, Tom and Hale, Owen (ed.), *The Encore Reader*, Methuen, London, 1965.
Nicoll, Allardyce, *The Theatre and Dramatic Theory*, Harrap, London, 1962.
Nietzsche, Friedrich, *Die Geburt der Tragödie aus dem Geiste der Musik* (1872), *Werke*, München Hanser, vol. 1 (no date).
Northam, John R., *Ibsen's Dramatic Method, a Study of the Prose Drama*, Faber, London, 1953.
Peacock, Ronald, *The Art of Drama*, Routledge and Kegan Paul, London, 1957.
The Poet in the Theatre (1946), MacGibbon and Kee, London, 1961.
Righter, Anne, *Shakespeare and the Idea of the Play*, Chatto and Windus, London, 1962.
Stanislavski, Constantin, *Building a Character* (transl. E. R. Hapwood), Reinhardt and Evans, London, 1949.
My Life in Art (transl. J. J. Robbins), Penguin Books, 1967.
Stein, Walter, 'Drama', in *The Twentieth Century Mind* (ed. C. B. Cox and A. E. Dyson), vol. 2, Oxford University Press, 1972.
Steiner, George, *The Death of Tragedy*, Faber and Faber, London, 1961.
Styan, J. L., *The Dark Comedy*, Cambridge University Press, 1962.
The Elements of Drama (1960), Cambridge University Press, 1967.
Taylor, John Russell, *Anger and After: a Guide to the New British Drama* (1962), 2nd revised ed., Methuen, London, 1969.
The Second Wave, British Drama for the Seventies, Methuen, London, 1971.
Tynan, Kenneth, *Curtains*, Longman, London, 1961.
Van Laan, Thomas F., *The Idiom of Drama*, Cornell University Press, 1970.
Watling, E. F., Introduction to *Electra and Other Plays*, Penguin Books, 1953.
Wellwarth, George E., *The Theatre of Protest and Paradox*, MacGibbon and Kee, London, 1965.
Whiting, John, *On Theatre*, London Magazine, 1966.
Wickham, Glynne, *Drama in a World of Science*, Routledge and Kegan Paul, London, 1962.
Williams, Raymond, *Drama from Ibsen to Eliot* (1952), revised ed., Penguin Books, 1964.
Drama from Ibsen to Brecht (expanded and extensively revised ed. of the above), Chatto and Windus, London, 1968.
Drama in Performance, C. A. Watts, London, 1968 (new ed.).
Modern Tragedy, Chatto and Windus, London, 1966.
Yeats, W. B., *Autobiographies*, Macmillan, London, 1955.
Essays and Introductions, Macmillan, London, 1961.
Explorations, Macmillan, London, 1962.
Selected Criticism, ed. by A. Norman Jeffares, Macmillan, London, 1964.

BIBLIOGRAPHY

SPECIAL ISSUES, COLLECTIONS OF ESSAYS

Contemporary Theatre (Stratford-upon-Avon Studies no. 4), ed. John Russell Brown and Bernard Harris, Edward Arnold, London, 1962.
Modern British Dramatists ('Twentieth Century Views'), ed. John Russell Brown, Englewood Cliffs, New Jersey, 1968.
Modern Drama, vol. 11, no. 3 (December 1968).
Tulane Drama Review, vol. 11, no. 2 (Winter 1966).
Twentieth Century, vol. 169, no. 1008 (February 1961).

ARTICLES NOT INCLUDED UNDER OTHER TITLES

Barish, Jonas A., 'Exhibitionism and the Anti-Theatrical Prejudice', *ELH, A Journal of English Literary History*, vol. 36, no. 1 (March 1969).
Brown, John Russell, 'Dialogue in Pinter and Others', *Critical Quarterly*, vol. 7, no. 3 (Autumn 1965).
Davison, Peter, 'Contemporary Drama and Popular Dramatic Forms', in *Aspects of Drama and the Theatre*, Sydney University Press, 1965, pp. 143–97.
Fry, Christopher, 'A Playwright Speaks', *The Listener*, 23 February 1950.
Frye, Northrop, 'A Conspectus of Dramatic Genres', *Kenyon Review*, vol. XIII (Autumn 1951).
Knight, G. Wilson, 'The Kitchen Sink', *Encounter*, vol. XXI, no. 6 (December 1963).
Lukács, Georg, 'Theatre and Environment', *The Times Literary Supplement*, 23 April 1964.
Rahv, Philip, 'Notes on the Decline of Naturalism', *Perspectives*, no. 2 (Winter 1953).
Reid, Douglas, 'The Failure of English Realism', *Tulane Drama Review*, vol. 7, no. 2 (Winter 1962).

STUDIES IN DRAMATIC LANGUAGE

(Where these are sections of books listed above only short titles are given)

Bentley, Eric, *The Life of the Drama*, Ch. 3.
*Brown, John Russell, *Theatre Language*, Ch. 1 especially.
Calderwood, J. L. and Toliver, H. E., *Perspectives on Drama*, pp. 337–86.
*Cohn, Ruby, *Dialogue in American Drama*, Indiana University Press, 1971.
Dawson, S. W., *Drama and the Dramatic*, Ch. 2.
Donoghue, Denis, *The Third Voice* (final chapter on 'Theatre Poetry').
Ewbank, Inga-Stina, 'Ibsen's Dramatic Language as a Link between his "Realism" and "Symbolism"'; 'Ibsen and "the far more difficult art of prose"', respectively in *Contemporary Approaches to Ibsen*, I and II, Universitetsforlaget, Oslo, 1966 and 1971.
Gascoigne, Bamber, *Twentieth Century Drama*, Ch. 5, 6 and 7.
Hawkes, Terence, *Shakespeare's Talking Animals, Language and Drama in Society*, Arnold, London, 1973.

* Published after the completion of this study.

*Larthomas, Pierre, *Le Langage dramatique*, Colin, Paris, 1972.
Nicoll, Allardyce, *The Theatre and Dramatic Theory*, Ch. 6.
Peacock, Ronald, *The Art of Drama*, Ch. 10.
Smith, R. D., 'Back to the Text', in *Contemporary Theatre*, Ch. 6.
Styan, J. L., *The Elements of Drama*, Ch. 1 and 2.
Van Laan, T. F., *The Idiom of Drama*, Ch. 1 and 5.
Vannier, Jean, 'A Theatre of Language', *Tulane Drama Review*, vol. 7, no. 3, Spring 1963.
Wardle, Irving, 'An Ear for English', *New Society*, 24 August 1967.

II. LINGUISTICS, STYLISTICS AND PHILOSOPHY OF LANGUAGE

GENERAL LINGUISTICS AND THE ENGLISH LANGUAGE

Barber, Charles, *Linguistic Change in Present-day English*, London, 1969.
Bernstein, Basil and Edge, David, 'The Role of Language', *The Listener*, 7 April 1966, pp. 501–3.
Bolton, W. F., and Crystal, D., *The English Language*, vol. 2, *Essays by Linguists and Men of Letters, 1858–1964*, Cambridge University Press, 1969.
Chomsky, Noam, *Language and Mind*, Harcourt Brace, New York, 1968.
Crystal, David, and Davy, Derek, *Investigating English Style*, Longman, London, 1969.
Lyons, John, *Chomsky*, Fontana, London, 1970.
Introduction to Theoretical Linguistics, Cambridge University Press, 1968.
Partridge, Eric, *A Dictionary of Clichés with an Introductory Essay*, 4th ed., Routledge and Kegan Paul, London, 1962.
Quirk, Randolph, *The Use of English*, Longman, London, 1962.

STYLISTICS AND THE LANGUAGE OF LITERATURE

Auerbach, Erich, *Mimesis*, Francke, Bern, 1946.
Barthes, Roland, 'Criticism as Language', *The Times Literary Supplement*, 27 September 1963.
'Style and its Language', in *Literary Style: A Symposium* (ed. S. Chatman), Oxford University Press, 1971.
Writing Degree Zero (1953) (transl. A. Lavers and C. Smith), Jonathan Cape, London, 1967.
Bateson, F. W., Replies to Roger Fowler's articles on 'Literature and Linguistics' and 'Language and Literature' (see under Fowler).
Blackmur, R. P., *Language as Gesture*, Allen and Unwin, London, 1954.
Brooke-Rose, Christine, *A Grammar of Metaphor*, Secker and Warburg, London, 1958.
Burke, Kenneth, *A Grammar of Motives and A Rhetoric of Motives* (1945, 1950), Meridian Books, New York, 1962.
Language as Symbolic Action, Berkeley, 1966.
Enkvist, N. E., Spencer, J., and Gregory, J., *Linguistics and Style*, Oxford University Press, 1962.

* Published after the completion of this study.

Fowler, Roger, *The Languages of Literature*, Routledge and Kegan Paul, London, 1971. (See also Bateson, F. W.)
Hough, Graham, *Style and Stylistics*, Routledge and Kegan Paul, 1969.
Jakobson, Roman, 'The Metaphoric and Metonymic Poles', in *Fundamentals of Language*, Mouton, Hague, 1956.
Levin, Samuel R., 'Poetry and Grammaticalness', in *Essays on the Language of Literature* (ed. S. Chatman and S. R. Levin), Mifflin, Boston, 1967.
Lodge, David, *Language of Fiction*, Routledge and Kegan Paul, London, 1962.
Richards, I. A., *The Philosophy of Rhetoric*, Oxford University Press, 1936.
So Much Nearer, Harcourt Brace, New York, 1968.
Riffaterre, Michael, 'Criteria of Style Analysis', *Word*, vol. 15, no. 4 (1959).
'Stylistic Context', *Word*, vol. 16, no. 2 (1960).
Seboek, Thomas A. (ed.), *Style and Language*, M.I.T. Press, Cambridge, Mass., 1960; especially the opening statement by I. A. Richards, the concluding statement by Roman Jakobson, and Sol Saporta's contribution.
Ullmann, Stephen, *Language and Style*, Blackwell, Oxford, 1964.
'Style and Personality', *Review of English Literature*, no. 6 (April 1965), pp. 21–31.
Watson, George (ed.), *Literary English since Shakespeare*, Oxford University Press, 1970.
Wellek, René and Warren, Austin, 'Style and Stylistics', Ch. 14 in *Theory of Literature* (1949), 3rd ed., Penguin Books, 1963.
Williams, C. B., *Style and Vocabulary, Numerical Studies*, Griffin, London, 1970.

PHILOSOPHY OF LANGUAGE

Alston, William P., *Philosophy of Language*, Prentice-Hall, Englewood Cliffs, New Jersey, 1964.
Austin, J. L., *How to Do Things with words*, Oxford, 1971.
Ayer, A. J., 'Can there be a Private Language?' – chapter in *Wittgenstein, The Philosophical Investigations* (ed. G. Pitcher), Macmillan, London, 1968.
Cassirer, Ernst, *Language and Myth*, New York, 1945.
Hampshire, Stuart, 'Vico and Language', *The New York Review of Books*, Feb. 13 1969, pp. 19ff.
Gellner, Ernest, *Words and Things*, Gollancz, London, 1959.
Pears, D. F., 'The Development of Wittgenstein's Philosophy', *New York Review of Books*, 16 Jan. 1969.
Wittgenstein, Fontana, London, 1971.
Russell, Bertrand, *An Inquiry into Meaning and Truth*, Allen and Unwin, London, 1940.
Vico, Giambattista, *The New Science* (1744), Anchor Books, New York, 1961.
Warnock, Geoffrey, 'Talks to Bryan Magee about G. E. Moore, J. L. Austin, and the relationship between them', *The Listener*, 14 Jan. 1971.
Weiler, Gerschon, *Mauthner's Critique of Language*, Cambridge, 1970.
Wittgenstein, Ludwig, *Tractatus Logico-Philosophicus* (1921), Routledge and Kegan Paul, London, 1961.
Philosophical Investigations, Blackwell, Oxford, 1953.

III. SHAW

PLAYS AND PREFACES

For reasons of convenience the fifteen volumes of the Penguin Shaw were used for the plays and prefaces available in that edition (18 full-length and 12 one-act plays). Where reference is made to this edition the date is always given.

Back to Methuselah, World's Classics edition (1945) with the revised Preface and Postscript.

The Standard Edition (Constable) was used for all the other plays.

SHAW'S CRITICAL WRITINGS

Our Theatres in the Nineties, three volumes in the Standard Edition.
Major Critical Essays (including the 1913 additions to *Quintessence of Ibsenism*), Standard Edition.
Shaw on Theatre (ed. E. J. West), MacGibbon and Kee, London, 1958.

PREFACES AND OTHER WORKS BY SHAW

The Complete Prefaces, Paul Hamlyn, London, 1965.
Preface to *Three Plays by Brieux*, Fifield, London, 1911.
Shaw on Shakespeare (ed. Edwin Wilson), Cassell, London, 1962 (now also published by Penguin Books).
Preface to *The Miraculous Birth of Language*, by Richard A. Wilson, Dent, London, 1942.
Shaw on Language (ed. Abraham Tauber and Sir James Pitman), Peter Owen, London, 1965.
'A Plea for Speech Nationalisation', *Morning Leader*, 16 August 1901, reprinted in W. F. Bolton and D. Crystal, *The English Language*, vol. 2, *Essays by Linguists and Men of Letters 1858–1964*, Cambridge University Press, 1969, pp. 80–5.

NOTE: Shaw's writings on language were found to be of relatively marginal interest for this study (so much of his energy went into spelling reform). The links between his linguistic ideology and dialect speech is summarised in note 34; his advocacy of pidgin English (ironic against Shaw's elaborate syntax and diction) is in the Preface to *The Miraculous Birth of Language*, pp. xx–xxi.

CRITICAL STUDIES

Adams, Elsie B., 'Bernard Shaw's Pre-Raphaelite Drama', *P.M.L.A.*, vol. LXXX (1966), pp. 428–38.
Barnes, T. R., 'Shaw and the London Theatre', in Boris Ford (ed.), *The Pelican Guide to English Literature*, vol. 7, *The Modern Age*, Penguin Books, 1961.
Bentley, Eric, *Bernard Shaw* (1947), Hale, London, 1950, and Methuen, London, 1967.

Crompton, Louis, *Shaw the Dramatist* (1969), Allen and Unwin, London, 1971.
Gibbs, A. M. *Shaw* ('Writers and Critics'), Oliver and Boyd, Edinburgh and London, 1969. (Contains a good bibliography of critical works.)
Jones, A. R., 'George Bernard Shaw', in *Contemporary Drama* (Stratford-upon-Avon Studies no. 4), Edward Arnold, London, 1962.
Kaufmann, R. J. (ed.), *G. B. Shaw, A Collection of Critical Essays* ('Twentieth Century Views'), Englewood Cliffs, New Jersey, 1965.
MacCarthy, Desmond, *Shaw*, MacGibbon and Kee, Prentice Hall, London, 1951.
Mayne, Fred, *The Wit and Satire of Bernard Shaw*, Edward Arnold, London, 1967.
Meisel, Martin, *Shaw and the Nineteenth-Century Theater*, Princeton University Press, 1963.
*Morgan, Margery M., *The Shavian Playground. An Exploration of the Art of George Bernard Shaw*, Methuen, London, 1972.
Ohmann, Richard M., *Shaw: the Style and the Man*, Wesleyan University Press, 1963.
Sidnell, M. J., '*John Bull's Other Island* – Yeats and Shaw', *Modern Drama*, vol. 11, no. 3 (December 1968).
Wilson, Edmund, 'Bernard Shaw at Eighty', in *The Triple Thinkers* (1938), Penguin Books, 1962.

BIOGRAPHICAL

Smith, J. Percy, *The Unrepentant Pilgrim*, Gollancz, London, 1966.

IV. ELIOT

THE PLAYS

Sweeney Agonistes and the Choruses from *The Rock* in *Collected Poems, 1909–35.*

Murder in the Cathedral, 4th edition, Faber, London, 1938, and 'Educational Edition' with an introduction and notes by Nevill Coghill, Faber, London, 1962.

All page references to the four later plays are, for convenience, to *Collected Plays*, Faber, London, 1962.

ELIOT'S CRITICISM

(In the text references are to individual essays as well as to volumes.)

After Strange Gods, Faber, London, 1934.
On Poetry and Poets, Faber, London, 1957.
The Sacred Wood (1920), 7th ed., Methuen, London, 1950. – 'The Possibility of a Poetic Drama'.
Selected Essays, 3rd enlarged ed., Faber, London, 1951.

* Published after the completion of this study.

Selected Prose, Penguin Books, 1953. (Though this selection contains nothing not found elsewhere, it highlights critical points, and has been used for double reference on occasions.)

The Use of Poetry and the Use of Criticism, 2nd ed., Faber, London, 1964. (Particularly the Conclusion, with the essential statement on drama, pp. 153–5.)

Articles and Introductions, etc.

'The Aims of Poetic Drama', *Adam*, no. 200, November 1949, pp. 10–16.

'The Beating of a Drum', *The Nation and the Athenaeum*, 6 October 1923, pp. 11–12.

'Five Points on Dramatic Writing' (a letter to Ezra Pound), *Townsman* vol. 1, July 1938, reprinted in Carol H. Smith, *T. S. Eliot's Dramatic Theory and Practice*, p. 53.

Introduction to *Shakespeare and the Popular Dramatic Tradition* by S. L. Bethell, King and Staples, London, 1944.

Introduction to *Savonarola: A Dramatic Poem*, by Charlotte Eliot, R. Cobden-Sanderson, London, 1926.

Introduction to *The Wheel of Fire*, by G. Wilson Knight, Oxford University Press, 1930.

'The Need for Poetic Drama', *The Listener*, 25 November 1936, pp. 994–5.

'Religious Drama: Mediaeval and Modern', *The University of Edinburgh Journal*, vol. IX, no. 1 (Autumn 1937), pp. 8–17.

'Ulysses, Order and Myth', *The Dial*, vol. LXXV (1923), reprinted in R. Ellmann and C. Feidelson, *The Modern Tradition*, New York, 1965, pp. 679–81.

CRITICAL STUDIES ON ELIOT

(Studies of Eliot's poetry alone – however distinguished – are not included in this list.)

*Bergonzi, Bernard, *T. S. Eliot*, Macmillan, London, 1972.

Brooks, Cleanth, *The Hidden God*, Ch. 5, Yale University Press, New Haven and London, 1963.

Browne, E. Martin, *The Making of a Play, T. S. Eliot's 'The Cocktail Party'*, Cambridge University Press, 1966.

The Making of T. S. Eliot's Plays, Cambridge University Press, 1969.

Donoghue, Denis, *The Third Voice: Modern British and American Verse Drama*, Princeton University Press, 1959.

'The Holy Language of Modernism', in *Literary English since Shakespeare* (ed. G. Watson), Oxford University Press, 1970.

Fergusson, Francis, *The Idea of a Theater* (1949), Doubleday, New York, 1953.

Frye, Northrop, *T. S. Eliot* ('Writers and Critics'), Oliver and Boyd, Edinburgh and London, 1963.

Gardner, Helen, *The Art of T. S. Eliot*, The Cresset Press, London, 1949.

* Published after the completion of this study.

Goldman, Michael, 'Fear in the Way: the Design of Eliot's Drama' in *Eliot in His Time* (ed. Waltonlitz), Princeton, N.J., 1973.
Jones, D. E., *The Plays of T. S. Eliot*, Routledge and Kegan Paul, London, 1960.
Kenner, Hugh, *The Invisible Poet: T. S. Eliot* (1959), W. H. Allen, London, 1960.
'Eliot and the Tradition of the Anonymous', *College English*, vol. 28, no. 8 (1966).
Leavis, F. R., '*Eliot's Classical Standing*', in *Lectures in America*, Chatto and Windus, London, 1969.
Lucy, Sean, *T. S. Eliot and the Idea of Tradition*, Cohen and West, London, 1960.
Matthiessen, F. O., *The Achievement of T. S. Eliot*, 3rd ed. (with a chapter on Eliot's later work by C. L. Barber), Oxford University Press, 1958.
Peacock, Ronald, *The Poet in the Theatre* (1949), MacGibbon and Kee, London, 1960 (pp. 3–25).
Smith, Carol H., *T. S. Eliot's Dramatic Theory and Practice*, Princeton University Press, 1963.
Smith, Grover, *T. S. Eliot's Poetry and Plays* (1950 and 1956), Phoenix ed., University of Chicago Press, 1960.
Winters, Yvor, 'T. S. Eliot or the Illusion of Reaction', reprinted in his *In Defence of Reason*, Swallow, Denver, 1947.
*Worth, Katharine, 'Eliot and the Living Theatre', in *Eliot in Perspective – A Symposium* (ed. G. Martin), Macmillan, London, 1970.
Williams, Raymond, *Drama from Ibsen to Eliot*, Chatto and Windus, London, 1952.

Essays in Collections

Kenner, Hugh (ed.), *T. S. Eliot, A Collection of Critical Essays* ('Twentieth Century Views'), Englewood Cliffs, New Jersey, 1962.
'*Murder in the Cathedral*' by John Peter.
Leavis, F. R. (compiled by), *A Selection from Scrutiny*, vol. 1, Cambridge University Press, 1968.
'*The Family Reunion*' by John Peter.
'Sin and Soda', *The Cocktail Party* reviewed by John Peter.
Unger, Leonard (ed.), *T. S. Eliot: A Selected Critique*, Rinehart and Co., New York, 1948.
'T. S. Eliot: From *Ash-Wednesday* to *Murder in the Cathedral*' by R. P. Blackmur (pp. 236–62).
'Strange Gods at T. S. Eliot's "The Family Reunion"' by C. L. Barber (pp. 415–43).

* Published after the completion of this study.

V. BECKETT

THE PLAYS

The Faber edition (seven volumes) contains all the dramatic work except *Come and Go*, A Dramaticule, Calder and Boyars, London, 1967. All English text references are to this edition (dates as given in the notes).

For comparison: *En attendant Godot*, Editions de Minuit, Paris, 1952, and (ed. Colin Duckworth) Harrap, London, 1966. *Fin de Partie*, Editions de Minuit, Paris, 1957.

NOTE: An indispensable chronological table (up to 1961) is given by Hugh Kenner in his *Samuel Beckett* (pp. 26–8) which sorts out the discrepancy between the dates of writing and publication, as well as the overlap between the French and English texts.

THE NOVELS

All references are to the English edition published by Calder and Boyars.

BECKETT'S CRITICISM

'Dante...Bruno...Vico...Joyce', in *Our Exagmination round his Factification for Incamination of Work in Progress* (first published 1929), Faber, London, 1961.

Proust and Three Dialogues with Georges Duthuit (first published 1931 and 1949 respectively), Calder and Boyars, London, 1965.

CRITICAL STUDIES ON BECKETT

Books (including shorter monographs and an extended introduction)

Alvarez, A., *Beckett*, Fontana, London, 1973.

Coe, Richard N., *Beckett* ('Writers and Critics'), Oliver and Boyd, Edinburgh and London, 1964.

Cohn, Ruby, *Samuel Beckett: The Comic Gamut*, Rutgers University Press, New Brunswick, New Jersey, 1962.

Duckworth, Colin, Introduction (pp. xvii–cxxxi) to *En attendant Godot*, Harrap, London, 1966.

Fletcher, John, *Samuel Beckett's Art*, Chatto and Windus, London, 1967.

and Spurling, John, *Beckett: a Study of his Plays*, Eyre and Spottiswoode, London, 1972.

Gessner, Niklaus, *Die Unzulänglichkeit der Sprache: Eine Untersuchung über Formzerfall und Beziehungslosigheit bei Samuel Beckett*. Juris-Verlag, Zürich, 1957.

Kenner, Hugh, *Samuel Beckett – A Critical Study*, Calder and Boyars, London, 1962.

A Reader's Guide to Samuel Beckett, Thames and Hudson, London, 1973.

Robinson, Michael, *The Long Sonata of the Dead*, Rupert Hart-Davis, London, 1969.

Schoell, Konrad, *Das Theater Samuel Becketts*, Fink, München, 1967.

* Published after the completion of this study.

Tindall, W. York, *Samuel Beckett* (Columbia Essays on Modern Writers, no. 4), Columbia University Press, 1964.
*Webb, Eugene, *The Plays of Samuel Beckett*, Peter Owen, London, 1972.

Articles, collected essays, special numbers

Atkins, Anselm, 'Lucky's Speech in Beckett's *Waiting for Godot*: A Punctuated Sense-Line Arrangement', *Educational Theatre Journal*, vol. XIX, no. 4 (December 1967), pp. 426–32.
Cleveland, Louise O., 'Trials in the Soundscape. The Radio Plays of Samuel Beckett', *Modern Drama*, vol. 11, no. 3 (December 1968), pp. 267–82.
Harvey, J. R., 'La Vieille Voix Faible: Writers on Beckett', *The Cambridge Quarterly*, vol. 1, no. 4 (Autumn 1966), pp. 384–95.
Ricks, Christopher, 'The Roots of Samuel Beckett', *The Listener*, 17 December 1964, pp. 963–4, 980.
Robinson, C. J. Bradbury, 'A Way with Words: 'Paradox, Silence and Samuel Beckett', *The Cambridge Quarterly*, vol. 5, no. 3 (Spring 1971), pp. 249–64.
Suvin, Darko, 'Beckett's Purgatory of the Individual', *Tulane Drama Review*, vol. 11, no. 4 (Summer 1967), pp. 23ff.
Walker, Roy, 'Love, Chess and Death', *Twentieth Century*, vol. 164, no. 982 (December 1958), pp. 358ff.
Samuel Beckett, A Collection of Critical Essays (ed. Martin Esslin), Prentice-Hall, Englewood Cliffs, New Jersey, 1965.
Configuration Critique (no. 8), *Samuel Beckett, La Revue des Lettres Modernes*, no. 100, Paris (1964). (Ed. Melvin J. Friedman.)
Modern Drama, vol. 9, no. 3 (December 1966). (Ed. Ruby Cohn.)
Perspective XI, no. 3, Washington University, Autumn 1959.
Casebook on 'Waiting for Godot' (ed. Ruby Cohn), Grove Press, New York, 1967.
Twentieth Century Interpretations of 'Endgame' (ed. Bell Gale Chevigny), Prentice-Hall, Englewood Cliffs, New Jersey, 1969.

VI. PINTER

THE PLAYS

The Methuen edition contains all the published dramatic work: sixteen plays and five revue sketches. Any textual differences between the first and second edition – as in *The Birthday Party* – are referred to in the notes.

POEMS

Poems by Harold Pinter: Enitharmon Press, 1968

PINTER'S WRITINGS ON DRAMA AND RELEVANT INTERVIEWS

'Harold Pinter Replies', *New Theatre Magazine*, vol. XI, 2 (January 1961), pp. 8–10.

* Published after the completion of this study.

'Writing for Myself' (Pinter in conversation with Richard Findlater), *Twentieth Century*, vol. CLXIX, no. 1008 (February 1961), pp. 172–5.

'Writing for the Theatre', *Evergreen Review*, no. 33 (August–September 1964). A revised version of Pinter's speech at the Seventh National Students' Drama Festival, Bristol, published in *The Sunday Times*, 4 March 1962, under the title 'Between the Lines'.

'The Art of the Theatre III', *The Paris Review*, no. 39, pp. 13–37. Interview with Harold Pinter by Lawrence M. Bensky. Reprinted in *Writers at Work, The Paris Review* Interviews, Secker and Warburg, London, 1968, and included in a selection (by Kay Dick) under the same title in Penguin Books, 1972.

'In an Empty Bandstand', Harold Pinter in conversation with Joan Bakewell, *The Listener*, 6 November 1969.

Pinter has also made a brief contribution to *Beckett at 60*, A Festschrift, Calder and Boyars, London, 1967.

CRITICAL STUDIES ON PINTER

Books (including shorter monographs)

Esslin, Martin, *The Peopled Wound, The Plays of Harold Pinter*, Methuen, London, 1970, published in a revised edition as *Pinter: A Study of His Plays*, Eyre Methuen, London, 1973.

*Ganz, Arthur, *Pinter – A Collection of Critical Essays*, Prentice-Hall, Englewood Cliffs, New Jersey, 1973.

Hayman, Ronald, *Harold Pinter*, in the series 'Contemporary Playwrights', Heinemann, London, 1969. (Second ed.)

Hinchcliffe, Arnold P., *Harold Pinter* in 'Twayne's English Authors Series', Twayne, New York, 1967.

Kerr, Walter, *Harold Pinter*, No. 27 in the series 'Columbia Essays on Modern Writers', Columbia University Press, New York and London, 1967.

*Trussler, Simon, *The Plays of Harold Pinter, An Assessment*, Gollancz, London, 1973.

Articles

Amend, Victor E., 'Harold Pinter – Some Credits and Debits', *Modern Drama*, vol. 10, no. 2 (September 1967), pp. 165–74.

Bernhard, F. J., 'Beyond Realism: The Plays of Harold Pinter', *Modern Drama*, vol. 8, no. 2 (September 1965).

Boulton, James T., '*The Caretaker* and Other Plays', *Modern Drama*, vol. 6, no. 2 (September 1963), pp. 131–40.

Brown, John Russell, 'Dialogue in Pinter and Others', *Critical Quarterly*, vol. 7, no. 3 (Autumn 1965), pp. 225–43. This is incorporated and expanded in *Theatre Language*, Allen Lane, The Penguin Press, 1972, Ch. 1.

Burkman, Katherine H., 'Pinter's *Slight Ache* as Ritual', *Modern Drama*, vol. 11, no. 3 (December 1968).

* Published after the completion of this study.

Cohn, Ruby, 'The World of Harold Pinter', *Tulane Drama Review*, vol. 6, no. 3 (March 1962), pp. 55–68.

Dukore, Bernard, 'The Theatre of Harold Pinter', *Tulane Drama Review*, vol. 6, no. 3 (March 1962), pp. 43–54.

Hinchcliffe, Arnold P., 'Mr Pinter's Belinda', *Modern Drama*, vol. 11, no. 2 (September 1968), pp. 173–9.

Knight, G. Wilson, 'The Kitchen Sink', *Encounter* (December 1963), pp. 48–54.

Lahr, John, 'Pinter and Chekhov: The Bond of Naturalism', *Tulane Drama Review*, vol. 13, no. 2 (Winter 1968), pp. 137–45.

Leech, Clifford, 'Two Romantics: Arnold Wesker and Harold Pinter', in *Contemporary Theatre* (Stratford-upon-Avon Studies no. 4, ed. J. R. Brown and B. Harris), Edward Arnold, London, 1962, pp. 11–32.

Morris, Kelly, '*The Homecoming*', *Tulane Drama Review*, vol. 11, no. 2 (Winter 1966), pp. 185–91.

Nelson, Hugh, '*The Homecoming*; Kith and Kin', first published in *Modern British Dramatists* (ed. John R. Brown), Prentice-Hall, Englewood Cliffs, New Jersey, 1968, pp. 145–63.

Schechner, Richard, 'Puzzling Pinter', *Tulane Drama Review*, vol. 11, no. 2 (Winter 1966), pp. 176–84.

Walker, Augusta, 'Messages from Pinter', *Modern Drama*, vol. 10, no. 1 (May 1967), pp. 1–10.

Unpublished dissertation

Ibsen, Elizabeth, *Blind Man's Buff* (a study in the theme of isolation in the first four plays of Pinter), Universitetsbiblioteket, Bergen, 1969.

VII. OSBORNE

THE PLAYS

The Faber edition contains all the published plays, and all page references are to this edition.

Full production details are given in Simon Trussler, *The Plays of John Osborne*, Gollancz, London, 1969, which also has the best bibliography for works on Osborne.

OSBORNE'S WRITINGS ON DRAMA AND RELEVANT PERSONAL STATEMENTS (a selection)

'Sex and Failure' (a review of Tennessee Williams), *The Observer*, 20 January 1957.

'The Writer in his Age', *The London Magazine*, vol. IV (May 1957), reprinted in *Casebook*, pp. 59–62. (For *Casebook* see below.)

'They Call it Cricket', in *Declaration* (ed. Tom Maschler), MacGibbon and Kee, London, 1957, pp. 61–84, reprinted – in part – in *Playwrights on Playwrighting* (ed. Toby Cole), MacGibbon and Kee, London, 1960, pp. 140–4.

'That Awful Museum', *Twentieth Century*, vol. CLXIX (February 1961), pp. 212–16, reprinted in *Casebook*, pp. 63–7.
'On Critics and Criticism', *Sunday Telegraph*, 28 August 1966, reprinted in *Casebook*, pp. 69–71.
'On the Thesis Business and the Seekers After the Bare Approximate', *The Times (Saturday Review)*, 14 October 1967.
Two interviews (with Kenneth Tynan), *The Observer*, 30 June and 7 July 1968.

CRITICAL STUDIES ON OSBORNE

Books (including shorter monographs)

Banham, Martin, *Osborne* ('Writers and Critics'), Oliver and Boyd, Edinburgh and London, 1969.
Carter, Alan, *John Osborne*, Oliver and Boyd, Edinburgh and London, 1969.
Hayman, Ronald, *John Osborne* ('Contemporary Playwrights'), Heinemann, London, 1968.
Trussler, Simon, *The Plays of John Osborne, An Assessment*, Gollancz, London, 1969.

Articles of special interest, and shorter studies

Corrigan, Robert W., Introduction to *The New Theatre in Europe 3*, Dell, New York, 1968. ('The Drama of the Disengaged Man', including a brief discussion of *Inadmissible Evidence*.)
Denning, Barbara, 'John Osborne's War Against the Philistines', *The Hudson Review*, vol. XI, no. 3 (Autumn 1958), pp. 411–19.
Dyson, A. E., 'Look Back in Anger', *Critical Quarterly*, vol. I, no. 4 (1959), pp. 318–26, reprinted in *Modern British Dramatists* (ed. John Russell Brown), Englewood Cliffs, New Jersey, 1968, pp. 47–57.
Gersh, Gabriel, 'The Theater of John Osborne', *Modern Drama*, vol. 10, no. 10 (September 1967), pp. 137–43.
Kennedy, Andrew, 'Old and New in London Now', *Modern Drama*, vol. 11, no. 4 (February 1969), including a discussion of Osborne's 1968 plays, pp. 442–5.
Kershaw, John, *The Present Stage*, Collins, London, 1966, Ch. 3.
McCarthy, Mary, 'Verdict on Osborne', *The Observer*, 4 July 1965.
Marowitz, Charles. 'The Ascension of John Osborne', *Tulane Drama Review*, vol. 7, no. 2, reprinted in *Modern British Dramatists*, pp. 117–21.
Rupp, Gordon E., 'Luther and Mr Osborne', *Cambridge Quarterly*, vol. I, no. I (1965).
Wardle, Irving, 'Looking Back on Osborne's Anger', *New Society*, I July 1965.
'Osborne and the Critics', *New Society*, 16 June 1966.
Worth, Katharine J., 'Shaw and John Osborne', *The Shavian*, vol. 2, no. 10 (October 1964), pp. 29–35.

Symposium

Taylor, John Russell (ed.), *John Osborne: Look Back in Anger: a Casebook*, Macmillan, London, 1968.

VIII. ARDEN

THE PLAYS

The Methuen edition contains all the plays, except *The Waters of Babylon, Live Like Pigs* and *The Happy Haven*, which are published by Penguin Books under the title *Three Plays*.

Ars Longa, Vita Brevis (a short, 'experimental' text) appeared in *Encore*, vol. 11, no. 2 (March–April 1964).

NOTE: The dates given in the main text refer to the first performance of the play.

ARDEN'S WRITINGS ON DRAMA AND RELEVANT PERSONAL STATEMENTS (in chronological order)

Letter concerning 'Vital Theatre', *Encore*, vol. 6, no. 3 (May–June 1959), pp. 41–3.

'Telling a True Tale', *Encore*, vol. 7, no. 3 (May–June 1960), reprinted in *The Encore Reader* (ed. Ch. Marowitz, T. Milne and O. Hale), Methuen, London, 1965, pp. 125–9.

'Delusions of Grandeur', *Twentieth Century*, vol. 169, no. 1008 (February 1961), pp. 200–6.

'Verse in the Theatre', *New Theatre Magazine*, vol. II, no. 3 (April 1961).

'Building the Play' (an interview)', *Encore*, vol. 8, no. 4 (July–August 1961), pp. 22–41.

'Arden of Chichester' (Arden talks to Frank Cox about *The Workhouse Donkey*), *Plays and Players* (August 1963), pp. 16–18.

'Shakespeare – to a Young Dramatist', *The Guardian*, 23 April 1964.

'Poetry and Theatre', *The Times Literary Supplement*, 6 August 1964.

'Who's for a Revolution?' (two interviews, with Walter Wager and Simon Trussler respectively), *Tulane Drama Review*, vol. 11, no. 2 (Winter 1966), pp. 41–53.

'John Arden' (an interview with Brendan Hennessy), *The Times Educational Supplement*, 9 April 1971.

CRITICAL STUDIES ON ARDEN

Blindheim, Joan T., 'John Arden's Use of the Stage', *Modern Drama*, vol. 11, no. 3 (December 1968).

Brandt, C. W., 'Realism and Parables: from Brecht to Arden', in *Contemporary Theatre* (Stratford-upon-Avon Studies, no. 4, ed. J. R. Brown and B. Harris), Edward Arnold, London, 1962.

Gilman, Richard, 'Arden's Unsteady Ground', *Tulane Drama Review*, vol. 11, no. 2 (Winter 1966), reprinted in *Modern British Drama* (ed. J. R. Brown), Englewood Cliffs, New Jersey, 1968.

Hahnloser-Ingold, Margrit, *Das englische Theater und B. Brecht*, Francke, Bern, 1970, Ch. 6.

Hainsworth, J. D., 'John Arden and the Absurd', *A Review of English Literature*, vol. 7, no. 4 (October 1966).
Hayman, Ronald, *John Arden* ('Contemporary Playwrights'), Heinemann, London, 1968.
Hunt, Albert, 'Arden's Stagecraft', in *Modern British Drama*, Englewood Cliffs, New Jersey, 1968.
Arden, a study of His Plays, Eyre Methuen, London, 1974.
Nightingale, Benedict, 'The Theatre of Bewilderment', *The Guardian*, 6 July 1965.
Shrapnel, Susan, 'John Arden and the Public Stage', *The Cambridge Quarterly*, vol. 4, no. 3 (Summer 1969).
Trussler, Simon, 'Arden – an Introduction', *Encore*, vol. 12, no. 5 (September–October 1965). (This number of *Encore* is devoted to Arden.)
Wardle, Irving, 'Arden: Intellectual Marauder', *New Society*, 9 December 1965.
Worth, Katharine J., 'Avant Garde at the Royal Court Theatre: John Arden and N. F. Simpson', in *Experimental Drama* (ed. William A. Armstrong), Bell, London, 1963, pp. 204–14.

* Published after the completion of this study.

INDEX

abstraction in dramatic language, 13, 14; in Beckett, 151, 152; imposed by incantatory rhythm, 10; liturgy as a move towards, 109; in Pinter, 175–7

absurd, the: Shaw and, 5, 50, 75–84; Shaw's use of word, 50n, 84–6

action: disjunction of speech and, 20, 22; speech as (Shaw), 38; spoken (Pirandello), 18, 54; doubleness in (Eliot), 95; *see also* stasis

actor-characters: in Elizabethan and Jacobean drama, 28; in Osborne, 32, 205–7

Aeschylus, 91, 97; first to employ duologue, 153

aestheticism: Shaw's recoil from, 42, 44, 46, 47; and Eliot, 98

alienation of man in Western society, Hegel–Marx theory of, 26

Archer, William, supports imitative language, 5–6

Arden, John: attempts to revitalise drama by use of pre-literary language, 30, 213–16; compared with Synge, 214; contrasted with Pinter, 228; exotic prose of, 227–8; interplay of languages in, 216–20, 228; language-consciousness of, 30; turns to situations with making of ballad plays, 220–7

Armstrong's Last Goodnight, 220, 223–6, 228

The Business of Good Government, 226

Friday's Hiding (mime play), 13n

The Hero Rises Up, 214n

Ironhand (adaptation of Goethe's *Götz*), 227n

The Island of the Mighty, 243

The Life of Man, 215

Live Like Pigs, 214, 218–20, 224n, 227

Serjeant Musgrave's Dance, 13, 80n, 220, 221–3, 228

Telling a True Tale (essay), 215–16

The Waters of Babylon, 217–18

The Workhouse Donkey, 214n

Aristophanes, 97, 100, 104, 214; *The Birds* by, 49, 104n

art, increasingly short cycles of decay and renewal in, 26

art/anti-art dilemma of Shaw, 41, 43, 46

Artaud, Antonin, on non-verbal language, 9, 29, 230, 231n

Index

Atkins, Anselm, on Lucky's speech, 140
Auden, W. H., on Shaw's devotion to music, 51
Auerbach, Erich, *Mimesis* by (direct speech), 35

ballads, Arden and, 30, 214, 215, 217–18, 219–20, 223–4
ballet, 8, 87, 88
Barish, Jonas A., on theatrical and anti-theatrical theatres, 30
Barthes, Roland, on the opposition of speech and writing, 242; extended idea of 'language', 8n
Baudelaire, C. P., 100
Beckett, Samuel, 130–8; and Berkeley's philosophy, 26; contrasted with Pinter, 137, 169–72, 190; dialogue in and out of monologue in, 20, 131, 136, 153–64; experiences language as 'abstracted to death', 231; inner development of languages of, 233–4; language of, recreated for each new play, 173; language of, recreated from ruins of language, 24, 128, 135, 137, 138–52; philosophical critique of language, 3, 4; potential convergence of Eliot and, 130–1; and shape of sentences, 109, 134; static-perennial cycle in plays of, 47, 171; theatricality of, 30, 143, 233; verbalism of, 133; wordless drama of, 11–12
  Act Without Words I and II (mimes), 11–12
  All that Fall, 2, 27; monologue into dialogue in, 154, 155, 157–9
  Cascando (radio play), 137, 141n, 152; monologue in, 154, 163–4
  Embers, 141; monologue into dialogue in, 154
  Endgame, 171; exploitation and parody of old-style tragedy in, 144–7; monologue into dialogue in, 156–7
  Happy Days, 135, 148, 149–51; counterpoint to speech in, 12; monologue into dialogue in, 154, 160–2
  Krapp's Last Tape, 12, 16, 147–8, 148–9; monologue into dialogue in, 154, 159–60
  Lessness (story), 136n, 237
  Molloy, 92n
  Not I, 236–7, 242
  Play, 15, 25, 153; monologue in, 154; triangle of contending voices in, 131, 132, 151–2
  Proust (essay), 131, 133, 139n
  Three Dialogues, 134
  The Unnamable, 134, 141n; monologue in, 155
  Waiting for Godot, 130; contrasted styles of dramatic speech in, 156; dialogue in, 154; dramatises breakdown of language, 24, 78, 139–44; elements of circus clown and *commedia dell'arte* in, 233; end of, 20; French version of, 143n; opening line of, 170; pressure of mime against words in, 11–12; reduction of thought to a broken machine in, 199–200
  Watt (novel), 154
  Words and Music (radio play), 13, 152; monologue in, 154, 163
Bentley, Eric, on Shaw, 63
Bergson, Henri, on verbal comedy and parody, 64
Berkeley, George, philosophy of, 26
Berne, Eric, *Games People Play* by, 178
Blackmur, R. P., language as gesture, 242
blank verse, Shakespearean: as an exhausted language, 92
Blin, Roger, on Beckett's gift for dialogue, 155
Bond, Edward, pluralism of styles in plays of, 234
Boulton, James, on Pinter, 168
Bradbury, Malcolm, in introduction to *Contemporary Criticism*, 243

Bradley, F. H., Eliot's study of, 110
Brecht, Bertolt: Arden on, 215n; attacks art-literature, 46; draws on Aristophanes, 104; *Galileo* by, 226; *The Messingkauf Dialogues* by, 29; range of languages used by, 28–9; *St Joan of the Stockyards* by, 59n; *Threepenny Opera* by, 49; uses Noh plays, 234
Brieux, Eugène, Shaw's preface to plays of, 56n
Brown, John Russell, *Theatre Language* by, 21n, 237n, 242n
Brustein, Robert, 20n (on Shaw), 67n, 234n
Büchner, Georg, *Woyzeck* by, 24
Bunyan, John, Shaw's use of style of, 44, 70, 76
Burke, Kenneth, on linguistic motives, 230–1

Castelvetro, Lodovico, on naturalism in drama, 17
Celtic tradition of epic writing, 217
Chekhov, Anton, 53; *The Cherry Orchard* by, 16, 56; classical naturalism in, 15, 38, 168; *The Seagull* by, 16, 21
chorus: Eliot's development of, 101, 102–8; Nietzsche on, 98
clowns, 10, 86; Beckett's use of elements from, 233
Cocteau, Jean, *La voix humaine* by, 163
Cohn, Ruby, on Beckett, 150
Coleridge, S. T., and ballads, 213–14, 215
comedy: of ideas (Shaw) 87; of manners, (Eliot) 96, (Pinter) 178, 188; of menace (Pinter) 176; parody as essential element in tradition of, 63; verbal, Bergson's definition of, 64
commedia dell'arte, 10; Beckett's debt to, 143, 233
communication: gap between speech and, 112, 168; language as a barrier to, 22; pressure towards scenes of real, in Eliot, 112, 113, 114, 116
confessional duologues, in Eliot, 116–23, 126
Congreve, William, 64; Eliot on, 88n
Conrad, Joseph, on everyday words, in *Heart of Darkness*, 235n
'conviction', Shaw's idea of inward relation between style and, 43, 44–5, 47n–48n
Cooke, Deryck, *The Language of Music* by, 14n
Cornford, Francis, *The Origin of Attic Comedy* by, 100, 102n
costume speech, *see under* speech
Coward, Noel, dialogue of, 111, 216
Craig, Gordon, *On the Art of the Theatre* by, 9
Creighton, Anthony, collaborator in *Epitaph for George Dillon*, 193
cricicism: and crisis, 1; flexible modes of language in drama call for flexible pluralistic body of, 237–9; possible contribution of verbal analysis to, 239–41

Dante, 138, 150
D'Arcy, Margaretta, co-author of *The Business of Good Government*, 226, and *The Island of the Mighty*, 243
Declaration (1957), Osborne's contribution to, 196
De Quincey, Thomas, on rhetoric and eloquence, 32
dialect of the tribe: in Eliot, 108–15, 175; Synge and, 26
dialogue, dramatic: between play and audience, 243; criticism of contexts and texture of, 239; in the gospels, 35–6, 37; and monologue (Beckett), 20, 131, 136, 153–64; in Osborne, 194–5, 197; in Pinter, 165, 166, 177, 187; *see also* language, spoken action, subtext
didactic drama, Shaw on, 41, 43
Dies Irae, 94, 105
documented language: in Osborne's

documented language (*cont.*)
Luther, 193; in Shaw's *Saint Joan*, 74; in Weiss's *The Investigation*, 36–7
Dryden, John, on serious plays, 53
'dumbness, cult of', 25

'eavesdropping' by dramatists, 26, 53, 169
Edel, Leon, on Henry James as dramatist, 7
Eliot, T. S., 87–94; Arden and, 216–17; confessional duologues in, 116–23, 126; 'dialect of the tribe' in, 108–15, 175; evolution of language of, 94–7; experiences language as exhausted, 231, and as inadequate, 3, 4; as experimenter and as preserver, 128–9; linguistic dualism of, 19, 109–10; liturgy in, 13, 15, 88, 89, 94; liturgy and ritual in, 97–109; lower-class speech in, 115–16; movement from liturgy to naturalism in, 95, 96–7, 109, 115, 128; potential convergence of Beckett and, 130–1; relation of poetry and plays of, 123; re-creates language for each new play, 173, 233; and Shakespearean blank verse, 92, 234; speech-of-appearance in, 31; the unsayable in, 19, 21n, 96, 104, 123–8
After Strange Gods (essay), 91
Ash Wednesday (poem), 123
The Cocktail Party, 130, 131–2, 171; confessional duologue in, 120–2, 126; language of, 111–13; liturgical echoes in, 108; the unsayable in, 125
The Confidential Clerk, 90; confessional duologue in, 119, 120; language of, 111, 113, 115; the unsayable in, 125
The Elder Statesman, 102; confessional duologue in, 116, 119, 120; language of, 111, 113–15; the unsayable in, 125
The Family Reunion: chorus in, 70n, 103–4, 107; confessional duologue in, 116, 117–19; Eliot's self-criticism of, 119n; liturgy and ritual in, 97, 99, 102; lower-class speech in, 115; at transition in Eliot's plays, 89n; the unsayable in, 124
Four Elizabethan Dramatists (essay), 5, 89
Four Quartets (poems), 97, 108, 121, 126
Murder in the Cathedral: Arden and, 217; choruses in, 99, 103, 104–6; confessional duologue in, 117; contemporary political jargon in, 33, 226; juxtaposed styles of speech in, 119; liturgy and ritual in, 93, 102, 107–8; rhythms of *Everyman* in, 3, 89, 91, 117; the unsayable in, 124
On Poetry and Poets (essays), 88n, 92, 119, 125, 129, 229
'Rhetoric' and Poetic Drama (essay), 88, 204–5
The Rock, 102
The Sacred Wood (essays), 87–8, 97
Sweeney Agonistes, 89, 91, 100–1, 130; affinity of, with Eliot's poetry, 123–4; dialogue in, based on everyday speech, 2, 26, 108–9, 175; elements of music hall in, 233; final chorus of, 103, 104, 108; parody of everyday speech in, 110
Sweeney Erect, 93
The Use of Poetry and the Use of Criticism (essay), 93n, 96
The Waste Land (poem), 80n, 93; new combination of known styles in, 34
Elizabethan drama, 28, 214; soliloquy in, 211–12
English language: Arden on (his writing of), 216; Beckett on relation of, to other European languages, 138; Pinter on obscenity and, 188n; Shaw on (accents), 54n

Eumenides: in Eliot, 99, 119; in Giraudoux, 99
Euripides: chorus from *The Bacchae* by, in *Major Barbara*, 49, 71
Everyman, 133; Eliot and, 3, 83, 91, 117
existentialism: in Pinter, 171n; theology and, 135n
expression: comedy and pathos of failure of, 16; as one pole of dramatic language, 13, 14
expressionist plays, 133
expressiveness: aesthetic, in implicit speech, 168; new kind of, in Pinter's theatre of language, 174; verbal, 2, 137

farce, Victorian, 30, 148
Fergusson, Francis, *The Idea of a Theater* by, 99, 229
'floating feelings', Eliot on, 94
Forster, E. M., *Howard's End* by, 235
fragments, aesthetics of, 144
Fry, Christopher, *The Dark is Light Enough* by, 210
Frye, Northrop: on archetypal masque, 132–3; on resources of verbal expression, 232–3

Gardner, Helen, on Eliot, 107
George, Stefan, Brecht on, 46
Gide, André, on Dada, 80
Gilbert, W. S., *Iolanthe* by, 104n
Giraudoux, Jean, Eumenides in, 99
Godard, J. L.: pastiche of Hollywood musicals in film by, 34
Goethe, Johann Wolfgang von, *Götz* by, 227
Goldsmith, Oliver, on style of Dr Johnson, 40
Gombrich, E. H., on cultural resonance, 34
Gorky, Maxim, *Lower Depths* by, 58
gospels, the: dialogue in, 35–6, 37

Harvey, J. B., on Beckett, 135
Hayman, Ronald, on everyday conversation in Pinter, 168
Hofmannsthal, Hugo von, 4–5
Huizinga, Johan, *Homo Ludens* by, 177
Hulme, T. E., influences Eliot, 90

Ibsen, Henrik: Arden on, 215; classical naturalism in, 15, 17–18, 38, 53; *The Doll's House* by, 13, 56; duologue in, between a character and voices from illusory past, 117; *Ghosts* by, 110; *Rosmersholm* by, 17; Shaw on, 40, 55–6, 85
idioms: in Pinter, 167; Shaw and, 48n
illumination: moments of, in Eliot, 124, 126–8
'imaginary museum', *see under* museum
Ionesco, Eugène, 61, 169; *The Bald Primadonna* by, 166
Irish speech: Beckett's heritage from, 141, 154, 157; as Shaw's mother tongue, 52n; *see also* Synge, Yeats

Jacobean drama, 28, 214, 236
Jakobson, Roman, on 'private' language, 232, 241n, 249
James, Henry: accepts ascendancy of language of imitation, 6, 7–8; dramatic attempts of, 5, 7, 40; exhaustion of artist in *The Middle Years* by, 231
jargon, in Pinter, 167, 184n
Joe Macbeth (gangster film), 11
John of the Cross, St, Eliot and, 124
Johnson, Dr, Goldsmith on style of, 40
Jonson, Ben, Shaw on *Volpone* by, 40
Joyce, James, 4; Beckett on *Finnegans Wake* by, 138, 139n; *Exiles* by, 75; on Shaw, 75
Jung, C. G., use of term *persona* by, 32n

Kafka, Franz, *The Trial* by, 182
Kenner, Hugh, on Eliot, 106
Knight, Wilson, on 'Dionysian' speech from below, 200
Koestler, Arthur: *Darkness at Noon* by, 181; on infolding of language, 25

Kott, Jan, on *King Lear*, 24

Lahr, John, on avant-garde theatre in USA, 231n
Lamb, Charles, *Specimens* by, 33
language, 8; as anaesthetic (Shaw), 83; as a barrier to communication, 22; crisis of, 1, 3–4, 26, 106; crisis of, as condition of creativity, 231; critical, progress from a limited language towards, 15, 20–2; 'documented', 36–7, 74, 193; of dramatic collage, 27–33, 71; exhausted, 92, 94; exhaustion not of language, but of particular writer in particular situation, 231; fragmented or minimal, 2; as gesture, 242; 'infolding' of, 25, 190, 233, 235; limited, of classical naturalism, 15–20, 29; a new dramatic, as a new combination of known styles, 34–5; non-verbal or anti-verbal, 8–13, 29, 230; opposition between written and spoken, 242; overtones and resonances of, 34; participatory and spectatorial, distinction between, 99–100; 'private', 131, 136, 232; re-mythologised, movement towards, 97; solipsistic, *see* solipsism; as sound (*Sweeney Agonistes*), 101; tension between spontaneity and design in, 175; as vision, 133; *see also* speech *and* dialogue
language-consciousness, 2–4, 31–2, 232; of Arden, 30; of Eliot, 90, 97
Lawrence, D. H., 188n
Leavis, F. R., on Eliot's poetry, 128
Lévi-Strauss, Claude, *bricoleur* of, 34
liturgy, in Eliot, 13, 15, 88, 89, 94, 97–108; formal, becomes an exhausted language, 94; intersection between naturalism and, 89; movement to naturalism from, 95, 96–7, 109, 115, 128; parodies or sanctifies everyday speech, 109
Living Theatre, 10
Lukács, Georg: on absence of confidants in new drama, 123; on the modern theatre of environment, 198; on the unspoken in dialogue, 28
Lyndsay, Sir David, *Thrie Estaits* by, 225
lyricism, old-style: used by Beckett, 141–2, 152

MacCarthy, Desmond, on Shaw, 71
McCarthy, Mary, on Osborne, 196, 204
Maeterlinck, Maurice, 133; Eliot and drama of, 87, 88, 98
Mallarmé, Stéphane, 98n; on speech as no more than a commercial approach to reality, 22–3
Malraux, André, and 'Le musée imaginaire', 28, 34
Mann, Thomas, *The Magic Mountain* by, 81
mannerism, 172; in Pinter, 172–4, 178, 182, 187
Marcuse, Herbert, defends aesthetic form, 231n
Marowitz, Charles, on the inarticulate, 25
Mauthner, Fritz, *Critique of Language* by, 4
meaning of meaning, for Beckett and for Pinter, 171
mechanistic thought, parodies of (by Shaw, Beckett, Osborne), 199–200
melodrama, Victorian, 30, 214; Arden and, 214; Eliot and, 104; Shaw and, 49, 57, 62
Miller, Arthur: Arden on, 215; *The Crucible* by, 36; on mime, 10
mime, 10–12
Molière: *Les précieuses ridicules* by, 63; Shaw on, 41, 86
monologue: dialogue in and out of (Beckett), 20, 131, 136, 153–

64; in Osborne, 193, 194, 198; *see also* soliloquy
Moralities, medieval, 214
Mummers' plays, 214
museum, imaginary: of drama, 214; of possible languages, 1, 33; of speech, 34, 39, (Eliot and) 89–90, 111; of style, 5, 28, 44, 232, 234; of style, as a mausoleum (Beckett), 137
music: relation between poetry and (Eliot), 98n; relation between words and, 13–14; Pinter and, 189–91 and n; *see also* Shaw (word-music)
'musicalising' of language, *see under* Symbolism
music hall, 30; Beckett's debt to, 143; Eliot and, 88, 101, 104, 233; 'folk art' of, in Osborne's *The Entertainer*, 193, 206
mysticism, 135; in Eliot, 3, 122, 124, 126
myths: in drama, 34; 're-mythologising', 98–9

National Theatre, couples Beckett's *Play* with Sophocles, 153
naturalism: bifurcation of Symbolism and (late 19th century), 15; classical, limited language of, 15–20, 29; Eliot's movement from liturgy to approximate, 95, 96–7, 109, 115, 128; as an exhausted style, 1, 2, 26; as one pole of dramatic language, 13, 14; Osborne thrusts histrionic rhetoric into, 192; persistent, of Osborne, 212; Pinter's mannerism and, 173; Shaw's distance from, 38, 40, 53–62; survival of, in parody, 234–5, and in simplification to minimal speech, 235; upholders of, 5–8
naturalist vision and non-naturalist language, in Shaw, 55–7, 63
'negative way', of mystics, 124, 135
neurosis: energies of, in plays of Tennessee Williams, 193
Nichols, Peter, plays of, 234
Nietzsche, Friedrich, on revival of chorus as anti-naturalist, 98
Noh plays, 234

obscene language, Pinter on, 188n
Ohman, R. M.: on Shaw's non-dramatic prose, 45; *Speech, Action, and Style* by, 242–3
Oh What a Lovely War, theatrical collage, 37
O'Neill, Eugene: *Hughie* by, 163; *Strange Interlude* by, 162
Osborne, John, 192–200, 202–4; his allegiance to words, 29, 204; Arden on, 215; comparison of Shaw and, 200–2; language of, 192, 195; rhetoric in, 192, 193, 197, 200, 204–12; shifts of style in, 233; two play forms and two languages of, 194
A Bond Honoured, 194; author's note to, 195n
Coriolanus (projected play set in African republic), 198
The Entertainer, 193, 206, 208, 210–11, 212; interplay between two modes of language in, 194
Epitaph for George Dillon, 193, 195, 205–6, 208, 209
Inadmissible Evidence, 207, 208–9, 212; monologue in, 193, 198, 211
Look Back in Anger, 192, 208, 209–10; rhetoric of odium in, 201–2
Luther, 193, 202–4; interplay between two modes of language in, 194
A Patriot for Me, 193
Time Present, 206–7, 212
West of Suez, 235

Park, B. R., on Shaw, 45
parody, 2, 33–4, 62–4; in Beckett, 141–2, 143; in Eliot, 92–3, 104; in Osborne, 193n, 195n; in

parody (*cont.*)
Shaw, 33, 39, 40, 64–73; in Stoppard, 33
pastiche, 63, 64; in Pinter, 187; in Shaw, 69–70, 71, 72, 85
Péguy, C. P., *Le mystère de la charité de Jeanne d'Arc* by, 107
persona, 31–2, 112
philosophy, critical: analysis of abstract into no-sense by, 26
Pinero, A. W.: accepts language of imitation, 5, 6, 7–8; defines spoken language, 54; on R. L. Stevenson as dramatist, 6–7
Pinter, Harold, 165; Arden on, 215; his conception of 'unverifiable' action, 20; contrasted with Arden, 228, with Beckett, 137, 169–72, 190, and with Ionesco, 166; experiences language as a source of nausea and paralysis, 4, 231; increasing self-consciousness of, 173–4; language as a smoke-screen in, 20, 167, 180; mannerism in, 172–4, 178, 182, 187; obsessed with words, 165–8; Osborne on, 192, 193, 194n; recreates language for each new play, 173; shaping of dialogue by, 174–8; spectrum of styles in major plays of, 178–88; subtext in, 21–2; and 'tape-recording' ear, 53, 109
The Basement, 178
The Birthday Party, 13, 167, 170n; two styles in, 178–82
The Caretaker, 16, 167, 169–70; fusion of linguistic and psychological pattern in, 177, 182–4; pathologically inarticulate speech in, 25; structure of, 171
The Collection, 167, 170–1, 178
The Dumb Waiter, 167, 170n, 176–7
The Homecoming, 166, 167, 177–8; shifts of language in, 184–8; structure of, 171
Landscape, 25, 172, 178, 189–90
The Lover, 167, 178
Night, 188
Old Times, 167, 178; fusion of 'infolding' language and theatrical collage in, 233
The Room, 167, 170n, 173
Silence, 25, 172, 178, 190
A Slight Ache, 167
The Tea Party, 178
Writing for the Theatre (article), 174–5
Pirandello, Luigi: modern theatricality in, 28; *Six Characters in Search of an Author* by, 18, 110; on spoken action, 18, 54
poetry, should help to prevent language from changing too rapidly (Eliot), 129
Pound, Ezra, 64, 98n; *ABC of Reading* by, 230; and Eliot, 106
Pre-Raphaelites, Shaw and, 43
Proust, Marcel, Beckett on, 131, 133, 139n
purgatory, as recurrent metaphor in Beckett, 139n

radio plays, 101; Beckett's, 152, 158, 188; *see also Cascando, under* Beckett
revue sketches, Pinter's, 175–6
rhetoric, 2, 32; in Eliot, 88n, 96; in Osborne, 192, 193, 197, 200, 201, 204–12; in politics, 31; in Shakespeare, 28, 88; in Shaw, 74, 75, 80, 83, 84; straight line of, in Shaw, 47
rhythm, Eliot and the idea of, 109
Rimbaud, Arthur, proclaims need for language of the soul, 22
ritual: and liturgy, in Eliot, 97–108; in Pinter, 177, 181–2
ritual drama, in Shaw, 48–9, 74; *see also* M. Morgan, 58n
role-enactment: language in, 31; parody in, 64
Rostand, Edmond, *Cyrano de Bergerac* by, 88, 205
Rudkin, David, use of West Midland dialects by, 26–7

Saporta, Sol, on 'linguistic features' and context, 240

Sardou, Victorien, Shaw and, 5, 72
Sartre, Jean-Paul: *Huis Clos* by, 131; *La Nausée* by, 210
Schiller, Friedrich, definition of 'naive' by, 18, 46, 89
Shakespeare, William: Arden invokes, 228; Beckett's allusions to, 144, 145, 146, 149; blank verse of, 92, 234; Eliot on, 88, 96; Eliot emulates final reconciliation scenes in, 125; leaves an image of wholeness, 229; modes of language used by, 3n, 216; Shaw on, 40, 51–3
  Antony and Cleopatra, Shaw on, 52n
  Hamlet, 11, 28, 110, 242
  King Lear, 52, 234, 240–1; Poor Tom's language in, 24
  Macbeth, un-mimable passage of, 11
  A Midsummer Night's Dream, interplay of styles in, 28, 63
  Othello, 186
  Romeo and Juliet, Eliot's analysis of balcony scene in, 116
Shaw, G. B., 38–40; the absurd in, 5, 50, 75–84; use of word 'absurd' by, 50n, 84–6; comedy of ideas in, 87; comparison of Osborne and, 200–2; his distance from naturalism, 40, 53–62; Eliot on, 87, 88n; on the gospel narrative, 36; hyperarticulateness of, 19, 38, 66, 81, 84; 'naive' and robust creativity of, 5; operatic approach to drama by, 13, 19, 40, 47, 49, 52, 53, 60–1, 72; parody and pastiche in, 33, 39, 40, 62–73; his propaganda on behalf of the published text of a play, 29; and Romeo, 117n; 'style' (ambiguities of) 41–7, (shifts in), 39, 58, 61–2, 75, 233; the theatre as temple for, 47–9; on theatricality of public and private life, 31, 74n; (Raymond) Williams on, 238; and word-music, 13, 49–53; Yeats on, 46, 51
  The Apple Cart, 49, 55n, 72
  Arms and the Man, 41, 62; parody in, 65–6
  Back to Methuselah: analogy to Wagner's *Ring* cycle in, 49; Automata in, 43, 77–9, 85; Automata as parody of mechanistic thought, 199, 200; pastiche in, 69, 70; postscript to, 86; preface to, 75n; speculative rhetoric in, 62; Speech-maker in, 76–7
  Candida, 43n, 55n
  Caesar and Cleopatra, 72
  Thd Dark Lady of the Sonnets, 52n
  The Doctor's Dilemma, 85; pastiche in, 69, 70, 71
  Don Juan in Hell, 50; conscious self-parody in, 67–8, 69, 70
  Geneva, 83
  Getting Married, 51
  In Good King Charles's Golden Days, 47, 83
  Heartbreak House, 52, 76; contrasts of natural and posed expression in, 59–61; interplay between voices of 'reality' and 'fantasy' in, 45; pastiche in, 69, 70, 71; supposed Chekhovian elements in, 56
  John Bull's Other Island, 44n, 55n, 71, 76
  Major Barbara, 13, 50, 76; chorus from Euripides in, 49, 71; superficial naturalism and melodramatic stage-Cockney in, 58–9; use of Bunyan's prose style in, 44, 70, 76
  The Man of Destiny, 72
  Man and Superman: the absurd in, 76, 85; conscious self-parody in, 45, 66–8, 69, 70; lower-class speech in, 55n; preface to, 42–3, 48, 67n; rhetoric in, 50, 201
  Mrs Warren's Profession, 49, 57
  The Music Cure, 86
  Music in London (articles), 50n
  Pygmalion, 78; Doolittle's speech in, 54–5

Shaw, G. B. (*cont.*)
The Quintessence of Ibsenism (essay), 55
Saint Joan, 36, 50, 202–3; collage of styles in, 45, 72–4; mystic voices in, 49, 226
Shakes versus Shaw (puppet play), 52–3
The Showing up of Blanco Posnet, 75
Too True to be Good, 80–3, 84, 85
Translations and Tomfooleries, 86
Village Wooing, 61–2
Widowers' Houses, 41, 57
You Never Can Tell, 38
Shelley, Percy B., pastiche-Jacobean in *The Cenci* by, 33
Sheridan, Richard B., patterned speech in plays of, 64
silences, in Pinter's plays, 172, 190
Smith, Grover, on Eliot, 93
Smith, J. Percy, on Shaw's 'ritual drama', 48
socialism, Osborne on dramatist's approach to, 196
society, Osborne on fragmentation of, 197
soliloquy: in Arden, 223; in Elizabethan dramatists, 211–12; *see also* monologue
solipsism in language, 30; Beckett's acceptance of, 131; Eliot's attempt to avoid, 123; externalised form of, in Osborne, 198; and language of tribe, 232
solitude: world of perpetual, in Eliot's poetry and Beckett's plays, 123, 130–2
Sophocles: Eliot emulates conclusion of *Oedipus at Colonus* by, 125; first to increase number of actors to three, 153
speech, 8; as action (Shaw), 38; -of-appearance, 31, 110, 112, 113, 119; 'costume', 32, 54, 63, 72, 193; dehumanised (Pinter), 177, 185, 187; disjunction of action and, 20, 22; gap between communication and, 112, 168; imaginary museum of, *see* museum; lower-class, in Eliot, 26, 108, 109, 110–16, and in Shaw, 55n, 58; natural, raised to dramatic poetry, 116, 118; opposition between written language and, 242; ordinary, Eliot's horror at meaninglessness of, 109; ordinary, literary debris in, 27; parody of ordinary, 2, 110; pathological breakdown of (*Waiting for Godot*), 139–40; pathologically inarticulate, 24–5, 76; *see also* language
spoken action (Pirandello), 18, 54
Stanislavski, Constantin: *Building a Character* by, 20; his 'production score' for *The Seagull*, 21
stasis, dramatic: in Beckett, 47, 131
Steiner, George, on pastiche in Shelley, 33n; linguistics and poetics, 239n
Stevenson, R. L., as dramatist: Pinero on, 6–7
Storey, David, 234; *Home* by, 235
Stravinsky, Igor, 34, 101n
Strindberg, August, 192, 195; pantomime in *Miss Julie* by, 11
structuralism, in study of drama, 241–2
Styan, J. L., *The Elements of Drama* by, 120, 242
style: imaginary museum of, *see* museum; montage of several different kinds of, 33; Shaw's idea of inward relation between 'conviction' and, 43, 44–5, 47n–48n
stylistics, and dramatic criticism, xii–xiii, 238–42; *see also* criticism
subtext (interaction of text and context), 20–2, 95; in Chekhov, 61; in Pinter, 174
Swift, Jonathan, Shaw on, 85–6
Swinburne, Algernon, 98n
Symbolism: Beckett's heritage from, 141; bifurcation of naturalism and (late 19th century), 15; distrust of public functions of

language in, 22–3; idea of 'musicalising' language in, 13, 47, 98, 109, 191
Synge, J. M., 53, 228n; Arden compared with, 214; on Ibsen's language, 18; preface to *The Playboy of the Western World* by, 26

Taylor, Tom, *Jeanne Darc* by, 73n
Te Deum, 74, 105
telephone, as instrument of anti-communication in Eliot, 110–11, 177
television plays, Pinter's, 173, 178
theatre: of the Absurd, 86; of environment (Lukács), 198; epic, of Brecht, 28; of happenings, Osborne's attacks on, 29; interaction of, with public life, 30; of language, 4, 174; non-verbal or anti-verbal, 230; of parables (Shaw), 70n, 77; popular, Arden and, 213; as temple, for Shaw, 47–8; in the theatre (Pirandello), 28
theatricality, 27–33; of public and private life (Shaw), 31, 74n; of Shaw, 40, 45; verbal, as a critical language, 33; verbal, difference between spoken action and, 54
Thomas, Dylan, *Under Milk Wood* by, 157
Tourneur, Cyril, *The Revenger's Tragedy* by, 94n
translation: of idiom (Pinter) 167n, (Shaw) 48n; of today into terms of poetry (Arden), 216, 217–18

unsayable, the: Eliot's effort to reach, 19, 21n, 96, 104, 123–8; Rimbaud's quest for, 22

Valéry, Paul, 22n; on Pascal, 30–1
Vannier, Jean, on Beckett and Ionesco, 168–9
verbal analysis, *see* criticism
verbal games, in Pinter, 169, 173, 178
verbalism, of Beckett, 133
Verlaine, Paul, *Art Poétique* by, 191
verse: Eliot on plays in, 121n; speaking in, as an oracular pronouncement (Arden), 221
Vico, Gian Battista: on language in *Scienza Nuova* (1725), 90; on language-cycle, 138

Wagner, Richard: Shaw on, 50n, 52; words of *Tristan und Isolde* by, 98
Walker, Roy, on Beckett, 162
Watling, E. F., on three dimensional drama of Sophocles, 153
Weil, Simone, on implicit love, 121
Weiss, Peter, *The Investigation* by, 36–7, 218n
Wesker, Arnold: Arden on, 215; non-verbal demonstrations in plays of, 12
Wilde, Oscar, patterned speech in plays of, 64, 111
Williams, Raymond, criticism of drama by, 21, 237–8
Williams, Tennessee, energies of neurosis in plays of, 193
Wilson, Edmund, criticism of drama by, 15, 72
Wittgenstein, Ludwig, 26; on 'private' language, 136n, 232
Woolf, Virginia, *The Waves* by, 191
word-music: in Eliot, 96; Shaw and, 5, 13, 49–53
Wordsworth, William, and ballads, 213–14
world war I: Gide and, 80; Shaw and, 75–6, 81–2
Worth, Katherine J., compares Shaw and Osborne, 200

Yeats, W. B.: early drama of, 98; Eliot on, 99; *Essays and Introductions* by, 23–4; *Explorations* by, 4, 213, 214; pins hopes for drama on naive naturalist, 27; *Purgatory* by, 127; on Shaw, 46, 51; uses Noh plays, 234; withdraws from public theatre, 128